Without Apology shares the stories of 24 ordinary, yet remarkable, women. Among them are:

- *Saundra, who volunteered in rural Mississippi during the height of the Civil Rights Movement.*

- *Ellie, who at age 92, continues to work part-time as a substance abuse counselor.*

- *Joann, who raised 17 children, five her own, five adopted, and seven fostered, many of whom were mentally and physically disabled, and now, with her partner, runs a group home.*

- *Gloria, whose entertainment career began when she was seven and earned $5 a night dancing at clubs, went on to spend years as a "nightclub girl," singing, dancing and doing comedy.*

- *Bessie, who was an incredible left-handed pitcher in the women's fastpitch softball leagues in Texas.*

- *Edie, who traveled on the Peace Train from Finland to Beijing, China, to attend the Fourth International Conference on Women.*

- *Shaba, who journeyed through Judaism, Islam, and Kabbalah as a black-skinned woman raised in the midst of racial segregation and Jim Crow laws.*

- *Arden, who lived a closeted life for almost 40 years before the death of her long-term partner motivated her to begin a life of activism.*

- *Helen, who entered the convent when she finished high school in hopes of sublimating her love for women.*

- *Kittu, who was born in India and raised high in the Himalayas, became fascinated by the concept of nourishment and later went on to be an integral part of developing the Recommended Daily Allowance rating system as well as WIC, a nutrition program for women, infants and children.*

- *Louise and Ruth, who after falling in love in college, were forcibly separated by school ⌐   ⌐er again after more than 30 years,   ⌐ter.*

D1636848

Praise for
the Old Lesbian Oral Herstory Project

- *This is truly an outstanding legacy that you have provided for all of us to enjoy!*

- *What you have done is so important that I think even you don't understand it. This will have a life of its own and be around way after we are gone. To have thought this up, seen the need, and assume the effort to get it done is phenomenal. I really do salute you.*

- *This is important history that would otherwise be too easily, and to our detriment, lost.*

- *Thank you for doing all this work for our Community and for those who might see the book. I am proud to say I knew some of these women and so happy that they shared their stories with us.*

- *The book and now the newsletter are full of all your spirits and the legacy of each woman whose lives you have touched. Your deep listening has brought your love of them and their remarkable transcendence to us each to learn from and cherish.*

- *The women who have been fortunate enough to be included in the book and the other plans you have for books will never be able to thank you enough for giving the story of life in the early 1930s to the younger members of our population.*

- *What a gift, to read all these life stories. We have come a long way in our society—need to go a lot further.*

- *Each bio from Lesbians around the US captures their joys and their travails, and inspires Lesbians of all ages to be true to our life's orientation despite homophobic challenges.*

- *Just knowing others went before me who are like myself, well, makes me feel less alone in this world.*

- *Thank you doesn't adequately express my deep gratitude for your loving, nurturing care for the stories of my sisters and me!*

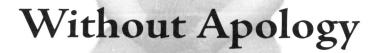

Without Apology

The Second Collection of Life Stories
Based on Interview Transcripts in the
Old Lesbian Oral Herstory Project

Without Apology:
Old Lesbian Life Stories
by Arden Eversmeyer and Margaret Purcell

© Copyright 2012
ISBN 978-0-9823669-0-5

Cost of a single copy within the United States: $19.95
Discounts available for bulk orders. Contact us for details.

Old Lesbian Oral Herstory Project:
    OLOHP
    PO Box 980422
    Houston, TX 77098
    e-mail: info@OLOHP.org
    website: www.olohp.org

Dedications

To the inspiring women who had the strength
and wisdom to know their stories are worth
telling, and trusted the Old Lesbian Oral
Herstory Project to honor their legacies.

A Confluence of Lesbians

Most of us are familiar with collective nouns such as a clutch
of eggs or a school of fish. Other collectives are fun, but seldom
used, such as a huddle of lawyers or a prickle of hedgehogs.
Collective nouns often tell you a bit about the object they modify.

Our experiences in bringing this book to fruition has lead us
to coin a new term: a confluence of lesbians. According to the
dictionary, a confluence is "a coming or flowing together, meeting,
or gathering." A confluence perfectly describes what occurred
in the writing of this book. The authors, and the women who
shared their stories for this book, were joined by Mary Henry,
Charlotte Avery, Sue Weinheimer, Marcia Perlstein, Pokey
Anderson and others, pooling their knowledge and skills,
becoming a force far stronger than its collective parts.

The Old Lesbian Oral Herstory Project has been blessed in
so many ways, and by so many people. Words of thanks seem
inadequate, but we'd like to offer them anyway. This particular
Confluence of Lesbians was truly amazing.

Photos on Cover

Photos in the graphics on the cover are all women whose stories are in this book. The same women appear in the same order on the front and back covers. From top to bottom: Dee Austin, Edie Daly, Joann Jones, Kittu Riddle, and Charlotte Avery

Photo on the Title Page

The image on the title page is Bessie Morris.

About the Book Title

The title of this book, *Without Apology*, is taken from Joann Jones' interview. The full quote is, "We are who we are, without apology." Her story is the last one in this book.

About the Images Throughout the Book

In an ideal world, we would have higher quality photos available to use in this book. But what we typically have to work with is photocopies and fading, damaged photographs. We used the best photos available to bring you a richer sense of these women's lives.

Contents

❧ ❦

The Stories

Addenda

Introduction

We had a plan. Before the ink was even dry on the first book, *A Gift of Age*, women were asking for more, and we knew we wanted to share more. So we decided that we'd do two more books. Instead of each book sharing a representative sample of the stories in the collection, we thought each book should speak to a theme. The next book would be made up of couples, each of whom had been interviewed for the Project. That would be followed by a book shaped around stories representing women who came out early in their lives, those who were late-bloomers, and the larger group of women who knew early in life, but, for their own reasons, lead a straight life for decades, only to come out again later.

For reasons we'll explain in a moment, this book includes couples and other women, as well. The stories run the gamut. You'll read the words of women who understood from the time they were children that they were different from almost everyone around them. There are stories of women who had their "aha" experience when they were in high school or college. Some married and tried to lead the life expected of them, and others managed to resist. *Without Apology* shares the story of two women who fell in love in college, only to go their separate ways before reconnecting decades later and staying together the rest of their lives. There are stories of women who truly had no hint of their difference until falling in love with another woman. There is even the story of a woman who was cognizant of who she was in her teens, but she married and didn't come out as a lesbian until she was well into her 70s.

Once we caught our breath after the completion of our first book and developing our big plan, we dove right in. The first step was to identify all the couples' stories in the collection. That wasn't a hard task, and it resulted in a lengthy list of names.

However, some of the air went out of our plan when we looked at the story contracts.

Each woman who shares her story has the option of signing an unconditional or a conditional contract. Both contracts establish that the woman is voluntarily sharing her story with the OLOHP, that she is aware that it will be used for research purposes, and that it might be used in various other ways to help promote the Project. The vast majority of the women have signed unconditional contracts. But if a woman isn't quite comfortable about how her story might be used, she can add stipulations. A few women prefer their stories not be used until after their death. Others ask that certain names and places be changed. There are even a few that ask that their story never be used in any way that might identify them.

Approaching our list of couples, from which we would be selecting stories for this book, we were surprised to see how many of them were not usable because one of the two contracts was conditional. The couples list was now much shorter, but we still thought we had plenty of stories with which to work. So, we began a more serious review of the potential stories. It didn't take long to realize that we'd made another false assumption. Our vision of doing a collection of stories from couples included being able to share how they became a couple, and some of their shared experiences from each person's point of view.

It was extremely interesting to find that, even with couples that had been together for decades, often their herstories didn't include much about each other! We quickly realized that it was an assumption on our part, not a failure on the part of the women telling their stories. With only one exception, all of the women had been interviewed independently. (The one exception was when one of the couple was struggling with memory loss, and her partner was able to help keep the story moving forward by providing an occasional name, date, or remind her of a story.)

Looking at the transcripts, it became clear that within a couple, each woman told her own tale in her own way. Some did share about their partners, and for that we are grateful. Otherwise we'd really have to go back to the drawing board!

Of the couples who are in this book, you'll see that we took two approaches. All were fascinating stories that we really wanted to share, but two sets of stories were extremely short. In that case, we combined their stories into one. In the others, we wrote their stories independently, but have positioned them next to each other in the book, so you can easily see how their lives fit together.

We hope you'll enjoy this book, and will share it with your friends and families. Each and every woman in this book has played an important role in our lives, and can in yours, too. They are **influential women**, in the everyday, most valuable sense of the term. By standing up and living the lives they wanted to, they have changed the world around them bit by bit, even when that wasn't their intention. They set an example for a student, provided a positive role model for nieces and nephews, broadened the thinking of someone serving dinner to them in a restaurant, and challenged the stereotypes often held by their employers, doctors, clergy and family members. Each of these women are pioneers, and we thank them all for living their lives and sharing them in a manner that has improved our lives.

About the Authors

Even though their homes are separated by over 2,000 miles, Arden Eversmeyer and Margaret Purcell have worked together as a team on several writing projects for the Old Lesbian Oral Herstory Project over the past decade.

Born in Wisconsin, Arden has lived her adult life in Texas. After retiring from a career teaching and counseling in the public schools, Arden began a second career, volunteering for a variety of organizations and causes. Her volunteer efforts included serving as a docent for the Houston Zoological Gardens for 20 years, acting as the mayor's appointee to the Area Agency on Aging, creating a safe social networking organization for older lesbians in the Houston area, as well as giving birth to and shepherding the Herstory Project.

Margaret has worked at a variety of professions over the years including: cook, farmer, greenhouse grower, retail manager, horticulturist, and writer. Her Pacific Northwest home reflects the gardening expertise of Margaret and her partner, Mary Henry. They have co-authored dozens of feature magazine articles and hundreds of newsletters on plant related topics. Like Arden, Margaret devotes much of her time to volunteer work, doing the desktop design and layout of brochures and newsletters for several organizations. Margaret is president of the Board of Directors of the OLOHP and works closely with Arden on various aspects of the Project.

A Note From Arden

It has been two years since *A Gift of Age: Old Lesbian Life Stories*, went from dream to reality. What a two years! We continue to meet ourselves coming and going, gathering and processing stories, and telling anyone who is willing to listen about the Old Lesbian Oral Herstory Project.

When you start reading through this book, you may be surprised to find my story included in it. Margaret had suggested it be in the first book, and I overruled her. To me, that felt self-serving. But she kept working on me until I've come to see that my willingness to let my story be a part of the book made the other women whose stories are included feel more comfortable. Since she wanted my partner Charlotte's story in this book, she convinced me it made sense to make room for mine. And I can see that including it may also offer the reader more insight into how the Old Lesbian Oral Herstory Project came to be.

The first book, *A Gift of Age*, has been a great addition to OLOHP in many ways, but it also had a complicating effect I hadn't expected. Now, when I initiate a conversation with a women about sharing her story, I often have to reassure her that we are not just gathering stories for another book. I'm afraid we may lose a few stories from women who are put off by our having produced books. We know we are gathering stories to preserve them, to insure their struggles, failures, and successes are there for generations to come. By no means are we capitalizing on their stories. However, explaining all that to potential interviewees has now been thrown into the mix.

Every woman whose story we share has given us full permission twice. The books are being done for one purpose only: in answer to the most common question we get year after year, "How can I read the transcripts?"

Reading actual transcripts will be possible at some point. The OLOHP collection is in the process of being moved from Texas, where I reside, to the Sophia Smith Collection, a preeminent archive of women's history at Smith College in Northampton, Massachusetts. Fifty-plus herstories are already there, and we anticipate the majority of the rest of the collection will be at Smith College by early 2012. Processing and cataloging takes time, but once that is accomplished, many of the transcripts will be available for reading there.

What we hope we have done by writing these books, is to do the research for you. We've read and reread, listened to the interviews, and then listened again. Margaret and I feel we've meticulously pulled pieces from each interview that conveys the essence of a woman's transcript in a story-telling fashion.

Working together on a project, such as writing a book, is a fascinating process. Luckily, the two of us complement each other's strengths and weaknesses, and we are able to resolve any disagreements easily. Maybe that's because Margaret and I have one very unusual fact in common: we were both struck by lightning, literally and figuratively. It may be an incredibly unlikely coincidence, or it may be that our ability to work on such a project together came from something beyond us both.

Given how much has happened in the two short years since *A Gift of Age* was published, I can't wait to see what the next few years will offer.

Arden Eversmeyer

A Note From Margaret

There are projects I take on in life that I can put my nose to the proverbial grindstone and stay with, on task, until completed. Working on this book is <u>not</u> one of those. In fact, going from one step to the next was typically such a circuitous route that I often found myself totally lost. Lost, but better for it.

For anyone who is even somewhat open and curious, the Old Lesbian Oral Herstory Project is rife with bits and pieces that lead one's mind off in one direction, and then another. For anyone trying to accomplish a goal, such as finishing this manuscript, I will testify that the stories can also act as quicksand, sucking you in and not letting go.

How many an afternoon has totally slipped from my grasp. An example was working with Edie Daly's story. Curiosity about things I'd never heard of before lured me off track to learn about: song pluggers in the 1920s, New York coat house models in the 1960s, and life in Sarajevo in the early 1990s. That last one was an eye-opener for me. What could possibly have been so important in my life then that I was barely aware of the conflicts in eastern Europe? The situation there had been so compelling to Edie that she solicited the support of friends and family in order to spend months living with local women in the midst of war-ravaged Bosnia. That led me to look back over other stories in this Project, to find more examples of women stepping outside of their comfort zones, going way beyond what was expected of them.

Working on this book has been such an incredible learning experience for me. I have learned about places, people, and events that I knew little or nothing about. Repeatedly, I was struck by how our early lives are shaped and directed by our families of origin, and just as often by circumstance. In each story, the woman came to one or two crossroads where she opted to take the road less traveled, the road her family and society would not have chosen for her. I am fascinated by the choices, the risks, and the paths these women have taken. The book is filled with stories that, if you let them, will lead you in directions you never thought of going. My advice is to go with them.

Hardly a week goes by that I don't stop to think about how incredibly lucky I am to be a part of this unique project, and to vicariously share such breadth of experiences through the stories. Each time someone asks how I became involved in the OLOHP, I am reminded how my work with Arden did <u>not</u> come out of any big decision I made. I simply happened to be in the right place at the right time. Maybe, as so many of the stories in the collection have shown, I was also in the right place in my life so I, too, could choose to spend the next decade of my life traveling down that road with Arden and the 250-plus women who have shared their stories with us.

I will be eternally grateful to Arden for inviting me to share this journey. Also, there aren't enough words to express how much I appreciate my partner Mary's generosity enabling my immersion in the OLOHP. On occasion, my immersion borders on obsession, and Mary does have to pull me back to reality, which she does gently. When her nephew, Sam, was young, and obsessed with all things baseball, his parents were trying to teach him that he had to listen to everyone else, too. As soon as there was a lapse in conversation, Sam would politely say, "Speaking of baseball…" When I get that way, bringing up some aspect of the book, or a transcription I'm working on, whenever there is a lull in the conversation, Mary will finally look at me and say, with a smile, "Speaking of baseball." She grounds me, and she reminds me that I <u>do</u> have a life beyond the Old Lesbian Oral Herstory Project, one that I need to pay attention to if I want to have a full, and interesting tale to tell when I reach 70!

Margaret Purcell

Is the Old Lesbian Oral Herstory Project New to You?

It occurred to us that not everyone picking up this book is familiar with the Old Lesbian Oral Herstory Project. If that is you, let us tell you a bit about it.

In 1990, Arden Eversmeyer was approached by a student doing graduate work in Texas. She was to do an oral history for a class, and asked Arden, whom she knew socially, if she would participate. Arden, who was then 59, shared her story, was given a copy of it, and stored it away in the back of a file drawer. She didn't even think about it again until someone asked her, years later, if she had ever shared her own story.

Arden had started LOAF, Lesbians Over Age Fifty, a social network for lesbians, in the Houston, Texas, area. As members began to have serious health challenges, she realized that if someone didn't do something, their stories would be forgotten when they died.

Looking around and realizing that she couldn't just wait for someone else to do something about it. Arden learned what she could about the process of gathering oral histories, convinced a friend to be her guinea pig, and jumped right in. There was a steep learning curve, as can be expected, but before long Arden had interviewed a handful of women she knew in the Houston area. Being referred to friends of women who had already shared their stories allowed her to cast a wider net. She took her recorder and began traveling outside the Houston area, and then beyond Texas.

Arden has also been involved in a national organization, Old Lesbians Organizing for Change, OLOC. Up until 2002, Arden had done all the work independently, gathering oral herstories, and absorbing all the expenses. She had shared information about what she was doing with OLOC on a regular basis, and this organization volunteered to act as her project's sponsor. At that point, it became officially known as the Old Lesbian Oral Herstory Project. With some financial support, and an introduction through OLOC's newsletter to women across the country, the OLOHP went from being a part-time hobby to a full-time job for Arden.

Other women have expressed an interest in helping with the Project over the years. Several have conducted some interviews. What they've been willing to do has been very helpful, but, unfortunately, most of them only stayed involved for a year or so. The Project continues to work with new transcribers in hopes that several will find it as compelling as Arden does.

Handling the Project a different way might have made it easier, but Arden has always held fast to her basic structure, believing that structure results in the experience and the story she wants to gather. Her basic structure is this:

- The goal of the project is to document the life stories of lesbians born early in the 1900s. The purpose of preserving the stories is so that those women are not forgotten, and their stories can be used for research in the future.
- Women sharing their stories all identify as women-loving-women at this point in their lives, whether they use the word 'lesbian' or not.
- With few exceptions, women sharing their stories should be 70 years of age and older.
- All the stories are collected through first person oral interviews that are then transcribed.
- Women sharing their stories orally will be given an opportunity to read their written transcripts and offer edits.
- Every woman will be given the option of signing either an unconditional contract, granting the Project use of their story as long as it is presented in a respectful manner, or a

conditional contract, granting some rights, but with some stipulations or exceptions.

* At a bare minimum, all women agree that their story will be included in the OLOHP collection.
* Women will be encouraged to share information about their whole lives, from birth on. They are urged to share as much about their lesbian lives as may be comfortable for them.
* Women are encouraged to provide support documents, such as photographs, articles, graduation programs, and such. Those items will be photocopied and returned to the women as soon as possible.
* All interviewers will have a basic outline of questions/topics from which to conduct the interview.
* Interviewers will all be old lesbians.

While the overall process has been changed slightly, it has basically remained the same. There have been younger lesbians, and even straight women, interested in conducting interviews. Arden believes that what an old lesbian is willing to share with another old lesbian is distinctly different from what would be shared with a younger interviewer, or a straight woman. She also believes it is important for anyone interested in being an interviewer to first be interviewed. The OLOHP continues to do its work in this manner. There are so many stories waiting to be told, as well as many ways to do it, so Arden encourages others who would approach it differently to seek out a better fit with another existing venue, or start a new one.

The Old Lesbian Oral Herstory Project will celebrate its fifteenth birthday in July 2012. In the past few years, it has incorporated, and it has received federal nonprofit status. It continues to have a strong working relationship with OLOC, and is very grateful for their ongoing support. Several new interviewers are now working to help gather the interviews. Arden continues to work hard to find women born in 1930 and earlier, before their stories are lost forever. More and more old lesbians have become aware of the OLOHP, and are reaching out to the Project to share their stories.

A major decision was reached in 2010 when, after two years of investigation, the OLOHP settled on a permanent home for the Project. All the stories and Project records will be archived in the Sophia Smith Collection at Smith College, in Massachusetts. That doesn't mean the Project is finished! We will continue to gather herstories as long as we can. As they accumulate, they are being sent to Smith College, where they will take their rightful place in women's history.

The Project is rapidly approaching a milestone we only dreamed we would see, to have preserved the stories of 250 old lesbians. As time marches on, there are now lesbians reaching 70, the age at which they qualify to be interviewed, who were born during World War II. They, too, have a unique tale to tell, and it is our sincere hope that the OLOHP will continue to thrive for years to come.

Here is an overview of some facts about the women who have shared their stories with the project:

+ There are now more than 250 herstories in the project.
+ The earliest birth date of a woman whose story is in the collection is February, 1916.
+ The oldest woman when interviewed was 90 years of age.
+ The oldest couple when they were interviewed were both 85 years of age.
+ The youngest woman to be interviewed was 65 years of age.*
+ Races represented to date in the collection are predominantly Caucasian/White, but also included are stories from African-American, Hispanic, and Native American women.
+ The women who have shared their stories live all across the United States. There are also a few stories of Canadian

women, and one story from Australia. Birthplace is an even wider distribution, with women born all across the US as well as in England, Russia, Canada, Panama, and India.

+ All classes of family background are represented, from growing up impoverished and on welfare to being raised with household servants.

+ Religions represented in the stories are various Protestant denominations, Catholic, Jewish, Buddhist, Wiccan, and pagan. There are also women who are agnostic and atheist.

+ Educational backgrounds run the gamut, from women who did not complete high school to women who achieved a Ph.D. or M.D.

+ Professions represented include teachers (yes, quite a few of them taught physical education), college professor, nurse, college dean, dancer, administrator, model, prison guard, writer, physician, researcher, probation officer, clerical worker, social worker, missionary, librarian, musician, nun, artist, building contractor, civil servant, and more.

+ A few of the women who shared their stories served in the military during, or shortly after, World War II.

+ Several women were subjected to psychiatric treatment, to "cure" them of their lesbian tendencies; quite a few spoke of seeking mental health help to deal with being a lesbian.

+ The vast majority of the women sharing their stories had been married at some point in their lives. Many had children.

+ The stories reflect wide variations in when the women became aware they were lesbians. Some knew when they were children; others didn't discover, or deal with, their lesbianism until late in life.

* Two slightly younger women were also interviewed as a part of their training to become interviewers. Arden's first interview (done by women outside the Project) was done when she was 59.

The Old Lesbian Oral Herstory Project and Old Lesbians Organizing for Change

OLOC, Old Lesbians Organizing for Change, is mentioned quite a few times in this book, for several reasons. OLOC is unique in its dedication to improving the lives of old lesbians for the past twenty years. For much of that time, it was the only organization devoted to old lesbians, so it isn't surprising that many of the women interviewed for the Old Lesbian Oral Herstory Project were a part of OLOC.

Arden served on the OLOC Steering Committee for 14 years, many of those years as a Co-Director. Although she had developed this project independently, OLOC was aware of her work. It was at an OLOC event in California in 1998 that Arden first sought advice from a woman who worked at a lesbian archive on structuring the project. As the project developed, Arden would occasionally submit excerpts from Herstories to the OLOC newsletter.

OLOC saw the importance of Arden's project, and in 2002, entered into a role of sponsorship of the OLOHP. In addition to providing financial support, OLOC has been able to assist Arden in identifying women who might be willing to share their stories.

The relationship between the two, OLOC and OLOHP, has been greatly beneficial to both.

The Stories

Katharine 'Kittu' Riddle

Born May 1919 in India
Interviewed in 2001, at age 82, in Texas

*It is the responsibility of each
one of us to nourish ourselves.*

*My parents were from rural areas of the United States,
and both of them had an interest in doing work overseas
as missionaries with the Presbyterian Church. In May of
1918, they married and sailed from Vancouver, British
Columbia, across the Pacific, landing in India about the time
of the Armistice, at the end of World War I. They went to
Allahabad where there is an agricultural institute. Daddy
was a teacher there.*

*When it got to be the hot weather the following year,
they went up into the Himalaya Mountains to study. It got
very, very hot in the plains. While they were up there, in the
boarding house studying the language, I was born.*

Kittu and her family returned to the plains region of India
when the rains returned, but when she was three or four, her

father was asked to become principal of Woodstock School, an international school located near where Kittu had been born.

When I was a baby in India, I was left in the care of an ayah, a women who took care of me. She found it very hard to say the name Katharine, and so she started calling me 'Kittu.' I found out it was like a little baby name, like a mom's pet name, and I have heard of one or two other people who are named 'Kittu' who are Indian persons. I have been called that from the time I was six months old, or maybe a year old.

My earliest memories were in the mountains there. I grew up as the daughter of the school principal, which meant that I was treated like a princess. The whole staff knew who I was. All of my childhood, I was aware of that. I was very seldom out of sight, or care, or oversight by someone connected to the school. I was a good little girl.

They all looked out for me, so I could roam the hillsides quite safely. There was usually somebody within earshot. That's what I really loved, time in the hills playing under the roofs of trees or bushes or making houses. We did all kinds of imaginative things.

Dysentery was prevalent in India, and there was no treatment. Sulfa drugs hadn't been developed, and it wasn't uncommon at all for children, who crawled everywhere, and put everything in their mouths, to contract it. Kittu originally had four sisters, but two, Patty and Dorothy, both died from dysentery when very young. Living conditions were less than ideal. Even so, the surroundings were idyllic, and Kittu loved living high in the Himalayas.

We had been living in one of the dormitories. The school had grown quite rapidly, and space was really limited. We finally decided it was time to build a principal's bungalow, and so my high school years were spent there. It was a very nice house. It had room for entertaining. All the parents of the students would come up to the hills during the summers. Mother entertained everybody who came up during the summer, and so we girls were involved in preparing and serving the teas, and helping out. We actually became used to having large groups of people in the house.

The Woodstock School was mainly for missionary children, and it was supported by the missionary board of the Presbyterian Church. But Daddy's vision, from early on, was that it become not only a girls' school. So it soon included boys, and then other religious denominations besides Presbyterian. Eventually it included other religions besides just the Christians, like Hindus, Muslims, and Parsees. There were Catholics, also, at our school. We truly became an international school.

My life there was really a very happy one, until I got older and into high school. Then I became more and more aware that being a principal's daughter sort of set me apart. There wasn't a boy that was going to date the principal's daughter. My classmates were mostly inclusive of me, but some of them just assumed that I was a level above them, and it was a very uncomfortable feeling.

The family had returned stateside twice during Kittu's childhood, once when she was in kindergarten, and again when she was in high school. The second trip was so that her father could pursue his master's degree in education. Otherwise, her entire childhood was spent in India.

I knew that when I graduated from high school, I would have to go back to the states to go to college. I had the choice of which college to go to, and chose Park College at Parkville, Missouri, because it was a Presbyterian school in which all of the students were employed. I liked that. I realized that no matter where I went, I probably would have to work part-time. Being in a place where everybody worked seemed to be more fun.

In the summertime, I had to earn some money. This was 1937-41. The opportunities weren't very great. I would be glad to take board and room at five dollars a month. During my junior year I heard about the YMCA in Estes Park, Colorado,

Kittu, age 17

which was interested in hiring students who were active in the YMCA. I applied and was accepted. It was a great experience, at the time, because we were not only paid well, a dollar a day, we were given leadership training in how to carry out programs.

While I was there, I met Chuck, my future husband, and so it was a wonderful summer. He was attending Oklahoma University and I had to go back to Park College for my senior year. My parents came back from India. Mother came and stayed in my college town. It was a wonderful time, except I had now been away from her for two years, and didn't feel the close bond that we used to have. I wasn't doing anything that she didn't approve of, but it was just that the distance was there. I was growing away from her, and I didn't like that.

I wanted to get married, and we talked about that. She said that she was sorry, very sorry, because she wouldn't be at my wedding. They had to go back to India.

Somehow, Kittu knew that when her mother left to return to India, she'd never see her again. A few months later, when she heard that her mother had died, she was devastated. There was no funeral service for her to attend. A grief-stricken Kittu traveled to where her sister was in college, and there, she received a true gift.

All of a sudden, in the mail came a card. Mother had bought an Indian silk sari for my wedding dress. When they got off the boat, she had arranged with the boat stewardess to deliver the sari to my aunt in Boston, when the boat docked there. That was the most wonderful gift my mother had ever sent me. She remembered!

She and Chuck Riddle married in 1941 in Chicago, where both of them were in college. Kittu was working on her graduate degree. They lived in a poor area of town, in a settlement house, and contributed to the neighborhood as social workers. They were in Chicago when Pearl Harbor was bombed. Kittu clearly remembered traveling in Japan, and it was difficult for her to reconcile the friendly, loving people she'd met with the atrocious acts of war that had just occurred. Men were being drafted and Chuck was given advice by the draft board that if he wanted to continue working as social worker, he needed to go into the seminary. So throughout World War II, Chuck both attended seminary and continued in social work.

By the time the war was over in 1945, Kittu was a mother, and Chuck wanted to be of some service to the country. His idea was to go to China, where he could work in construction. Kittu had been adamant that she did not want to be a minister's wife, or a missionary wife. Next thing you know, they joined the Presbyterian Board of Missions, and headed to California to learn as much Chinese as they could before Chuck went on ahead to China.

I stayed with the parents of my stepmother, and they were very kind to us. I started right in, trying to get passage to China. At that time, they didn't allow wives and children in the country to accompany their husbands, because China was still recovering from the war. By September, I had managed to book passage on one of the ships scheduled to leave October 1st. So I did all the packing that we needed to do and got things loaded up and taken over to the ship. On the night of September 30th, a maritime strike was called, so nothing left the West Coast, and I had to go collect my stuff at the ship and take it back. I didn't know how long the strike would last. They said the ship would leave within four days after the end of the strike. I was stuck waiting. If I went anywhere for two days, I might get back and find that the ship had left without me.

Boarding a ship and leaving was just the beginning. The ship was overloaded. Kittu and her children shared a cabin with 16 other women, and no one got much rest. There were other children on board, but hers were the youngest, and people were helpful. Even so, juggling her children, and all their possessions through the endless lines when they arrived in Shanghai, was exhausting. Chuck was there waiting, and they began the next leg of their journey into China.

Shanghai was in terrible condition, with very cold buildings, and we still had to get to Beijing. The night before we were to leave, three planes crashed at the airport because of fog. So again, our departure was delayed. We finally left about a week later. We were met at Beijing, and taken to the mission compound. In our house, we felt like there were ghosts, as other families had lived there, and their belongings were strewn around. I don't know who occupied the house during the war.

I had studied the language, but I could not speak it well. I began trying to find out how to become more fluent, and I decided to create an experience where all I would hear was Chinese. I invited women whom I had met, nurses

and teachers, to come to tea. I spoke to them in English
and halting Chinese, saying, "I would appreciate it if you
would have all your conversation in Chinese, and just let
me listen." I would speak when I could. They started in and
talked about their homes, their children, and their work.
This was a wonderful experience for me, because that was a
way to become fluent in the Chinese language.

We became a group that met once a month, and I felt that
I was really accepted into their lives as a friend. So that was
my first experience of what is now called a 'support group.' We
really did help each other in solving problems at home.

Kittu and Chuck didn't fully realize what was going on in
China. The Communists and Nationalists were locked in a battle
for control of the country. No one knew, from day to day, which
way the political winds were blowing.

One day, when Chuck and I were having lunch with friends,
a man came to the door with a big black book. He said,
"Every American here must read this." On Tuesday, there
was to be an evacuation of Americans out of Beijing, and we
should be ready by 8 a.m. the next day to be sent back to the
states. If we did not agree, we would be on our own and we
would sign away our rights to the protection of the United
States. We went back to the house, and we were laughing to
ourselves, saying, "We don't want to leave; the Chinese are
our friends, so we need to stay here and help."

The principal of the school, where they were teaching, asked
what the Riddles were going to do. When they said that they
really wanted to stay, he explained that their presence would
put everyone in danger. Understanding the issue in a new light,
they packed what they could take with them, and left. Kittu and
her family reluctantly fled the area, taking a train to where they
could get on a military transport to take them down river.

Chuck was assigned a cot down below, and the children and I were assigned bunks in the officers' quarters. Before we sailed that afternoon, there were crowds of people on the dock. They were Europeans who had fled the Communists once before. They were standing on the docks asking to go, too. Our captain decided to take a hundred of them on board, and the women were assigned to our unit. Of course, we were very glad to accommodate everybody, but it meant that the quarters were very crowded, and we were on that ship for two days.

The ship's officers kept asking us, "Where do you want to go?" We said, "We need to go to Shanghai. Our orders are to go to Shanghai." "We will just have to come to Shanghai and rescue you," they said. "You are just making life more difficult for us."

The family did finally make it to Shanghai, but it, too, was in turmoil, and they spent the next month living like refugees, while trying to decide what to do. The Riddles managed to communicate with a family member back in India. Even though they weren't technically missionaries, they managed to get an invitation and the necessary paperwork to join her. They ended up making their way to India, to start a new chapter of their grand adventure.

We had several invitations from institutions and schools, and accepted an invitation to go to Moga, in the Punjab region, where educators had set up a new school curriculum. It was a school for village children, and also a training school for teachers of village children. The curriculum was such that they learned plants, about crops, planting, seasonings, gardening, about fruits and vegetables, sewing, and how to make shoes. The idea was they were to return to the village. There were many ways in which we could help. We were very happy there.

Suddenly, I realized that my children would be going to the same school that I had gone to up in the mountains. It was an English-speaking school. I was to spend four or five summer months up in the mountains with them. I did not want them to be boarding there, so, for a number of years, I was in charge of all the houses in the mountains, which a lot of the missionary people used. There were thirty different residences. With the help of the watchmen, who were the hill men who actually did the work, I did the supervision of the repairs. Those were interesting years, quite different than anything that I had ever envisioned doing, except that I knew what it was like, because I grew up there. My children all graduated from that school in 1960, 1964, and 1965. We then decided to return to the United States permanently.

Family portrait in 1958

Feelings had begun to change in the Indian government, and non-Indian churches were no longer as welcome. Kittu and her family left India for the last time, and settled in New York. Once there, Kittu dropped in at the Interchurch Center in Manhattan, with the intention of applying for a secretarial position.

That is where I found Gertrude Nyce, who was personnel officer for the Presbyterian board. She said, "Kittu, you've got a master's degree in nutrition, why do you want to be a secretary?" I said, "I don't know what other kind of job to apply for." "Well, there is a job under Agricultural Missions with the National Council of Churches. Why don't you go ask them what they are looking for?" she replied. I did that, and it was a good thing.

Agricultural Missions had for years helped men, by teaching farming to those who did labor on improvement projects in other countries. They had thought about a Home Economist, but never hired one. So I was the first Home Economist hired there, and was asked to respond to requests from all over the world for help in training teachers, getting money, and developing a curriculum.

I went first to Nigeria, in order to meet people and to talk to them about what kind of needs they had in the area of Home Economics and Nutrition. It was my first trip abroad on my own, and I met some very remarkable people. I also got all kinds of ideas as to what could be done.

Kittu spent her time evaluating situations, and helping the different entities that could fill various needs to connect with each other. During her years in India and China, she had garnered a host of skills, and a breadth of knowledge. Now she was putting every bit of it to use, traveling in Nigeria and beyond. In addition to working directly with the native peoples in an area, Kittu also began helping other home economists develop strategies on how to effect change in incredibly challenging conditions. With her guidance, a group of dietitians was able to evaluate what it would take to feed the over-whelming number of Chinese refugees who flooded into Hong Kong after Communist forces won the Chinese Civil War. They brought that information to the government, and got enough food allocated to keep the people nourished, and taught them how to stay healthy.

1967

During this time, her family moved to Morehead, Kentucky, and, as much as she hated to do so, she had to give up her job. When that proverbial door was closed, another opened. President Nixon announced that there would be a White House Conference on Food, Nutrition, and Health, and Kittu was asked to be a conference advisor to the Task Force on Women. It was an amazing experience that connected Kittu with leaders from national organizations, and gave her another chance to impress upon people the over-arching importance of nutrition.

Other doors opened as well. She and another nutritionist were given the opportunity to lead a delegation of U. S. women to the Women's Asian Conference on Hunger, meeting in India. Kittu was also to become involved in shaping the WIC program, a nutritional program for low-income women with young children in the United States. In addition, she worked at evaluating foods for the nutrition they offer. That work was later part of the basis for the RDA, Recommended Daily Allowance, information now found on every package of food marketed in the United States.

The move to Kentucky was also the impetus for periods of personal growth for Kittu. It was becoming more clear that she had spent her life following Chuck, putting his needs ahead of her own.

When we left New York City, and went to Morehead, Kentucky, and I did not have a job, a position linked to what I had experienced, I was discouraged. I had done the right thing, following my husband where he was teaching, and somehow the world didn't seem very fair.

It was a matter of scrounging around and starting over again, and yet it also was a time of spiritual searching. I went up to Grailville, and there I met Mary Daly, this Catholic woman who was a Boston University Professor. She used the concept of 'graduation,' meaning she did not deny that she had been raised in the church, and she had grown beyond that. She said to me, "I hear you have been a missionary." I said, "Yes, and I am considering graduation."

I really felt that the church was no longer useful to me in the way that it had been. I had grown up, had grown beyond the church. Even though I was an elder in the Church at that time, I didn't intend to be there. There was more learning that I had to do. When I went back to Morehead, I was supposed to be at a meeting, and I could not bring myself to go. I got in the car and drove and found myself down the road in the other direction. I said to myself, "Kittu, you better pay attention to what is going on in your life."

Kittu had been thinking a lot about her own spirituality. Her varied life had already exposed her to a diversity of faiths. She had seen all sorts of people who weren't Christian, and nevertheless, were leading admirable lives. Kittu realized that there were lots of ways to live, and to believe, and that every religion has some part of what we look for. She came to believe that, "what we really need isn't religion, it's each other," and that we need to learn from each other.

In 1972, when she found out about an independent studies program she wanted to pursue. Before she could get started, she discovered she had breast cancer. At age 52, Kittu had absolutely no idea what this would mean in her life.

In a little hospital there in Kentucky, not a soul came to talk to me about the operation. I had no knowledge about it. The only people that I knew who had had breast cancer had died. They only kept me in the hospital three or four days, and when I was to go home, I had no idea about what to do with my stitches, or care for myself, or anything. After I recovered, I went to the National Cancer Society for help. Even then, the doctors didn't want us, as volunteers, to talk to women with breast cancer before their operations, because we would get them upset. We said that was exactly the point, that women needed more information. We really had to work hard, and show them that we had something to say. That was very important work that grew out of my dilemma.

I was accepted into graduate school, and started working on how nourishment happens in a living system. That became my study for two years. I was able to read, write papers, and attend seminars. I studied with a professor at the University of Kentucky. I also met with a psychologist who taught group psychology. It was a very important time in my life.

Then I knew I had to go to apply for a job and I really was at a loss, because I didn't want to. I realized that I would have to go to Washington, D.C., as I had worked very closely with the International Agriculture Department of the United States. I went there, and saw Helen Strouv, whom I had worked with. She said, "Well, before we even talk, I'm just heading over right now to Ruth Leverton's retirement party,"

Ruth Leverton is a Nutritionist who I met while I was doing my master's degree in Chicago. She had helped me on a number of different occasions. She was retiring as the second in command of the United States Department of Agriculture, so this was a big step.

I went there and I realized, when I went up to see her, that I was walking through a crowd of all the nutritionists whose doors I had thought I would have to knock for inter-views, or intended to send copies of my resume. I went up to Ruth and she said, "Well, what brings you to Washington right now?" I said "I have just finished my Ph.D." "You want a job?" she asked. "Yes." So she turned to the entire crowd and said, "Quiet everybody, quiet, quiet. Here is Katharine Riddle, just finished with her Ph.D., and she needs a job. Who's got a job for Katharine Riddle?"

That's how I got a job. Just like that. I didn't have to fill out an application, or anything. You couldn't have a better recommendation.

Next stop, Penn State College. Kittu was now to be teach-ing courses, and serving as the college nutritionist. The move meant that she would, once again, be living apart from Chuck. The job, and the time away, gave Kittu time to turn her question-ing mind to another idea that had been working away inside her.

During my doctoral work, I had it pointed out to me that women historically nourish others, they do not nourish themselves. It is the responsibility of each one of us to nourish ourselves, and there is a lot more to it than that. We do have to take responsibility for ourselves, our bodies. I had been thinking, "I really do wish that there was a place that women could meet to talk with other women about this."

While she was living and working in Pennsylvania, spending time pondering the concept of women nourishing themselves, one of her daughters, who lived in nearby New York City, called, needing her.

My oldest daughter, Dorothy, who had been teaching at Staten Island College, a part of the University of New York, had become quite ill, and I went to take care of her. She had said that there were three groups of women on the faculty: one was married women who left the campus at five o'clock to go home to care for their families, one was radical leftists, who wouldn't help, and one was the lesbians. She said, "Out of all those groups, the only group that has been helpful to me is the lesbians."

I realized that, in going there, I was probably going to meet the lesbians, and I had not consciously ever met a lesbian before, that I could remember. I had been there two or three days, and I was sitting in the living room talking to some of the women. I looked around the room and thought to myself, "Oh my goodness, I'll bet every women in this room with me is a lesbian. What do I do?" I was scared. I was afraid of saying the wrong thing. I was afraid of doing the wrong thing. I had no idea what to say. I was just scared. I didn't know what to expect.

I tell this story, because I want people to know that that was my beginning with lesbians. I felt sorry for lesbians. I really thought that their lives must be very miserable, because they did not fit into society. I didn't know whether I could do anything about how they felt. That was my introduction to it.

That idea surfaced again, about women nourishing themselves. Now that she saw how that group of lesbians had cared for her daughter and also nourished each other at the same time, Kittu began to imagine a place where women could go to learn from each other, and teach each other, a nourishing place. And the idea kept growing.

Chuck had continued working in Kentucky, and decided it was time for him to make a change, too. Together, they sold their home there, and began to think about what came next. Kittu had saved some money, and, along with the funds from selling their house, they began looking for land, land that would be the home for Kittu's dream, A Nourishing Place.

That was the beginning of our eventually getting a divorce, because having a man on women's land wouldn't work. Within the year, we did get divorced. I went back and taught at Penn State College, for awhile. When I came back, Esther Pashek and I rode back together.

I was there on that land in the desert of Arizona for three years. About 1,000 women came and went, learning to nourish themselves. It was while I was there, that I was attracted to a woman named Cathy, and found that being with her was very enjoyable. Being on the land was a kind of eye opener for a lot of different women.

We did succeed, I feel, in having women, heterosexuals and homosexuals, get to know each other, and be able to contribute to Nourishing Space. One of the things we talked about a lot, important to all of us, was how we thought about our lives and how we thought about people who were different from ourselves. I had a lot to learn about the business of unity.

One woman introduced me to Margot, who was looking for something. Her marriage was unhappy, and there came a time when she moved in with me. She and I were there together for about a year, before I ran out of money. I had not found a partner to help with the finances for the land, and that was one of the major obstacles to having the land. So I had to tell the Advising Committee that, unless somebody else was going to help, within six months I would have to sell.

At the end of 1978, we sold the land. Margot and I moved to Tucson and found a house that we could buy. Living there, we needed to get jobs. I was not ready to go back to teaching. When I looked back on it, I did have three wonderful years living with women, and there was nothing quite as wonderful as that. To get back into the grind of realistic life was something that I wasn't ready for—yet.

Instead of going directly back into teaching, Kittu opted to spend some time working as a nutritionist. One of the projects that captured her attention was the sharp decline in the number of women who breastfed their babies. In 1940, almost all women breastfed, but, now, it was down to less than one out of four who did. Kittu helped develop programs on the Papago Indian reservations that would begin to change that trend.

When her daughter contacted her about a job opening at the University of Nebraska, Kittu made another career change. She took a position where 25% of her time was spent working with women in the International Program. Word had come out of Washington, D.C., that more effort needed to go toward women and their role in agricultural programs in other countries. It challenged Kittu, who felt this wasn't really her field of expertise. Again, applying the various lessons she'd learned over the years served her well.

Fortunately, Margot was also able to transfer to Lincoln, Nebraska. Kittu stayed at the University of Nebraska and worked on the program for a few years before retiring, but recognizing that she wasn't done yet, she reached out in another direction.

I still felt the need for getting together with women, but there was no place where they could go. I made up some flyers, and tacked them around the campus saying, "Tea and Talk for Any International Women, come to my house." I gave an address, and signed it, and women came on Friday afternoons, just to share experiences. It was, of course, open to any women who wanted to be there. You didn't have to be international. "Tea and Talk" really filled a great need, and we developed a common bond.

Margot's job required her to relocate to San Antonio, Texas, so she and Kittu moved again. By now, developing community wherever she was had become a priority. Kittu had been thinking about women sharing their stories with each other, so she started a project called Story Letters.

When she was 68, Kittu heard about a conference being held specifically for old lesbians on the west coast, and off she went. There she met Shevy Healey. Over the next few years, as Old Lesbians Organizing for Change, OLOC, started to grow, Shevy kept in touch with Kittu, and got her involved. Shevy also introduced her to friends from OLOC who lived in Houston, Arden and Charlotte. "How do you find other lesbians? One

Margot and Kittu in 1991

leads to another! You never quite know who you're going to meet next." That works for Kittu, because she doesn't think others look at her and identify her as a lesbian.

I never felt that people could identify me, and I probably feel safer that way. I do know that when I go to certain groups, I am pointed out that way. One of those groups is the reunions of Woodstock School, which are held annually, someplace in the United States. I have been to two or three of those over the years, and I am sure that all of my friends there know of the change in orientation I have been through. That doesn't mean that I have lost friends. It just means they don't know how to talk to me anymore, or they think that I have changed. But it makes it interesting.

Last summer, when I went to the school reunion in Fort Collins, and wanted to sell copies of my autobiography, A Nourishing Life, *I wondered what might happen. I sold fifty copies, so that was pretty good! Pretty good acceptance, and nobody came up to me and said, "How dare you!" or anything like that. Actually it's a pretty accepting group, and I am really pleased about that. I did have people come up to me and say secretly, "Changed my lifestyle, too." They were not out, but it was nice to be the recipient of that confidence, too.*

Retirement didn't mean slowing down in other areas of her life, either. When she got an invitation from People to People International to join a women's study group that was going to South Africa, she quickly signed on. She and Margot both went as delegates, meeting leaders in the African National Congress of South Africa and touring the area, learning of various women's projects.

We found that the women were doing a great deal of supporting each other. We discovered, of course, that there were four or five lesbians in the group and we certainly did enjoy them.

One of the women who looked the most dyke-ish, with a flat hair top, was the one who was the most loving and giving person in the whole delegation. I don't know if she was aware of it, but she did more to raise friendliness towards lesbians than anybody I know. She was so understanding of people, took time to talk to them, and to listen to them. It surprised me, because it changed my idea about dykes. It was very much a learning experience for me.

A variety of projects keep Kittu busy now. She's doing her best to divest herself of personal files and materials that will go to archives, and moving other items along to family and friends who are interested. As those types of projects do, they've led her to think a lot about how the world runs, about living systems, and different kinds of nourishment. She wonders about food being processed in a system, and how it is turned over into something new. That something new might be seeds within the body, or ideas that are there, unformed.

People don't realize, with every bite you eat, you are a different person. Information you take in makes you a different person. You are a different person, or should be, with every social contact. Part of the process is getting rid of what you don't need. If you don't get rid of what you don't need, there is no room for anything new.

Kittu now lives in Arizona with her partner, Margot.
You can learn much more about Kittu's life in her autobiography,
A Nourishing Life. It can be obtained through various vendors
found on the internet. ISBN #978-1571971838

Interviewer: Arden Eversmeyer

Shaba Barnes

Born December 1935 in New York
Interviewed in 2003, at age 68, in Arizona

There was no mistaking me now. I was free.

I remember growing up during the time of the Second World War. The country and my surroundings, for sure, were experiencing a depression. I was born and raised in Brooklyn, New York. We lived in a three-story tenement. Sometimes I heard my folks speak about 'The Depression,' about the hard times we were living in. I did not feel the effect of it because I had nothing to compare it to, and because I never went hungry. We had clothes to wear, a comfortable place to live, and lots of love.

My grandparents had thirteen children. Eight of them lived within four blocks of us. My mother was the oldest daughter, and our home was a meeting place. Our home was usually noisy, filled with laughter, children crying, and people talking. There was never a place to be quiet, or alone.

A unique thing about our family was that we were black Jews. As I remember the story, my grandparents were servants to a wealthy Jewish family name Lapidus, who lived in Elizabeth City, North Carolina. My grandfather was a lumberjack, and my grandmother did domestic work. Because she had lots of children, many of them were allowed in the main house, to be near her during the day. The family was Orthodox, and my grandmother learned to cook and clean the Orthodox way. She learned to keep a kosher household, observe the Jewish holidays and the Sabbath.

The Lapidus family did not stop at teaching my grandmother their way of cooking and cleaning. They also taught the entire family the history of their religion, and why they did most things. They taught my grandmother that, based on her looks and stature, we were a part of a tribe of black Jews called Yemenites. My grandfather was Native American and white, so they addressed my grandmother specifically about her history. They told the family that her people were a Bedouin tribe from the Middle East who raised sheep, and traveled far. They were traveling in the northern parts of Africa, when some of our ancestors were captured, and brought to this country. Because our ancestors were in the wrong place at the wrong time, they were caught by those who wished to prosper by selling slaves in the New World.

My grandparents worked for the Lapidus family in the South during the early twentieth century, in the midst of racial segregation and Jim Crow laws. They learned that our skin color, and heritage, was not something to be ashamed of, that families must work and stay together. They also practiced love and godliness. They taught my grandparents and my aunts and uncles that freedom is internalized, and we did not have to believe the ugly lies of others about us.

In hindsight, I thank the Lapidus family, because they did give my family a sense of pride that many blacks did not experience, at that time. They taught my folks the Hebrew language, we practiced the religion, the spiritual beliefs, and

*especially all of the kosher dietary laws. Besides my grand-
parents, the jewels of the teachings fell on the ears and hearts
of my mother, the oldest child, and my Uncle Fred, the oldest
son, who became a rabbi. He later became the spiritual leader
of a synagogue called The Temple of Israel, in Brooklyn, New
York, in the early 1950s.*

*When my mother and many of her siblings married,
they all moved to Brooklyn. This was the family that I was
born into. Friday nights, the house was full of people. It was
a spotlessly clean apartment, candles were burning, and
prayer and food filled us all. The women and children wore
clothing to cover their entire bodies, except their faces. The
men wore black pants and white long-sleeved shirts. They
also wore black and white shawls, and something around
their waists similar to a scarf, or belt, with strings hanging.
As a small child, it was lots of fun. When I got older, it was
embarrassing.*

In some ways, Shaba's life was like most children of that era.
Her father was a gentile, what non-Jewish people were called.
He was a laborer who worked in a factory, and was gone to work
most days. Her mother did most of her work in the home, and
took on extra jobs to help out even more. Shaba was the middle
of three children, with a brother ten years her senior, and a
sister five years younger than herself. She came from this strong
family, and her childhood presented some serious challenges.
Her mother's rules were very strict, and her family's lifestyle
kept Shaba from feeling like she fit in with her peers. Even when
going to her public school, she wore long dresses, had a kerchief
tied under her chin, her legs were covered, and she wore closed-
toed shoes.

*By the time I was eleven or twelve years of age, my mother
and father had separated. My father began taking me out
to his home to spend some time with him. I never saw it*

going on, but I believed that he was also a gambler. He had rolls of money, and his was the newest car in the neighborhood. He liked to take my sister and me, with our friends, to Coney Island, an amusement park in Brooklyn. He would buy us sweets until we got sick. He taught me to tap dance, unbeknownst to my mother, and then he would show me off to his friends by having me tap dance for them. I loved it.

My mother used to get angry, and say that he spoiled me. He danced in clubs and theaters. My mother never attended a movie in her life, so she would not let any of us children frequent such a place, even with our father. They were such opposites. I don't know how they stayed together as long as they did.

All of the cleaning and housework was not done by my mother. I spent many days on my knees, cleaning woodwork and floors. I often felt like Thursday's child, full of woe. As the oldest daughter, I had to help my mother with a lot of household chores, learning to cook and to do things that I had not the slightest interest in, from the beginning.

Then there were Saturdays, when many of the kids on my block got to go to parks and movies, or just play in the street. Not me. That was our Sabbath, and we stayed in temple all day. It might have been okay, but we lived in a neighborhood where we were the only black Jews, and you know how other children treat you when you appear different. I tried my best to blend in.

After awhile, my mother gave in. I cried constantly. I was so unhappy that I had to look so funny all the time, and the kids made fun of me. I even got a few girls together. We formed a quartet, and began singing at different churches.

My mother finally allowed me to attend various churches with my friends on Sundays, so I could socialize with them a little. I was not interested in the religions. It was just fun and a social time for me. I went to Catholic, Baptist, and

Pentecostal churches, and others, all that had services on Sundays. Saturdays, of course, I attended our temple.

After a while, her mother loosened the rules a bit, but she still had to wear long dresses, and keep most of her self covered. Shaba was now able to go without a scarf on her head, and that made things better.

As I got older, it became harder and harder to hide my shape, even under all the clothing. I did think of kissing a girl in my first grade class, but I never told her.

I heard my mother and uncle talking one day, about a boy that attended the temple. They were saying that he was a good boy, and would make a fine husband for me one day. I grew up with that boy, and wasn't about to marry him. He was like a brother to me.

When Shaba was high school age, there was another young man spending lots of time in their home. His mother worked, and Shaba's family took care of him after school.

One day, we were home alone, and he showed me some cleaning fluid. He told me to sniff it. I was inquisitive, so I did. I passed out. When I came to, I realized that something had happened. My clothes were disheveled, and I felt unclean. I wasn't sure what he had done, but I knew that it was wrong. I also knew that my mother would kill him, and me, if I told her what I suspected. So I said nothing.

I liked him before that happened, but afterwards I was so ashamed and angry that I couldn't stand to see him. He left the neighborhood when his family moved. My mother had not taught me anything about sex or pregnancy. When I got morning sickness, I thought my mother was trying to poison me. I tried not to eat, and cried constantly.

Shaba was pregnant, severely depressed throughout, and for weeks after the baby was born. Lying in bed one morning when the baby was about three months old, she remembers hearing a booming voice, which she later realized had come from within herself, commanding her to get out of bed. Galvanized into action, Shaba got an aunt who lived down the street to watch the baby, and went out and found a job at the telephone company that very day.

With various family members pitching in to help care for her son, Clifford, Shaba became close friends with the nursing student, Betty, from her mother's workplace, Kings County Hospital. They began spending time together, and one day, when they were supposedly going to learn to play golf, the guys took them, instead, to the Muslim mosque. Shaba said, "In many ways, it was similar to the Jewish temple. The women wore long-sleeved dresses to the floor. Some even wore white uniforms." The teachings were similar to what she knew from Judaism, Arabic sounded similar to Yiddish, their books were read from back to front, and the foods were similar. They did not eat pork or shellfish and they prayed six to eight times a day, facing east. It felt welcoming to Shaba. "My favorite part was that the women and men were separated, and even went in separate doors," she explained. Shaba and her best friend, Betty Shabazz, began attending the mosque regularly.

When Shaba was 18 years of age, she moved out of her mother's home, and she found a room nearby. Her aunt kept Clifford during the week days, her mother kept him evenings, and Shaba had him on the weekends, and on her days off. Life settled into a routine of working, going to the mosque, and raising her son.

This went on for a few years. In the meantime, Betty married the minister of the temple, Malcolm X. Then there was a push to marry me off. I had enjoyed hiding my feelings for

*women, while spending all of my time with the sisters from
the mosque. We took trips together, we slept in the same bed,
and showered together. I thought that was the best it could
get. It never occurred to me that I could have a relationship
with a woman.*

Members of the mosque introduced Shaba to a man they
thought would make a good husband for her, and she saw him
several times. At a point when they'd talked on the phone often
but were barely dating, he asked her to marry him. "I accepted
his proposal of marriage. Why? Because I wanted to get away, to
have a new experience," she said. Thinking that he would be good
to her, that she would finally have a home, and be able to care for
her own son, she moved to Philadelphia, where he lived and had
a business. She began planning for her wedding, and thought
every woman's dream was about to come true for her.

*After the wedding, when we went home, he took me to the
room he stayed in. I had never kissed this person, and now
I was expected to sleep with him. Not only that, he owned
a service station, and I smelled gasoline. I had not even
changed my clothes, and still had my wedding outfit on.
When he went into the bathroom, I bolted. I simply turned
around, grabbed my suitcase, and ran. "This is not right,"
I thought. No way was I getting involved with this person
who I did not know. I was not attracted to him. We had
nothing in common. What had I done? I was embarrassed,
bewildered, and in shock. I didn't know where to run.*

In a town that was new to her, and without any friends,
Shaba ended up wandering the streets until she was so tired that
she stopped, and fell asleep on a park bench. Luckily, a woman
found her the next morning, and directed her to a nearby shelter.

*I didn't know it at the time, but a religious group that helped
young people owned it. Everyone was nice. The place was*

clean. The men stayed on one floor, and the women on another. The rates were reasonable, and the food was good. What I couldn't stand were the sermons piped into my room.

Eventually, with her marriage annulled, Shaba returned to the mosque in Philadelphia. She could face the gossip and stares there, but wasn't ready to go back to the questions and the stares of New York. She did some bookkeeping in Philadelphia, but when a friend told her she could get back into the telephone company, she went back to New York. She also picked up another bookkeeping position for awhile.

I quit my bookkeeping job to work at the post office for the Christmas holidays. I remember the first night that I reported to the parcel post station, located on 3rd Avenue at the waterfront. It was during the Christmas rush. I wore a business suit, stockings, and two-inch high heels. The men had a good laugh. I had to lift boxes my size, learn how to drive a crane, and stay alive and warm. The men resented me, the first woman on their shift, and challenged me constantly. I had to become one of them to gain their support and have someone to watch my back when needed.

Shaba had also returned to the Muslim mosque she'd been attending earlier. She had gotten a taste of teaching classes, at the mosque while in Philadelphia. Enjoying it, she began to do the same back in New York. As part of the teaching, she participated in trips. On an excursion to Chicago, Shaba struck up a conversation with Louis, a Muslim man that was a fellow teacher, and was surprised when he made a comment about her sexuality.

He said, "I know that you have a little boy in you." I was shocked, and relieved. I had tried to bury my feelings for women so deep that it was burdensome. When he said that, even before I replied, I felt relief. I did not deny it.

People had been after Louis to marry, and he suggested he and Shaba marry to keep others from pressuring them. Shaba wanted another child, and this man liked her son. Shaba felt he'd be a good husband, and agreed. A few months after they were married, Shaba was pregnant, and Louis, her husband, was off to Cuba, where he had a job working with Fidel Castro. He tried to get her to go with him, but she wasn't interested. Instead, she stayed home, working, pregnant, and caring for Clifford. Louis returned about a week before Shaba's baby was born.

The love I thought I had for him was gone, but I was determined to make the most of this marriage. Muslims do not believe in separation or divorce. I did not want to disappoint my family anymore. So here I was, taking care of the house and children by day, working for the phone company at night.

He began to mistreat me. I was constantly tired. I had to make eight course dinners every day. I made bread for every meal, home-made soup, never anything from a can.

Once, my brother came over to wash the windows and clean the floors for me. Louis came home and started a scene. Men were not allowed in the presence of a woman alone, unless they were married. Not even family members. It was embarrassing, and hurtful. My brother never returned.

I began to stand up for myself. We started arguing, and once he slapped me. That was the last straw. I hit him back. I pushed him down the stairs. He wasn't badly hurt. I knew what I had to do. He left the house one morning. When he returned, I was gone. I had found an apartment, and arranged for someone to move me. I told no one, at first, where I was moving, to make sure he could not find me. I could not go back to the mosque because they would take his side, and I would not be allowed to speak or associate with any members for a year or more.

Around the same time this was happening, my father died. It was too much for me. I became very depressed. I had another aunt keep my children while I worked. Other than that, I did not even visit my mother, who blamed me for my marriage not working. I grieved for several months. I had lost my father, whom I adored, my marriage, and even my religion had turned against me.

I didn't know it at the time, but my mother was very worried about me. One day, my butch cousin called, and said she was coming to visit. I remember being afraid of her when I was a child. She never looked like the women I knew. She smoked, drank, talked loud, said bad words, and wore t-shirts and pants, like men. I had not seen her for many years, except at my father's funeral, so I thought it was odd when she called.

She brought a bottle of Mogen David kosher wine, the kind we drank at Passover. She spent the entire weekend with me. At first we talked about my dad, then other members of the family. I fixed a nice dinner, and she played with my children. I was enjoying her company. I began to lighten up. The next day she told me the purpose of her visit.

My mother had called and told her that she thought it was time for her to have 'that' talk with me. My father had asked my cousin to be there for me when I needed her. My mother and father both knew that I was a lesbian long before I could even grasp such a concept. All of these years, I had suppressed my feelings, and covered them up with situations that victimized me. My cousin also shared with me about the other family members who had lesbian relationships. I couldn't believe it.

The saddest thing was that my mother and father knew about me all this time. My mother watched me struggling to figure out my life, and said nothing. I became very angry.

Shaba, third from left, out with friends at age 28

An aunt had also made a comment to Shaba that indicated she recognized Shaba as a lesbian, but she wouldn't talk about it further. Shaba's life changed drastically, as she dealt with what she saw as her family's lack of help, and began to spend time with her cousin.

My cousin introduced me to one of her friends. My entire persona changed. No longer was I the Muslim housewife and mommy. There was no mistaking me now. I was free. Of course, it pained my mother to witness this metamorphosis, but she stuck by me. She cried when she saw that I had cut off all my hair.

Finding the gay community turned out to be easy for Shaba. "I think that it found me. Since I was usually dressed in the butch style, it was easy for women to approach me," she said. Shaba's first serious involvement came quite by chance.

I began to spend time with a coworker. One evening, after work, she came home with me. We had dinner, and a few drinks. It was getting very late, and I was tired. She talked and talked. Finally, I said that she was invited to spend the night with me, but I only had one bed, so she had to sleep with me. She said that was okay. She was my first live-in relationship.

Over the next few years, Shaba was in and out of a couple of relationships, and decided she didn't want anything serious again. But as things happen, life didn't go according to her plans. Once again, Shaba started spending time with a coworker.

Sandy, a friend, came to my house one day with one of her coworkers, Terra. She told me right away that Terra was not gay, that she was married with children. They were doing a door-to-door survey for the University of Chicago on sanitation. I barely talked to Sandy, because I couldn't help watching Terra. Terra seemed to be attracted to me, also. Later that evening I heard a knock on my door. It was Terra. "Why not? I know that it cannot be serious, as I don't want a relationship. We will just have some fun," I thought. Wrong again.

We fell in love. It was the deep, aching "can't-live-with-out-you" love. We spent all of our free time together. We were both working the second shift. She would spend the night at my house, and go home in the morning, after her husband had gone to work, to care for her children.

She and Shaba were together almost constantly. But things fell apart when Terra's husband had her followed, found out what was going on, and insisted Terra take her kids with her. "She brought them to my house for several days. Those three boys, and one girl, were the most unruly children I had ever met," Shaba felt. Shaba's own kids were spending much of their time with her mother, or Lillie, a friend of her mother's, who lived nearby. Nothing was easy. Terra kept coming and going in Shaba's life until she finally showed up pregnant. Terra wanted to stay with Shaba. Despite pressure from her friends, Shaba took Terra in. Once the baby was born, Terra's husband began stalking Shaba, threatening her life.

Shaba at age 40.

The stress was just too much. In addition to working, raising her own children, and the corrosive relationship she was in, Shaba had also been trying to complete some college courses. It just wasn't working. Shaba knew that as long as she stayed in New York, it would not get any better.

An opportunity arose, and Shaba moved to Los Angeles to finish her education. She was working for an airline at the time, and left thinking she would come back frequently. Her mother took it hard, and when Shaba told her she was taking her children, her mother was devastated. But it was something Shaba had to do. "A new me began to emerge. I took speech classes to get rid of my Brooklyn accent. I softened my wardrobe, and I took evening classes at UCLA."

Lillie had cared for Shaba's children in New York, along with her own two daughters. When she moved to California, Shaba's mother talked Lillie into moving with Shaba. Lillie was a nurse who had befriended Shaba's mother, and also took care of Shaba's grandmother from time to time. Shaba's mother reasoned that they could have their children there together, and help each other. Even though it didn't start out that way, over time a relationship developed between them.

Shaba was befriended by a feminist college instructor, and became very involved in the women's movement, to the extent that school fell to the wayside for a while. She became secretary to the local chapter of NOW, a member of the Feminist Theatre, a radical acting group, and joined a writer's group.

As part of the Feminist Theatre, Shaba starred in a play called *Angela's Happening*, a play designed to raise awareness of imprisoned activist Angela Davis' situation, and to raise funds to help free her. Shaba went one step further, pressuring NOW to throw their support behind Angela Davis' fight for freedom. This experience led her in a new direction.

A few years later, I went back to school. This time, I attended Santa Monica City College, a two year college, where I majored in Criminal Justice. I graduated from there. I had it in my mind to become a law officer, as I wanted to help right the wrongs of the criminal justice system. I wanted to have a positive influence on the women in the system. I felt I could do that from the inside. The things that motivated me were the several bad experiences that I had had with police.

When I graduated from the Police Academy, I was assigned to Sybil Brand, the Los Angeles county jail for women. I soon learned that I was not going to make a difference in that way. The women inmates quickly learned that they could play me for sympathy. Someone was always sick, crying with pain, reaching out, and begging me for help. Just about everyone I worked with warned me to ignore them. I began having nightmares every night, constantly hearing the doors being slammed shut, and keys rattling. The poor treatment of the women was overwhelming. I couldn't take it. I resigned.

Shaba had maintained a habit of having two jobs at once. When she quit her jail job, she was still working with the airlines. Going back to a more peaceful routine, Shaba didn't know she was about to experience another pivotal moment in her life.

Graduating as president of her ministry school class in 1980

I went to a church on a Wednesday evening with a friend. As I listened to the speaker, I realized, for the first time in my life, someone was articulating exactly what I had come to believe. I became excited. I started going to church at every opportunity. There were speakers from all denominations and callings. Although it came under the heading of Christianity, it embraced a philosophy that accepted all truths. It is the metaphysical teaching called Religious Science, or Science of Mind. It is also commonly known as a New Thought religion.

After many years, I had found a teaching that I wanted to share. I studied everything that I could about this teaching. I took every class, and attended all the meetings. I enjoyed taking people with me to church. I wanted to introduce them to the teachings. I became a practitioner, a two-year training process. The only classes that I did not plan to take were classes for the ministry. I didn't plan on becoming a minister at that time, but I wanted to learn more. So, after three more years of in-depth training, being voted president of the class for the last two years, being made the first woman sergeant at arms at our yearly conferences, earning the honor of being valedictorian for the 1980 graduation, I became Reverend S.A. Barnes, Minister at Large.

I was assigned the title of Minister at Large, because I wanted to be able to travel, move around, and meet different people. I had a study group, and took over a church prior to graduating. The experience was good, but I realized that I did not want to be tied down week-after-week at the same church. As a Minister at Large, I was able to go on assignments to cities where they needed an interim minister for various reasons. I loved it. I was sent to Hawaii to help start a church on the windward side of Honolulu.

I thought that this was a dream, and I enjoyed it for a while. I stayed in Hawaii for three months. I went alone. Maybe it was the combination of missing my family, the quiet living near the great Pacific Ocean water edge, or the humongous bugs, but I was glad to get back to the mainland. During this time, I was still on the books at the airlines. Once, I even took a leave of absence for a year. I was getting tired of it though.

Looking for another change, and another challenge, Shaba took a new job that paid her $14 less per hour than her airline position. The job spoke to her. Lillie had introduced Shaba to the director of nursing at Kaiser Permanente, where Lillie worked. The woman believed Shaba, as a minister, could bring some peace to an embattled work atmosphere.

Shaba stepped out of her financially secure life, into the unknown. She was given the job of assistant to the administrator, which included acting as their chaplain. The administrator was new to the job. The previous person to hold that position had been shot and killed at her desk by a disgruntled employee.

There was a time in my life when I felt that I was a protector of women. I would escort them to public arenas, where the controversy might become physical. I once escorted Aileen Hernandez, then the President of NOW. The new hospital administrator knew this, and I also became her escort.

Shaba stayed with Kaiser for the next 15 years, and her responsibilities changed over the years. This fit into a pattern that developed in Shaba's life: 15 years at the phone company, 15 years at the airline and 15 years at Kaiser.

As long as her mother was alive, Shaba made regular trips back to New York. She took her mother on trips to San Francisco, Hawaii, and Jamaica, and even had her come live with her in California for six months every year.

Despite plans to return to New York on a regular basis, that wasn't how things turned out. Shaba went back only once after her mother died, and that was to a family reunion.

Shaba had been estranged from her sister for years. "My sister stopped speaking to me when I started dressing masculine, and cutting my hair short. She did not approve of my lifestyle, and that was her way of showing it," Shaba explained. When their mother fell ill and was dying, she made the two promise they would be there for each other as sisters. Despite agreeing, they didn't stay in touch after the funeral.

Totally unexpected, a family wedding finally brought Shaba and her sister back together. "It wasn't until my daughter's wedding that I saw her again," she said. The mother of the groom, a born-again Christian, acted out, refusing to set foot in Shaba's house, when she was told Shaba was a lesbian.

My sister, who not too many years before had snubbed me for the same reason, spoke to the groom's mother, and questioned her righteousness in shunning her sister, who only wanted everyone to feel welcomed. I learned about this later in the day. After that, my sister and I became close. We talked on the phone each week, sent cards, and bridged the gap that had existed for so many years.

Through all her career moves, relationships, and spiritual studies, activism had always played a role in Shaba's life. But not always in the expected way. She'd been active in union leadership while at the phone company, and had been part of a class action suit against United Airlines when she'd been told, "only men could hold a certain position."

As soon as she'd gotten to California, Shaba had become very active in NOW, serving in leadership on a local level, and attending an International Conference for Women held in Mexico City in 1975. Despite limited knowledge of Spanish, she was able to use her skills in centering one's thoughts and energies to help resolve conflicts between the Spanish-speaking women and others. Months after returning home, Shaba received a letter, in Spanish, on official government letterhead, nominating her to serve as representative to the World Conference of the International Federation for the Formation of the Permanent Integration of Women in Mexico! Shaba said, "I was over-whelmed. I found lots of excuses for not accepting it, and I graciously turned them down. I was honored."

Slowly, her activism also came to include advocating for lesbian rights. Her first step into that arena came about the same time Shaba had become a minister, and was working hard at her new job at Kaiser.

The gossip mill is very active in most hospitals. Once I had a secretary who was pretty new at the medical center ask me if I was gay. My response to her was, "Are you interested?" She took that as a 'yes' from me.

Sometime later, maybe a week or more, I spoke to her about being away from her desk, and taking longer breaks. She got angry, and went to the administration. She told the administrator that I was a lesbian, and that I had a lot of women coming to my office. The administrator told her that she was hired to do a job, not to cause trouble.

She still was not satisfied, so, in the cafeteria, she began talking about me again, telling others that I was a lesbian. My personal physician was there, and responded by telling her how vicious she sounded talking about me that way.

Some others, who heard, let her know that they did not appreciate her gossiping about me that way. I never said a word to her about it. Many people stopped speaking to her. They put a freeze on her, and ignored her to the point that she resigned.

I did not know, until I got a new secretary, that she had written a hate letter about the hiring of lesbians and gays in the hospital. She left it in the computer. The new secretary found it. Totally outing me like that worked to my advantage. It became hard to do my administrative work, because I spent so much time counseling employees, gay and straight.

Shaba's job at the hospital also drew her into other forms of activism. She was in charge of the volunteer program, as well as blood drives, the gift shop, the chaplain program, the senior center, and more. She also established a lesbian and gay group. "Lillie and I were active in the growth of that organization. We like to feel that we were instrumental in getting the domestic partnership benefits for all of Kaiser's members," Shaba said.

Over the years, Shaba sometimes questioned her own involvement with NOW, and other organizations she belonged to. NOW was perceived as an organization of primarily white, middle class women. Some of her African-American friends questioned the less-than-diverse places she lived, and people with whom she associated. There were other groups she worked with that didn't offer much diversity. But Shaba was comfortable with her choices, and has been able to think her way through the issues.

I feel comfortable living my life from the inside out, doing what my heart and mind dictates. My response to those who question me is, "If you go to heaven, and the people there are not your color, are you going to leave?" I am not going to make myself 'a victim.' When I look at myself and see my limitations, it's not my skin color. My limitations are what I limit myself to.

When Shaba retired from Kaiser Permanente, she also retired from the ministry. She and Lillie moved to Taos, New Mexico, where, before long, she was doing pottery, writing stories and poetry, and finding outlets for her activism. She found Taos a nourishing place to live, surrounded by kind, intelligent people.

Reflecting on her life, Shaba talks of when she had been in the seminary. She'd become fascinated with a building she often drove past. It looked like a white castle, and was always well cared for. She knew it was something spiritual, but couldn't find out anything about it. She called, found out that she was welcome to attend the Sunday service, and went, note pad in hand, thinking she would write about it as part of her studies.

When I walked through the door, I was awe struck. The room was colorfully decorated with Tarot cards around the walls. The card in the middle of the room was exactly like the room I was entering. The prayers and chants were in Hebrew. It was the Temple of Kabbalah.

Years later, at the church she was then attending, Shaba was asked to teach a class on the Tarot. She taught a 10 week class on the Kabbalah, the study of the mystical aspects of the Jewish philosophy.

So, you see, where I started is where I returned. I have enjoyed a rich, amazing life. I count my blessings every day.

Shaba now lives in Albuquerque, New Mexico. In the eight years since her interview, Shaba has continued to devote much of her time to her activist, artistic, and spiritual lives. Among her many contributions, she served for several years as Co-Director of Old Lesbians Organizing for Change.

Interviewer: Arden Eversmeyer

Edie Daly
and
Jackie Mirkin

Edith 'Edie' Daly

Born January 1937 in Florida
Interviewed in 2004, at age 68, in Florida

*For me every woman, what ever
way she is, is beautiful.*

Born to mid-westerners who were driven by the Depression
to emigrate to Florida for work and a lower cost of living, Edie
began her life in Miami, Florida. Back in Chicago, her father had
been a songwriter and "song-plugger," skills that were not in great
demand once the Depression gripped the country. Her mother
had a myriad of talents and interests, but little outlet for them
early in her life. Edie's early memories are of growing up when
everything was unsettled, during the decade between the worst
of the Depression and the beginning of World War II. Everyone
was struggling to get back on their feet.

*We came from a musical family. My dad started to own bars.
When I was two, he would take me to the bar at night, and
sometimes in the afternoon, I guess to baby-sit me while my*

mom would do errands. He'd stand me up on the bar, and I'd sing. The men would throw pennies. I learned really early in my life to perform, and to be in that kind of place.

At home, her father sang all the time, instilling a love of music. Her father also taught Edie and her sister all the old songs and how to sing harmony.

Age 5

My folks were divorced when I was five, when the war started, during the defense era. My dad did not go into the service, because he was classified 4-F, not physically fit enough to go. They divorced, and he moved north someplace. Then my mom went north and worked in New Jersey in a defense plant. She took my sister and me. That was probably the happiest part of my mom's life. She was happy to be working, doing a man's job as a draftsman.

It was her first time 'out-of-the-box,' free to live her own life. She had a lot of women friends, and I had a very strong woman-oriented youth. After the war, we went back to Florida. She married her childhood sweetheart, and we moved to St. Petersburg, Florida. My mom became involved with Girl Scouts, and she was my Girl Scout leader. That was both good and bad. Every summer I went to Girl Scout Camp for eight weeks. Summer camps were the places I became a strong woman, with a sense of knowing who I was as a girl, having no influence of boys over me.

I saw boys only in school. I didn't do very well in school, as I was dyslexic. I couldn't read or do math. Camp was the place where I found success with myself. There I found the energy from inside me that told me I was okay, even though

*I always made very poor grades in school, and I couldn't do
academic work. I really found myself in camp.*

*I lived for summers when I could be at camp. I learned to
chop wood, build fires, erect tents, do all the outdoor camp-
craft, and all outdoor things. I absolutely loved it, and I was
a star pupil. I was always one of the best at camp craft. I
swam and learned boating. I just loved the outdoors and
it really was a joy in my life, one that has been carried on
throughout my life. I always say, I began my women's circles
in the Brownies, when I was six. Every year, women and
girls sharing their stories, and later, women sharing together,
were the most powerful things in my life.*

Edie returned to St. Petersburg, Florida, after the war when
her mother remarried. Her stepfather was a jack-of-all-trades,
and they embarked on a new venture. They built a trailer park.
Working with her stepfather, ten year old Edie learned about
carpentry, plumbing, and electricity as she helped.

*We bought land across from the Veteran's Administration
Hospital out in Seminole. He cleared the land first with bull-
dozers, and then he dug the trenches. I can remember helping
him dig the trenches, laying the pipes for the sewer and water,
and then doing the electrical work. The electrical wires, at
that time, were all overhead. I learned how to thread the
pipes. The electrical work was always more difficult, and I
have a healthy respect for electricity.*

In addition to learning skills from her stepfather that would
serve Edie her whole life, she did manage to attend the local
public schools, but it wasn't easy for her.

*When we moved from Miami, I was in the second grade,
going into the third grade. They decided to put me back into
the second grade again, because of my dyslexia. They didn't
know about dyslexia then, they just thought I was slow. I*

Eleven-year-old "Freckles" at
Camp Juliette Lowe

didn't fare well with that, because I was not in my age range. I was always the oldest in the class. I think that made a big difference.

The stigma of being considered slow by her classmates and teachers was compounded by Edie's parents having been divorced. Even though her mother had remarried, divorcing was something that was way out of the norm at that time. Edie always felt out of place at school, but summer camp was her refuge.

That's where camp came in. I knew I was smart, and all of my friends were the smartest kids in the class. So I knew there was something wrong, but I didn't know what it was. I thought it was my fault, because I knew that I was smart enough to know that I wasn't dumb.

As Edie progressed to high school age, her feeling of being different from everyone else led to acting out. Her mother had divorced Edie's stepfather, and Edie was living as a latchkey kid, coming and going unsupervised while her mother worked. To keep things from getting even worse, Edie's parents enrolled her in a boarding school near where her father then lived in West Palm Beach, Florida.

One of my father's good friends was the secretary to the principal of the school. It was a Roman Catholic boarding school, run by Dominican nuns. That was where I went for the last three years of high school, tenth through twelfth grades. It was really my saving grace, because they discovered my learning disability. It was comforting to know where I was going to be for a while, also. Every year of my school years, up until the tenth grade, I was in a different school. That's very hard on children.

My mom loved to travel, and she used to say, "Well, they never do anything in the first couple weeks of school." She and I traveled those weeks, so I was always behind. When we would return, it was always a new school situation. I learned how to make friends fast, if I was going to have any friends at all!

I never had really deep friendships. The other thing was that I never wanted to say goodbye. I would be away at summer camp, and my mom would have moved us to a new house. When I came home, I wouldn't have any friends in that neighborhood, and I hadn't said goodbye to my old friends. I didn't realize until later in life that that was one of those things that played into my inability to say goodbye, hanging on when it should be over, and I should have moved on. I sometimes call that tenacity, and sometimes call that just plain hanging on.

Though Edie did stay in one place through high school until she graduated, the very next day she made her way to New York, determined to make her way in the big city by herself. The only person she knew there was her sister, who had just gotten married.

I lived in the Studio Club, which was a residence for girls run by the YWCA. My sister had lived there for a short time when she first went to New York, so that's how I knew about it. I went, I didn't have a job, and I didn't have any skills. I didn't know how to type or how to do anything. But I went anyway, as I was getting away from home. I was leaving Florida, and I was never coming back.

I pounded the pavement for about two weeks, and finally found a job as a model. I modeled coats in July. I was a junior model on 7th Avenue, in the garment district. I worked for Highlander Coat Company. I didn't realize that when you work in the garment business, there are seasons. Of course, they only made coats up until January. In January, they are finished making coats for the season, and this company did not make swimsuits. So I was out on the sidewalk again.

Next, I found a job with General Electric as a file clerk. I eventually got a job in the mailroom, delivering mail to the 52 floors of the General Electric Building. I had the top floors, where the president, Ralph Cordner, and his buddies were located. I used to be able to stop and talk to the secretaries a little bit as I delivered the mail. I delivered the mail every hour, and there were probably about six or seven of us mail girls.

I went to New York with sheer determination that I was going to be able to get a job. In those days, the rent was only $12 a week for the room, and I think there was a $10 charge for the food coupons. By eating breakfast and dinner everyday on my food coupon, I could get through the week and end up with some savings. I've always been a person who likes to save. I ended up saving $10 a week out of my salary, even though I only made $42. I knew that eventually I did want to go back to school, even though I had thought I'd never go back.

Of course, Edie's plans didn't go the way she had thought. One of the other mail girls was part of a club that did things with men from another club. The group had a moonlight cruise on the Hudson River planned, and Edie's friend invited her to go, and got her a blind date. Her friend was dating Phil, and Edie would go with Phil's roommate.

There were four of us together on this cruise up the Hudson River. With the moonlight on the water and the music, it was very romantic. We were all singing on the back deck of the boat, having a good time. After the boat ride, we went to somebody's house in Brooklyn and danced all night long. Phil said that I shouldn't go home alone all the way back to Manhattan. He needed to take me on the subway and make sure I got home okay. He got me home early, early in the morning. At 1 p.m. that afternoon, the phone rang and it was Phil. He said, "I thought maybe you'd like to go rowing in Central Park." I got up and dressed, and he took me rowing. We fell in love just like that, it was like love at first sight. We became engaged in two days, and married within about nine months.

Once she was married, Edie gave birth to three boys in rapid succession, and entered into a very difficult time in her life. Raising the three children was exhausting, and her marriage to an alcoholic husband made it even more stressful. She'd start out each day by telling herself to forget yesterday, and that each new day would be different. That helped her get through day-to-day, but she was also disengaging from life itself, leaving her lonely.

He was very abusive. At one point I even called the police. I had the three kids, and he would come home late at night and fly off the handle for no reason and hit me. Finally I just called the police. They said, "Are you sure you are going to want to press charges?" This must have been in 1962. I said, "Yes, I will," and he stayed in jail overnight.

I called my Episcopal priest, because we did go to church then, and he went with me to press charges the next day.

Phil got released, basically, in the custody of the priest. So the priest was now in charge of counseling us, but it didn't do any good, and we moved away from there very quickly.

When we moved, it was kind of like 'out of the frying pan into the fire.' We moved to a suburb of New York City, Yorktown Heights, which was a bedroom community. All the men went to work in the city. Phil was gone from seven in the morning until seven at night. I was there with all the other moms, but they were very different than I was. My interests were in art, music, dance, plays, things like that.

I had very little in common with the other moms. I was very isolated, and I felt really depressed. This was now 1966. One of the outlets that I found there was my music.

I found one of the other mothers, who played the guitar and sang. I had been teaching myself to play the guitar, during the folk music era, so I was really into being able to sing, and to find my way out of my depression.

This woman, Vicki Lucas, who sang with me, had a beautiful soprano voice. It gave me the chance to sing alto, which is what I loved anyway. I could sing harmony to anything. She taught me a lot more about the guitar, and I taught her a lot more about music, and about singing. We had a duo, and we called ourselves The Patchwork Singers, because I made patchwork jumpers that we could wear when we went to sing.

That was the age of the mini-skirt, and if you sat on stage in a mini-skirt, you know how hard that was to keep your knees covered. I was not into showing my knees. I made up these long jumpers that were a patchwork material. We sang songs from around the world. We did bar mitzvahs, and we went around to the schools and sang for the school kids. Vicki was Jewish, so we went to Hadassah, and we went to temples. We had a wonderful time.

The Patchwork Singers stayed together for about four years, before Edie's youngest son was old enough to enter first grade. To be more involved, Edie volunteered to ride on the school bus that first day, to help with the children. When they reached the school, she found out there really wasn't room for more students, and they had moved the kindergarten class to a church. Since they didn't have a teacher's aide for that class, Edie stayed, starting out as a volunteer.

There were four separate classes of kindergarten. They hired me as a part-time teacher's aide, and I worked in the middle of the day, when the morning kids left and the afternoon kids came. That was the most important time. The other time that I was there, I was able to do the mimeographing that they needed, to get their supplies, and to do all the things that the teacher's aide needs to do for the kindergarten. That job lasted for 12 years. It paid basically minimum wage, but I had a job that was the same days off that my kids had off. It was perfect for me and I didn't have to get up early and supervise. Also, I didn't have to get up too early and leave before my own kids left. I was on their schedule, so that was very good for me.

Edie stayed in her marriage for 17 years. She was able to do it because he was gone 12 hours of the day. She was, essentially, a single mom with time to develop a good relationship with her boys.

Something remarkable happened to Edie while she was working for the school system.

The school started something new that they called a 'resource room.' It was for kids with learning disabilities. That teacher was interviewing for teacher-aides, and she chose me. It was wonderful because that was exactly what I needed to do, to learn to read again. I had been teaching myself to read.

I started with the little books with my own children, and began reading to them. That increased my skill a little. But because I was now teaching kids with dyslexia, I learned what the problems were, how to teach them. I had to learn it to teach reading.

It was a revelation, and a huge relief for Edie, to finally understand why reading was so easy for others and so difficult for her. She saw the tests that they gave the kids, and suddenly she saw her own problems, spelling words backwards and skipping the first letter, or a whole word.

I was a teacher's aide in that school district for 12 years and then I fell in love with one of the first grade teachers. I was that teacher's aide. Between us, we had two husbands and seven kids. How to deal with that?

Doreen and I began to divest ourselves of both our husbands. My kids and her kids grew up together, but they were arch enemies at school. We knew we could never live in the same house together with our kids. They would not do well. We decided that we would wait until they were off to college.

My last kid was still a high school senior. Doreen said to me, "You know, after 12 years of working in the school, you need to have something that pays you more than $5.50 an hour. Besides that, you can't be a teacher's aide all your life." She said, "The only reason I'm a teacher is that my mom always told me that I needed

Age 40, in 1977

something to fall back on if my husband got sick, or some-thing happened." Doreen taught me that same ethic, of how to be my own person.

I took an aptitude test, and found out that I'd be good as a nurse. I loved science, and even though I hadn't been good in school, I felt that I would be able to do this. When I took the pre-test that they gave to find out what I would be good in, my lowest scores were in reading, but I made high scores in science.

During all those years of struggling to get through school, Edie had developed her listening skills, and that's how she got by. She not only had trouble reading, but she was dysgraphic, so she rarely took notes. Yet, here she was, in college.

Edie earned her Licensed Practical Nurse (LPN) degree and now had a marketable skill that started her out at a base pay that it had taken her 12 years to work up to in the school system. If she'd had some better guidance, Edie would have gone for her Registered Nurse (RN) degree. She hadn't been aware that financial assistance would have made more schooling possible, or was even available. By now, her husband was long gone, and had failed to provide any kind of support for her and their children. Relying on welfare and a Pell grant to get them through, Edie wanted to get a job that would support her family as soon as she could.

Welfare gave me $350 for myself and my three kids to live on. I went to the bank, and I said, "Look, I don't know where my husband is, and he's left me with these kids. I can go to school this year. I can learn enough so that I'll have a good job when I get out." And I said, "I want to keep my kids in the same school, so I need you to work with me about my mortgage." I had more than 50% paid off from the original mortgage, so they let me pay interest only. At that time, it was around $100 a month.

When I graduated with my class, I had a 93 point grade average. I was really surprised, and very happy with myself. That gave me a lot of self-esteem, and the ability to just be myself. I had decided on nursing, because I really wanted to have something I could take wherever I went. I knew that I wanted to travel. That was really one of the things I wanted to do in my life.

I started to work that year in the local area. Then the school board offered all of their teachers early retirement packages, three years salary to quit early, with some other benefits.

Edie's budding nursing career took a slight detour when Doreen decided to take the offered early retirement package.

Their children were now grown, so without anything tying them to New York, they moved together to Florida. Edie quickly put her training to work on the evening shift, which afforded her the time to go back to school, during the day, to get her RN.

Doreen was wonderful, because not only did I have to do a lot of studying and reading, but I had to do writing as well. I was in college, and I was expected to do writing. I would write my paper out in long hand, and she would type it and correct it as she typed. So she really helped me. She was wonderful.

They had moved to Florida in 1981, and Edie earned her RN four years later. Because of her love of science, and her mechanical skills, Edie became an Intensive Care Unit (ICU) nurse for the next 12 years, before transitioning to work as a home health care nurse.

I went to opposite ends. I went from where people were on life support systems, to being able to help them not be in that position. I went into their homes, to be able to help them to die with dignity, to know what their meds were, and how to

*take them. A teaching job was really what it was. So, at the
end of my working career, I was able to use my teaching and
my nursing, together, for the last four years before retirement.
I really enjoyed that. That was really the best part, as far as
my working career.*

There was much more than working in Edie and Doreen's
life in Florida. They hadn't been there long when they began to
wonder why they couldn't find a women's community. Back when
they lived in New York, Doreen was still working, and they felt
they had to stay closeted. They had to be extremely careful in
seeking out other women like themselves.

*We were able to go to New York City. It was 1974, the
year of* Lavender Jane Loves Women.* *We went down to
Greenwich Village, and we saw this little sign. I said, "Look
at this, Doreen. This says something about upstate New
York. It seems to be a house for women, and it seems to be a
collective of women." We were in the Oscar Wilde Bookstore,
and we wondered what it was. So we decided we would go
and check it out.*

*On one of the weekends that the kids were being taken
care of, we went up to this place in the Catskills. It was near
Woodstock, New York. It was a house for women, and it
was a lesbian commune. We got there the day after Labor
Day, and they had just finished having their big Labor Day
gathering.*

Edie and Doreen were disappointed, but looked around
anyway. It was there that they found Alix Dobkin's record,
*Lavender Jane Loves Women.** They listened to it, and had to

---

** Lavender Jane Loves Women was a ground breaking album of music
created by and for lesbians. Released in 1973, the original recording is
no longer available but the music was re-released as part of a two-CD
set by Alix Dobkin entitled* **Living With Lavender Jane.**

buy a copy for themselves. They may not have connected with the women yet, but now they at least knew that the women were out there. They did, eventually, find a group in New York that met for ballgames, picnics, and such and most importantly, met far enough from where they lived that they felt safe getting together before they moved.

Living in Florida, they knew other women had to be out there, too. They just couldn't seem to find them. They tried a gay bar, but found it so noisy you couldn't talk, even if you did meet someone. As they left the bar one night, they noticed the shop space next door was available to rent.

I almost couldn't sleep for the whole night. I was up early in the morning, and when Doreen got up I said, "I have this wonderful idea." We had about $1,500 from selling our houses, and moving to the South, that we thought we were going to invest in the stock market. I said, "What if we opened a women's bookstore with that $1,500? We could meet other women that way."

Sure enough, we opened a women's bookstore next to this gay bar. We figured that's the place women would go. We said, "What should we name it?" We decided it needed to be a name that lesbians would be able to relate to. What would they know? They would know The Well of Loneliness,* so we named it The Well of Happiness. We knew that women would still catch on to what that name meant.

So there we were, we opened up the bookstore. Publisher Barbara Grier** was here for what is now called 'Florida Equality,' or 'Equality Florida.' It used to be called the 'Task

---

*For many lesbians living during this era, The Well of Loneliness, a 1928 lesbian novel by the British author Radclyffe Hall, was the only lesbian book available, so many women recognized the name.
** Barbara Grier, was editor of the pioneering lesbian periodical, The Ladder, and publisher at Naiad Press, the largest publisher of lesbian books during that era.

Force.' They had a statewide meeting, and Barbara Grier was
there to sell books. She had three cartons of books left over,
and said we could have them; she would donate them. So we
opened the store with those three cartons of books.

We painted the store lavender. I can remember being
up on the ladder, putting up a big sign on Gulf Boulevard
that said, 'Women's Books.' That was a radical act at that
time, and that is really where I became politicized. I didn't
think I was political, but when you have a book store, and as
people come in the door it says 'Women's Books' and 'Well of
Happiness,' people know who you are, and it's a political act.

Within two months, we knew 250 women. We knew,
also, that a bookstore cannot survive without a community.
And we knew that it was not going to be able to make money.

To complicate matters, Doreen and Edie were still heading back north for three months each year. They left care of the
bookstore with people they had to pay. Edie and Doreen had
been working without compensation, so this added a financial
burden. Another complicating factor was that despite being two
women who owned and operated a women's bookstore named
after the iconic lesbian work by Radcliffe Hall, *The Well of
Loneliness*, Edie and Doreen were still in the closet.

We decided to have some kind of a women's meeting. We
thought it was going to be a book club, because we needed
to sell books. We had one of those black composition books,
and we called it our 'little black book.' When people came
in and bought books, we asked them if they would sign their
names and addresses in the book. We promised we would
never show it to anybody else, and we'd never sell the list.
We told them that they didn't need to worry, because any
communication they got from us would be totally without any
identifying words on the outside. We would hand address
them, and they would be totally incognito.

Reluctantly, about a hundred women signed our little black book. We decided to send out invitations, and we would have something that we would call a 'salon.' We named it 'The Salon,' after Natalie Barney in France who had a salon. Gertrude Stein had 'salons' in Paris, as well. So we named it after those women who had salons at the turn of the 20th century in Paris.

Fifty women came to our first meeting of 'The Salon.' We started out as a feminist run organization. I was so nervous. I had prepared a short biography of Natalie Barney to read to the women, to explain to them why we were naming it 'The Salon,' what we were going to do, and so forth. My paper was shaking so much that I could hardly see the words.

My voice was cracking, and Doreen and I both said, "You see us standing up here in front, leading this, but there are 50 women here tonight. There are more than enough women so that we will not be standing in front of you again until eleven months from now. There are enough women to take responsibility for every monthly meeting—a different woman, or several women, up here every month."

Developing a structure for the group was the first task. They decided it was important to avoid having a hierarchy, so they adopted a consensus model. Another challenge was finding a place for that many women to meet. They started meeting at a community house. But since it was located next door to the police station, many of the women weren't comfortable there. Next, they tried the clubhouse at the condo complex where Edie and Doreen lived.

One of the nights when we were having our meeting in the condo clubhouse, we were doing massage. One of our massage therapists was teaching us all how to give massage, so half of our women were lying on tables, and half of the women were massaging them. Then the president of the condo association walked in. We got a letter the very next day saying that we could no longer meet there. So we found another place to meet, the Girl's Club of Pinellas Park. Pretty soon they found out we were lesbians, and they said we couldn't meet there. They didn't want their kids to come in contact with us. I don't know what that was about, but I do know they didn't want lesbians there. So they kicked us out of that place.

The group continued to cast about for a safe place to meet. Libraries were out, because meetings there had to be open to the public. Churches were out, because many of the women had had bad experiences with religion. Then they were contacted by a local group of Quakers.

The Friends, the Quakers, found out that we were looking for a meeting place, and they invited us. Then, not only did we have a place that was welcoming, by a group that was peaceful, they had run their organization by consensus for 400 years. They knew how to do it, and knew how to teach and nurture us to get us through the hard times. Now it's been 21 years, and we're still operating by consensus. We still get some mentoring when we get into tough times. The Quakers are able to mentor us, and they never push any kind of religion on us. You know, when we meet at the meeting house, it's a totally peaceful place.

Finding the Quakers not only solved the immediate need for a safe meeting space, it led Edie into a new phase of her life. Through the Quakers, Edie became aware of the planned Women's Peace Encampment at Seneca Falls, New York, in 1983. Attending that was a mind-expanding experience for Edie. It was also the first year she attended the Michigan Womyn's Music Festival, and she went to the March on Washington.

These experiences changed Edie in a very basic way. She now wanted to speak out for women, and to be out for herself. Along with this awakening, came a desire to become more political. Ultimately, these two elemental changes to Edie's needs brought her relationship with Doreen to an end.

> *Doreen and I realized that we were not going to be together anymore. It wasn't that we didn't love each other, it was like we grew apart. I began to be really out, and really wanting to be an activist, and she was not. That wasn't what she wanted to do. That was going to be my path, and she didn't want to walk that path. We were nine years apart in age. I think that played a part in our separation. I see that with other women.*
>
> *That's not really a large difference in age, but I was coming into my own, and she was ready for retirement. Also, I was a late bloomer, and I was just learning how to speak in front of people. She already knew how to do that. She was a teacher and could do that very easily. But that wasn't an easy part for me.*
>
> *I was really quite shy. I was just learning how to be assertive. I learned that skill in 1983, when I went to Seneca, to the Women's Peace Encampment, which was to protest the missiles.*

One focus of the event in Seneca, was to protest the United States sending cruise missiles to England. At the same time the women were protesting in Seneca, women were protesting in Greenham, England, where the missiles were going. The two sides held simultaneous 24 hour protests.

> *We had that connection between the women of Greenham Common and the women in the United States. That was where I learned about civil disobedience. At that time, we had what we called WEBS, run in a egalitarian, non-hierarchical way. We called them 'learn togethers,' not workshops. In learning together, there were those who could teach, those who could share what they knew, and those of us who didn't know about the subject yet. I began to look at*

Edie in the center, at a 1994 New York City Dyke March

*these women and think, "They are no different than I am,
and I am no different than they are. They just know what to
say, and I just have to learn what to say."*

*I learned by watching those women, putting myself out
there, and making myself say what I was thinking. I guess
that's how you learn any kind of skill. For me, that was my
activism. And that's how I can go down the main street
of town in a Martin Luther King parade, and be out and
proud, and talk to people on the side of the street about the
issues. I started then.*

Her first foray into activism was when Edie gathered the
courage to step off the curb at a Pride march in New York, and
join some women she knew. She was overwhelmed by the feeling
of being one of thousands, proudly and loudly declaring their
sexuality, and chanting, "Out of the closet and into the streets!"
That taste of what it felt like to stand up and demand to be

counted, fed into a part of Edie that had been dormant and waiting, and it was only the beginning.

One of the many things Edie is appreciative of is the role she has played in the formation, and ongoing efforts, of the Women's Energy Bank. WEB started to fill a need for feminists to connect, share, and learn. It focuses on a wide spectrum of issues that affect women's lives, both locally and globally. WEB began in the early 1980s, has involved hundreds of women during its history, and has published a monthly newsletter for more than twenty years, without fail.

Edie's dedication to working on behalf of women everywhere took her to Sarajevo with a group called Peace Now. She didn't have the money for the trip, but when she shared what she wanted to do with others, they pitched in. Edie spent three months living with the local women, at a time when war was crushing the country. Sarajevo is the capital city of Bosnia and Herzegovina, which had recently declared their independence from Yugoslavia. Sarajevo was under siege by the Serbs for four years, 1992-1996, during which time at least 10,000 people, including more than 1,000 children, were killed.

Amidst the turmoil and danger, Edie stayed in support of the local women. While there, Edie was involved in a group that provided local children with art supplies, so that they could draw pictures of what they saw all around them. Back in the United States, Edie and the other women who had gone, went to schools, talking to students

Age 58

about what the children of Sarajevo were experiencing on a daily basis, trying to show them that violence is not the answer.

Two years later, in 1995, Edie traveled abroad once again, this time with the Women's International League for Peace and Freedom. She joined the Peace Train, filled with women heading from Helsinki, Finland, to the Fourth International Conference on Women being held in Beijing, China. Over 21 days, the train went through nine countries, with WILPF members speaking to women at stops along the way.

In two of the train cars, they took out all the seats, and they just put vinyl down on the floor of the train. We held seminars while the train was in motion, every day, except for the days that we stopped. There were 250 women from 42 countries on that train. We had all day conversations on all different kinds of topics. We talked about economics, women's economics, and about how women in all different countries were doing things outside of the patriarchy. They taught us how to start a bank, how to start a business, and how to help people in other countries that were not so fortunate to be able to help themselves. And we talked about how to create change.

I learned, for instance, about what my idea of feminism was at that time. The focus of feminism in the United States was how many women can we get into college. In Africa, it's how do you get fresh water into your village. That's a feminist issue, because the women are the ones who have to go get the water. They have to get up an hour early, to go to the next village to get water to bring back to use for that day. Every single day they have to do that. So water is a women's issue. I changed my whole idea, in that time, about what feminism is.

As with her earlier trip to Sarajevo, Edie had depended on support from friends and family to make this once in a lifetime journey. And, as she did after her return from Sarajevo, she made sure to share what she had experienced when she got back home.

A year later, Edie discovered Old Lesbians Organizing for Change, an organization that limits its membership to women 60 and older.

I began to look at these old women, and I said, "That's where I want to be. When I grow up, that's what I want to be." I could see that they had been activists all their lives. And now they're old, and their activism is against ageism as well.

Before long, Edie also found Jackie, someone who is as much an activist as she is herself. Together, they've gone on to speak up, speak out, picket, protest, march, and write on behalf of women everywhere.

After years of living as a totally out activist, political lesbian, Edie is able to recognize the steps she took as she first stuck a toe out of the closet.

The first, maybe half a year after I knew Doreen, and we were still in our jobs, we were still closeted, and we didn't know anybody else. I thought I was bisexual. I really thought that it wasn't who Doreen was and our sexuality, it was just that I loved her. I thought that I could love anybody.

I thought that I would probably call myself bisexual, although I don't know that I was truly aware of what that meant. I knew that I always loved women. This, finally, felt like coming

Jackie with Edie in 1998

home. This was a place where I was finally able to figure out, "Yes. This is what it is." Within that year, I changed from, "I can love anybody," to "I love women." That made me know that I was a lesbian, and now I always call myself a lesbian.

People question. They stereotype. People look at us, and they know what Jackie and I are. We're not able to hide. In my other two relationships, we were both able to pass. When I walk down the street with Jackie, you know we're a lesbian couple. There's no doubt about it. We're out, we're proud, and that took a little getting used to. And I love it.

When Edie came out to her sister, she was surprised to find out that her sister's first two relationships had both been with women. Sadly, she had decided she couldn't handle the social stigma of being a lesbian, and married to raise a family. Years later, Edie's sister divorced, and became a third order Episcopal nun. When her sister fell ill with a rare form of cancer and was dying, her life took an unexpected turn. Edie's sister fell in love with the woman who was her social worker, and was helping her while she was in hospice.

She fell in love when she had only two or three more months to live. She came out to me at that time. I was so excited, and happy for her. But all of those years, when she hid and denied her sexuality, made me so sad. Because all of those years she lived without that part of her life, the love part of her life, being expressed, or with a wonderful partner. But she seemed to be okay. That was how she dealt with it.

In retrospect, Edie also thinks her mother may have been a lesbian. In going through some family papers, Edie found photos of her mother with another woman. Edie's 'gaydar' immediately went off.

I could tell that these two women loved one another. I knew the woman in the photo at that time. She was a Girl Scout leader. I knew that there was something very special between them, even though I was maybe ten, eleven, twelve years old. I knew that this woman was a very special woman to my mother, and I knew that she was more than just a best friend. Those are the kinds of role models I had as a child, and because strong women have always been in my family, I knew that it was okay. That's one of the things I treasure.

When I went to boarding school, it was an all-girl's school. I never had to be in that teenage place in school with boys. I never had to have that competition with boys. I never had to hang back because boys in high school always get called on more, and always are the ones that are telling you how it is supposed to be. I was lucky in that way.

It was simply my luck not having to have that oppression in my life. I've always been able to see women as strong, independent, knowing who they are, and doing whatever they want to be doing in their lives.

The sense of empowerment, when I'm with women, is more than just loving Jackie or loving my friends. There's a deep love that I have for all women. I always say, all women are beautiful. There's no woman that isn't beautiful. And so, that sense of youth and beauty—everything that's imposed on us by men, I totally reject every part of that oppression. For me every woman, whatever way she is, is beautiful.

Edie continues to live in Florida, where she loves working with clay, loves sewing, loves music, and loves her involvement in various organizations. She now facilitates workshops in the Alternatives to Violence Program with women in Federal Prison. Edie loves women… especially Jackie.

Interviewer: Arden Eversmeyer

Jacqueline 'Jackie' Mirkin

Born January 1931 in Massachusetts
Interviewed in 2004, at age 73, in Florida

You've done the right thing. This is right.

*I went to public schools from first grade through high school.
I should have gone to kindergarten, but my mother decided I
was too smart, and enrolled me in the first grade, lying about
my age. I passed the first grade. Kids were talking in the
school yard and saying how old they were going to be on their
next birthday. Some of those kids squealed to the teacher that
I was only five-and-a-half, and the school administration
decided that I had to repeat first grade.*

Jackie loved school from early on, relishing the positive
recognition she got there. She may have only been five-and-a-
half when she started her formal education, but she'd already
learned an abundance of life lessons and many of them were
confusing to a young, precocious child who soaked up everything
that went on around her.

My mother and father had a very stormy marriage, and my father was a violent man. Though she never told me, I knew that he beat her sometimes. When I was six or seven years old, and I would see bruises on her, I would ask her where they came from. One time her nose was all swollen, and I asked her about that. She said, "Oh, I was washing the dishes and something fell off the kitchen shelf and hit me in the nose." Even at six, that seemed strange to me.

Her parents had married very young, and against their families' wishes. At 17, her mother had been a very talented artist, and was offered a scholarship to attend The Museum of Fine Arts School in Boston. At 19, her father was following in his father's footsteps, working for the Singer Sewing Machine Company as a salesman. In an era when birth control was almost non-existent, they married too young and had Jackie two years later.

I was born at 1:56 PM on New Year's Day. The reason I know the exact time, is that my mother, who was twenty, complained bitterly that I ruined her New Year's Eve party. She had to leave the party, and I wasn't born, dammit, until two o'clock the next day. I was her first child, and she went into a long labor. So she could've stayed for the whole party.

Jackie and her parents started out living with her maternal grandmother. This was also home to her mother's fourteen year old sister, Jackie's aunt. It was the fourteen year-old who nurtured Jackie, and was always there for her, offering her a sense of stability and being loved. As her father's job transferred him around New England, Jackie's life was continually changing. Then her mother became pregnant again.

Sometime during that pregnancy, or right afterwards, my parents separated, and they were then divorced. We were living in Springfield, Massachusetts. We moved back to

Boston to be closer to my mother's family, though we didn't live with them. My grandmother and my aunt were living with my mother's middle sister, so there wasn't any room.

When I look back, my mother had a job, and the move was very traumatic. We had spent the whole summer in Springfield. We didn't know that my parents were separated. My sister didn't know anyway, as she was an infant. They left us with my paternal grandmother and some of my aunts that were still at home, and we stayed there throughout the summer. I started school in Springfield.

In October, suddenly my mother and father appeared and took us to Boston, to a boarding home. In those days, there weren't the kind with regulations that there are now. If somebody wanted to take care of babies, they could just take babies in. And so they found a place that would take in me and my sister. My mother had a room in a place down the street. She'd come and see us as often as she could. After a while, she just couldn't stand having us in this situation. So she stopped working and went on welfare, and then moved us to another kind of boarding home, where parents and kids lived together.

Jackie's was a middle-class upbringing, filled with conflicting messages. She knew they were on welfare, and that they were poor, but her mother worked to give Jackie a sense that she was no different from the people around her.

My mother knew she was different, as she didn't have the same values as the working class people. She always had this affinity for people who were worse off than she was. Some of it was just genuine caring, but some of it was that she never had a very good self image until the day she died. She was more comfortable with people with whom she didn't feel she had to live up to higher standards.

She never was really accepted by her mother and her sisters. Some of that was that she looked a lot like my grandfather, and she was his favorite child. My grandparents had married each other and divorced each other twice! We're not talking about a great deal of stability there. When you think about that era, it was all very different. Every time I had to fill out a form at school, there was no place for divorce. Your parents were either alive or dead. It was like, "What do I put there? Do I cross it out?"

Even though her life didn't look like those of her friends, and she didn't have what they had, her mother worked hard to instill an appreciation of what they did have. Also, she emphasized the importance of taking care of yourself.

She used to talk about food for the soul, and what that meant. Even if we were on welfare, she could find a way to save enough, maybe 50¢ for each of us, to go and eat in a cafeteria once a week so that we ate out. I knew other people in similar circumstances that never did anything like that. It was a fine time eating in the cafeteria. You got to choose what you liked to eat, and you knew what your budget was, so you never went over it. It was fun, and she was relaxed, and we would have real conversations at times like that.

Her mother also helped her develop a strong sense of acceptance of people who were different from them. Unfortunately, this came with a dose of punishment, which played a leading role in Jackie's upbringing.

My first awareness that I was being insensitive was when I was about seven years old. We had a part-time cleaning woman that came, probably once a week, for a couple of hours, to help my mother clean the house. Some kids came by, and they called through the window and said, "Mrs. Mirkin, can Jackie come out to play?" I was there, and I said, "Oh I'll be out, but I can't come right away because I'm supposed to be helping the maid." Then, I wasn't allowed to go out.

My mother closed the window, and she reprimanded me. She said, "We don't have maids. This is a person who works for a living. And your father does a different kind of work. He gets paid for that." Then she said, "You're staying in. You can't go out because what you said was wrong, and you need to stay in here and think about that." Of course, at that time, I got the message. It's still with me. I didn't quite understand, but I think what she did in her own way was extremely important.

Another occurrence that strongly influenced Jackie involved a woman who did some work for their family.

My grandmother worked with this woman all day, sewing bandages for World War II. She happened to be an African-American woman, and, in order to earn additional income, did some housecleaning. She would do it after work, like at five o'clock for a few hours, or on a Saturday. So as my mother was also working full-time again, or almost full-time, because my sister was only in kindergarten, she would come to our house to clean.

We had an attic apartment that had a huge bedroom with two big beds in it. My sister and I, at that point, shared a bed at one end of the room, and my mother slept alone in a bed at the other end of the room. When this woman came to clean, she'd stay and visit. She had to be to work very early the next morning, so she would sleep over. She'd share the bed with my mother. And there was never any discussion of this. It was just what she did. She was a friend.

I think that those were two kinds of powerful messages for me, so that I never questioned that there was room for all different kinds of people.

In her early years, there wasn't any formal religious upbringing, but Jackie was aware her family was Jewish. When she'd visit her paternal grandmother, she'd go with her to the orthodox synagogue, where only the men were allowed in the sanctuary, and the women had to sit upstairs. Her mother's family was also Jewish, and had come to America fluent in Russian and Yiddish. Other than attending synagogue now and then, her Jewish heritage wasn't a part of Jackie's everyday life until she reached junior high school.

Jackie at age 13

When I was in seventh grade, my mother thought that I should go to Hebrew School, and so I did. I learned Hebrew. I didn't really learn much about the religion, but I learned more about the language and history, something that's always interested me. In that way, I got more connected with some of the more formal aspects. But we weren't religious. My mother later remarried. My stepfather belonged to a conservative temple. That was where the Hebrew School was. We went on the high holidays. But we were definitely not observant.

During her early teens, Jackie began to become aware of the women and girls around her, and aware that what she was feeling might not be how other people felt about their friends.

In junior high, I became gradually aware that I was 'different.' Nothing excited me more than my first pair of dungarees. In 1941, these were only made for men and boys. My grandmother disgustedly muttered 'mitekehs,' the Yiddish

*word for pants, whenever I wore them. My favorite aunt
began giving me her used, more 'feminine' clothes, which I
dutifully accepted, as poor relatives on welfare do, but had
no interest in wearing. In those years, my happiest times
occurred at a summer girls' camp. I began to have crushes on
my camp counselors, all of whom were female.*

*That was probably the beginning of my entering 'the
closet.' I never shared my feelings or fantasies with anyone. I
knew no language in which to express them. No one told me
I was wrong, or different. I just knew that I was, and that it
was not a safe subject for discussion.*

Indirectly, it ended up being to Jackie's benefit that her
mother had such a contentious relationship with her own
parents. When Jackie was about to start high school, opinions
about her schooling were swirling around her. Her mother's
family thought she should take business courses, so she could
get a job immediately after graduation and help support her
mother. But a teacher at Jackie's grammar school had said that
Jackie should go on to college, so that's what her mother decided.
Whether it was to rebel against her family's wishes, or because
she felt college was the best option for her daughter, it worked
out well for Jackie.

Jackie attended the college preparatory Girls Latin School
in Boston, and found she loved the atmosphere of an all-girls
school. "I felt at home in this place where young women were
respected for their abilities to achieve in the academic world."
The school had a history that went back to the 1600s, but it
had traditionally been exclusive socially, and exclusively for
boys. Even when a separate school for girls was established
in the 1880s, the student population continued to be children from college-educated families. Even though Jackie felt
accepted, she knew her background didn't match those of the
other students.

*Once again, I was different, because every other student at
the school had come from families where people had gone
to college. I was the first in my family to do that. So there
wasn't anybody in my family who could give me guidance,
and I really needed to get it from school. They had a part-
time guidance counselor who three-quarters of the time
taught Latin. She didn't quite know what to do with me,
because she really didn't have to do that much work for other
students. Their families knew how to get them into college.
So, it got really late, and I didn't have a college placement.*

Jackie was advised to apply to Boston Teachers' College,
but decided against it. Even though there weren't a lot of career
options open to women, Jackie wasn't sure she wanted to be a
teacher. Besides, she also knew more about the college than most
high-schoolers would. Boston Teachers' College was physically
connected to the Girls' Latin School. Jackie knew she didn't
want to face another four years in what was essentially the same
building, but she also had some more serious concerns.

*I was aware enough about my education to know that they
were doing some rather strange things at Boston Teachers'
College. Like in their Biology course they had torn out the
chapter on reproduction, and that wasn't being taught. In
Boston, even though it was public school, most of my teachers
were Catholic—Irish Catholics. They read from the Douay
version of the Bible, and the New Testament in class every
morning. There was supposed to be separation of church and
state. So Boston Teacher's College would have been a last
resort choice for me.*

The day before her high school classes ended, the guidance
counselor called Jackie's mother to tell her that Jackie was
being offered a scholarship to Suffolk University. It had been
an evening law school, but had recently added a day liberal arts

program. It had also been an all-male school. In an early affirmative action-style program, the school was now offering some scholarships to women.

> *I didn't find out until my senior year at Suffolk that the school was not accredited. I spent a year working before I went to graduate school. Sometime during that year, they got their accreditation, so that saved me.*
>
> *It didn't matter, because it was so great for me. Even though I was commuting from home, and it was a small school, still in Boston, it was still a light for me. It just opened me up to new possibilities and new friends. I had a wonderful relationship with the faculty. It changed my life.*

While at Suffolk, Jackie formed a close friendship with one of the few African-American women in her class. There were so few women at Suffolk that they formed a Women's Association to get together and form bonds. Jackie's friend was president of the Association. At one point, her friend bought some holiday gifts, and dropped them off at Jackie's home when Jackie was not there. Later, Jackie was lectured by her stepfather for letting "her" put Jackie in a terrible position by coming to their all white neighborhood. After all, what would the neighbors think about having someone of color who expected to be invited in. Her mother stayed quiet through this, even when Jackie's stepfather implied that, since the woman didn't come in, it would look like she was just delivering something. Jackie was horribly hurt that her mother didn't speak up.

Jackie's friend later invited her to a party on Martha's Vineyard, where her family lived, and she jumped at the chance. When she told her parents where she was going, and with whom, her stepfather put his foot down and forbade her to go.

> *I was twenty, but I was still living at home. I was dependent at that time. So my sense was, "If I assert myself, and do*

what I know is right in my heart, it's going to make the rest of the family miserable. And I'll be out of here as soon as I can." So I didn't go to the party, and I had to tell my friend. She accepted it, and it didn't ruin our friendship.

In fact, she invited me and my best friend, who was also white, and two male white students that we were dating, to a party where we were the only white people. It was a big, fashionable party. That was my first experience at being totally in the minority. The other people were so accepting and gracious. It made the contrast stand out even more, in comparison, how our white family, and society, was so the opposite. It made my family uncomfortable, just having her presence at the door.

Even though it caused me sadness to see my mother not stand up for what I knew she really believed, no one could ever take away those values that she had given me.

Straight out of college, Jackie went to work for the Jewish Community Center. To get a full-time position, you needed to have a Master's Degree in Social Work, which Jackie didn't have. Instead, she was hired as part-time, meaning she was working twice as hard as her MSW counterparts for only $23 a week! She loved the work, and, best of all, it enabled her to move out of her home.

1963, at a social workers camp

Jackie had, technically, lived at home all through her first four years at college, but spent most of her time staying with her best friend. Her home life was still difficult. Her mother had remarried into a miserable relationship.

I got into a boarding house within walking distance of Harvard University, where there were graduate students from all over the world also living there. I was not very far away from a friend from college who had an apartment, and she helped me. I finally got away from my family life, and my mother's oppressiveness.

When I graduated from college, I had majored in English Literature, and minored in German. I was thinking about teaching English on the college level, because I loved it. I think a lot of my interest then was because I was so close to the English faculty, and my friends were all in that department.

I applied to Boston University, and was accepted in a master's degree program. There were some money issues, and I wasn't sure if I could get a scholarship. Also, I wasn't sure which I wanted to do more, Social Work or English Literature, in graduate school. That's why I decided to work at the community center, which would give me a chance to test out my interest.

From the age of 17, I had been a camp counselor. I loved working with kids. I seemed to have a talent for it. So that's what eventually won out. I applied to Wayne State University in Detroit, Michigan, and was accepted. You're supposed to apply to three schools. I couldn't stand having to write all those autobiographies. You couldn't write one and make copies of it. They all skewed their questions in a different way, so you had to write each one differently. I just decided to put all my eggs in one basket.

My supervisor at the community center helped me, because she was already in a graduate program. She said,

"Don't stay in Boston unless you have to. I'm here because my husband is here." She helped me meet some new friends, and they suggested a couple of schools. I chose what they said and got accepted. I don't know what I would have done if I hadn't! It was really a relief, to be totally on my own.

Within two years, Jackie had a Master's Degree in Social Work, with a major in group work. Her first field placement was with the B'nai B'rith Youth Organization, and her second field placement was at a settlement house in an all black, transitional neighborhood in Detroit. Jackie liked both jobs, and gained valuable experience that helped her get her next job with a local Girl Scout council.

Jackie had gotten some financial assistance from the United Way while she was in graduate school, and her only obligation to repay the money was to work at least one year in an agency that received United Way funds. The Girl Scouts fit the bill. After a bit of research, Jackie found that the Detroit council was bigger and more bureaucratic than she wanted. Through some connections, she got hired at a smaller, suburban council.

I got out of school in May, and started working in July. They didn't know what to do with me during the summer. They were so focused on day camp and summer camp. Otherwise, staff members took vacation during that time. So, as a new employee, they decided to send me to camp, since I'd already done some of that before.

The camp director, who was my college professor's room-mate, and I became involved, and that was my first lesbian experience. We've been friends ever since.

That wasn't my first awareness, but it was my first time sleeping with a woman. I recognized from some time in my teens that I would form these crushes on older women. My relationship with my mother was so difficult, that I had convinced myself that what I couldn't get from my mother, I was trying to get from these other women. I had just enough information to make my own diagnosis. At the same time, it always seemed to me there was something different operating, as these feelings were so intense. But those were the days when there wasn't anybody to talk to.

Jackie became depressed, and a friend referred her to a psychiatrist. She talked openly with him, and he indicated that her problems "stemmed from being a homosexual, arrested at the oral stage of my emotional development." He also told her that even psychoanalysis five times a week wouldn't cure her. Jackie told him she wasn't looking for a cure, and, for the first time in her life, she was comfortable with herself. She wanted relief from the depression, however.

Without any other resources to consult about this aspect of her life, Jackie had to figure things out by herself.

Now that she was aware of the nature of her feelings for other women, Jackie began to notice the behavior of many of the women in her daily life. As part of her job, Jackie would go to conferences for social workers. In this era, almost every social worker was female. After a conference session, it wasn't unusual to be invited to someone's room, with a bunch of other women, to socialize.

I'd walk into a room, and I'd see a 'heap' of women, and I mean a 'heap.' They would be heaped on a bed, just being together. And when I would walk into the room, I always felt like the process stopped. Nobody identified who they were or what they were. There was no passing on of information about the culture, or anything. I liked being with these people, but I felt there was some kind of unspoken mystery. It was like this was a club, and you had to have a secret password, which everybody knew but me. That's how I used to feel in their company.

That same reaction of caution may have happened anytime someone new entered the room, but to Jackie it felt personal. Because of that, she didn't develop any strong friendships among these women. When they were together, conversations were casual, and the words 'lesbian' or 'homosexual' were never mentioned. Jackie had heard the words since she was a child, and knew they were considered bad. Homosexuality was just not talked about.

After five years working with the Southern Oakland Girl Scout council, Jackie decided to move back east. Her sister now had a child, and Jackie wanted to be part of their lives. Wanting to avoid being too close to her mother, who was still in Boston, Jackie opted to move to New York.

Trying to connect with the complex social service system in New York City while living in Michigan was very difficult. In 1960, Jackie applied to the National Headquarters of the Girl Scouts. She succeeded in getting what seemed like a dream job, in the Camping Division, but quickly learned that it was not right for her. Jackie found the job too remote from the people to be served, mostly policy-making and article writing assignments. The office was filled with women, most of them older than Jackie. Even though Jackie was sure most of them were lesbians, no one was 'out.'

One of the other motivations behind Jackie's move to New York, was a woman now working at the YWCA, living nearby in Stamford, Connecticut. Jackie was in love with her. They lived together for two years, but Jackie always felt something wasn't quite right. She was also growing restless with her work with the Girl Scouts. To Jackie, it felt like the organization was wanting qualified social workers on their staff, but not capitalizing on what they offered. Instead, the agency worked hard to make the social workers conform to the ways things had always been done. It was a stifling atmosphere for her.

Jackie's lover had also been a co-worker at one point, and she knew Jackie was well qualified for a wide variety of jobs, so she helped her get an interview. After two years with the Girl Scouts, Jackie moved on to working as a supervisor of social services for 40 boys and girls at a facility that cared for children who didn't fit into the foster care system. It was an extremely challenging job, during a time when laws and regulations weren't in place to protect this unique group of individuals.

The agency taking these kids announced to the community, and to the funding people, that it was a residential facility for emotionally disturbed kids. However, the staff were doing all kinds of old fashioned parenting such as hitting them, and punishing them with confinement. It was a real test of my skill to work with the executive, to get him to see the problems.

It was like we were running two programs. In the daytime, I would be working with the kids, building trust, and using all kinds of techniques to help strengthen them. Then at night, they'd get punished for the very self-expressions I was teaching them how to do. Finally, the administrator saw that this was the case and he worked very well with me. But then, behind the scenes the Board was putting pressure on him to get rid of me, because they felt that the kids were acting out more.

The administrator didn't have to get rid of Jackie, because she'd had enough, and after two very challenging years, she took a position elsewhere. But she just couldn't walk away.

I found out the administrator was carrying around a letter. He had my letter of resignation in his left pocket. In his right pocket, he had a letter from the Board, instructing him to get rid of me. He hadn't had a chance to open my letter yet, and was feeling guilty knowing he had to do what they said, and he didn't want to. So he opened my letter, and was happily relieved of that responsibility.

Two younger Board members took me out to lunch, and said, "We need you to know that you're being asked to leave here. If that should happen, it has nothing to do with the quality of your work. It's because you're Jewish, and they have never had a Jew in any kind of authority position here." That was the first time in my life that I ever knew, openly, that I was encountering anti-Semitism.

On the job in 1970

I was so glad I had turned in my resignation. The executive wrote me an excellent letter of recommendation, and we stayed good friends. Then the staff wanted to resign in support of me. They were furious when they heard what was going on, and they were very unhappy that I was leaving. They were happy for me, but not happy for themselves. And I said, "No, you can't abandon these kids. What can we do to help them?"

What we did was to strategize. I called every agency that had placed a kid in the institution, and told them that great change was going on, and the Board had not committed to doing the kind of work that was necessary for these children. I told them that I had no control over who, if anyone, would be brought in to replace me. I did this, not because I thought I was the beginning and the end, but I thought that the Board would try to get someone who would just buckle under, and return the agency to its former state.

"I can't, in good conscience, any longer recommend to you that this is a good placement for this child." I said. "I *think there are other places in this state that would be more appropriate." So, by the time I left, the population was almost non-existent. I had formed such positive working relationships with these agencies that they knew my work, and they trusted me. They knew that if they left those kids there, they would leave them in danger. So we cleaned out the place. After that, they gradually changed their whole focus. Within the next few years, they became a foundation, and stopped trying to be a residence. So even though it didn't happen immediately, I think I began an important process.*

After leaving the agency, Jackie got a faculty position in the graduate School of Social Work at Rutgers University. This was during the Lyndon B. Johnson administration, when there was heightened awareness of the need for certification programs, and more extensive education opportunities for social workers. Jackie stayed there for six years, helping structure and develop programs that would improve the availability and effectiveness of social workers.

After six years, the question of tenure came up. Jackie was considered to be working at the University on "soft money," money from grants. Therefore, getting tenure wasn't a straight-forward process. Jackie had just started steps toward breaking into their tenure system, when she had a change of heart.

In the process of doing this, I suddenly realized I didn't want to be here anymore. It was the 1960s, and I wanted to see if I could do what I was asking my students to do. These were dangerous times, you know. It was when the race riots were going on in Newark, New Jersey, and all kinds of things were changing in the world. Students were demonstrating on college campuses, including ours, although it was pretty mild at Rutgers. So, going up for tenure was a wonderful thing for me, because it helped me to clarify that I didn't really want to stay at the university.

Jackie left her position at Rutgers without another job in hand, but that didn't worry her. After a few calls, she was offered a job that would allow her to be back working directly with clients. This transition wasn't easy though. Her new co-workers saw her as over-qualified, and were suspicious as to why she had left a university job to join their ranks. At the same time, her university connections couldn't understand what she was doing either. It didn't take long for Jackie to know it had been the best career move she'd ever made.

She wasn't alone through all of these career changes. She had a long-term partnership, and the two of them often worked together on projects where their fields intersected.

In 1990, as she neared 60 years of age, Jackie opted for an early retirement, as she'd accumulated enough years in social work to draw a pension, and she wanted to try something new. Jackie had left her long-term, closeted relationship, and was beginning to connect with the larger LGBT community. She had started a part-time counseling practice on the side. Retiring from social work early allowed Jackie to expand it, taking on contracts to work as a consultant with the schools, and to work with the AIDS community. This helped her move one step closer to her goal to come further out of the closet.

Toward the last, after I left my relationship, I was now out much more. I was in the gay community. I was now going to meetings, and my name was appearing in the newspaper, indicating that I was on this and that committee. I never did come out officially in the school district. Working in a high school as a consultant, every time a young woman walked into my office, there was already suspicion of what I was doing. Whatever anybody knew was fine. They knew that Chayke and I lived together. They all knew that we were lesbians. However, except for whatever kind of gossip went on, there was no confirmation of it.

In later years, I had books in my office and stuff on my bulletin board, so the kids would know that it was a safe place to come.

Several years later, after she was no longer working in the schools, Jackie was viewing the AIDS Quilt while it was at Rutgers, and saw two women teachers she recognized from the last school where she had worked. They had always been together, and Jackie had wondered about them, but they had never talked with each other. When Jackie spotted the two together, her earlier suspicions were confirmed. Once they saw Jackie, they immediately left. "I was dangerous," she felt. There were people, like this couple, who were even afraid to be seen associating with her.

Jackie hadn't fully realized how lonely she was, and how she had limited herself by not coming out. By not being out, finding other lesbians wasn't easy. She had made some connections through a lesbian friend or two, but her circle was very limited. When she had entered her 22-year relationship, it was with a woman who was homophobic, and most of their friends were straight. When they did connect with other lesbians, nothing was ever admitted openly. It was always a big secret. Even with the women's movement happening all around them, they stayed isolated.

When she was working in a large high school in the 1970s, Jackie made friends with a home-economics teacher, who encouraged her and her partner to travel to Cape Cod for their vacation. "That friendship is what really opened me up," said Jackie. That summer offered several opportunities for Jackie and her partner to build connections, and to see that it was possible to lead a fuller lesbian life. When the same group had a big party in New Jersey, Jackie had another revelation.

I walked into this party, and I had never seen so many lesbians, you know. They were sitting on each other's laps.

They were hugging each other. They were kissing each other. They were talking. My first reaction was aaaah, and then I realized that this is where I belong. That began to change things.

It didn't happen immediately, but when friends came to visit them months later, the dam of silence finally broke. It seems that the other women had decided that they had had enough of avoiding the subject, so they asked straight out, "How long have you two been together?" That was the first time that anyone had directly asked Jackie the question. Not only did she feel safe enough to answer, it was never the same afterwards.

Along with a growing sense of comfort and pride about being a lesbian, Jackie's activism also kicked into high gear. Activism wasn't something new to her, but it had always been motivated by a personal experience. Her earliest awareness of being part of an action was an incident in college. In Detroit, in 1953, Jackie had had an African-American classmate with whom she and two other women had worked closely on a large project. The woman contributed equally to the project, and other classwork, yet the professor insisted on making remarks about "how good she was doing for a Negro." She and the other two project-mates tried first to get the professor to understand his error, but ended up having to go to the dean with their concerns. They were essentially patted on the head and sent on their way.

For Jackie, it was her first conscious act of trying to bring about change. It wasn't her last. Throughout her career, she capitalized on opportunities to stand against what she perceived as injustice, and to create and support programs to improve the lives of the disadvantaged. During the early seventies, Jackie was part of the longest running teachers' strike ever to have happened in the United States, in Newark, New Jersey.

As she stepped out of the closet, Jackie turned some of her activist drive to gay and lesbian issues. She started small, helping to pull together a directory to aid guidance counselors in finding help for kids questioning their sexual identity. Before long, she assumed more active roles on committees and kept going from there. In her acts of LGBT activism, Jackie was very involved in AIDS work, specifically with people who were HIV positive and homeless.

Jackie found that the activist work she did at this stage of her life taught her several very important lessons, and opened up her way of thinking. As a social worker, she'd always worked under the basic tenet that you can't counsel someone when they are under the influence. Suddenly, she began to see that while you might not be able to counsel them into making better decisions for themselves when they are under the influence, you can help them meet some of their other needs. Perhaps that will move them to a point where they can benefit from counseling. It takes a change in thinking to work with people, not from where you want them to be, but from where they are.

Another of Jackie's activist passions revolved around SONG, Southerners On New Ground. SONG works for

In the early 90s

LGBTQ liberation across all lines of race, class, abilities, age, culture, gender, and sexuality in the southern United States.

I was fortunate to go to a meeting of Equality Florida at which SONG did one of their trainings. After that, my life just changed. When I moved down here to Florida, I really went into some kind of culture shock. All of my early life involved bi-racial and inter-racial contacts at work, and in my friendships. When I got here and found out how segregated it was, and I wasn't working, I had no way of meeting people of color. I went to a meeting where SONG's board of directors spoke, and I heard what they were about, and watched them work, and I thought, "There's a place where I can connect."

This period in her life also brought Jackie another new adventure, the opportunity to focus on nurturing a new life with Edie. Getting to the place in her lesbian life where she could have a full and healthy relationship hadn't been a smooth road. Her first few relationships had been brief, very closeted, and her long-term relationship also brought lots of challenges.

It was twenty-two years in the closet. Ten of those years we didn't live together, and twelve we did. Whenever I would get close to thinking we should be more open, it was too threatening to her. This was partly because she was still work-ing in the city in which she grew up. We were both working there. She had a very large extended Jewish Orthodox family, and was very fearful of what her reputation would become.

The impact on our relationship was tremendous stress. Everything had to come from the relationship, because we knew we wouldn't have community. We had friends, many of whom were also in closeted relationships, but we never talked about that.

How do you find people? It's very difficult. I loved my first partner dearly, and I loved the things that we did together. We did a lot of traveling and enjoyed so many of the same things like classical music, jazz, art, the theatre, eating in interesting ethnic restaurants, and just walking in New York. We would park the car and say, "Well, we haven't been on this block before. Let's walk around the block and see what it has to offer." She had a zest for life which was wonderful, but I always had this sense of loneliness.

I could never figure out what it was about until I met a woman at work that I hadn't known before, a teacher who had referred someone to me as a client. Later, she told me that she had done her best to seduce me. She finally succeeded, and we had an affair that lasted for about three and a half years.

It wasn't until I ended the affair, and, by then, had left my partner, that I moved into the lesbian and gay community in a major way. I found a therapist, a lesbian feminist, who really helped me understand what was going on inside me, and what getting involved in the affair had meant for me. This was a woman who was actually more closeted than I am now, but she was 'out' compared to what I was then. She had real positive feelings about being a lesbian, and could talk about it, which was very attractive to me.

So, beyond the obvious initial sexual attraction, it was me really grasping for community and being open. I'm a very open person, and was in every other way. It was really crippling to hide this part of me, particularly once I got beyond the stage of thinking that I was sick. There was a time I had believed what I had been told, that if you are a homosexual you are mentally ill. But I had no evidence of having a mental illness. I finally got to that point where I realized that it wasn't true, that my sexuality was a part of me, and that it was right. From my first sexual experience with Ann, I felt like this is what I am supposed to be. This is what has been missing in my life. I felt whole. Then to have this void, and feeling of loneliness that just was with me wherever I went, was very difficult.

After I ended that affair, I stayed in therapy and also became much more active in the community. First, I was in a SAGE over-50 support group, with women from 50 to 90, and some women were just coming out in their 80s! Their stories varied from much more closeted than I had been, to having been out in the bars and arrested in that whole scene in New York. I heard every kind of story, and I really got a taste of women's history in a way, especially lesbian women's history, than I'd ever known before. It all just kept saying to me, "You've done the right thing. This is right."

I made friends, and it just changed my whole outlook. As a result of that, and my political activities in the lesbian and gay community in New Jersey, I even gradually changed the focus of my private practice. I started to advertise in lesbian and gay publications, so that I started to have more adult clients than kids, and was ready for that.

I had spent my whole life working with kids, and it felt good to be working with adults for a change. Then I started to have almost only lesbians and gay men as clients, along with a couple of bisexual women. The more I worked with gay people, the more natural that felt and the healthier I felt.

After leaving that affair, I was single for eight years. I dated some. I really learned how to live by myself, which was a very important relationship. Also, I learned the difference between 'being alone' and 'being lonely.'

It was from that base, then, that I met Edie. I came to this relationship in a way that I had never come to a relationship before. All of me came to the relationship, with a woman who was also able to bring all of herself to me. This has been the healthiest and most wholesome relationship I've ever been in, because it is also the most conscious.

We came together and talked about the fact that neither of us wanted to be in a relationship just for the sake of a relationship. We wanted to add something to our lives. We didn't have to be in a relationship. We wanted to be enriched. We wanted to be with another person because we liked her, we enjoyed being intimate, and we wanted to be with someone who was willing to work on the relationship.

Neither of us had really had that in our relationships before. To say that it was easy would be a lie. It was very, very difficult. Especially when you get two old women who are set in their ways, and who know what's right. But it's been a period that's been total joy.

If I could say one thing to other lesbians out there, or anybody who feels sexually different, it's to just be yourself and be open. Don't stay in the closet. It's dangerous, and it's harmful to your mental health. So these years of retirement have been the happiest, and the most productive, of my life. Learning on a personal level has made it possible for me to learn on many other levels. So, that's what I wanted to share.

Jackie loves, learns, plays (and indulges in her passion of perusing catalogs) in Florida with her partner, Edie, where they are both involved in a myriad of projects and causes.

Interviewer: Arden Eversmeyer

Jess
McVey

**Born February 1918 in Massachusetts
Interviewed in 2003, and 2008
at age 85, and 90, in California**

I needed to think about myself.

Most people have a healthy dose of curiosity and wonder, but Jess received a double dose early in life, of curiosity, wonder, and audacity. Named at birth Jane McVey Walker, the McVey part came from her family connection to the McVey's in Scotland, who were skilled designers of patterns used to weave tartan plaids. She later dropped the "Walker" and went with her nickname, Jess.

Born into a working class family, some of Jess' earliest memories are of riding along with the men who helped her father deliver coal. The wagon was drawn by a draft horse and when they got to their destination, bags of coal were dumped into metal chutes that carried them down into the cellars of homes and buildings.

*I loved doing that. I got to know the guys and went with
them all over town delivering coal. I played with the kids
in the public school. They were Italian, Polish, and French
Canadian. I was never invited to their houses, but played
with them. It was an interesting place to grow up, because I
saw the whole structure, from capitalism right on down to the
poor people.*

Jess' only sibling was less than four years older than she,
but their personalities were very different, and they seldom
played together. Neither did she play much with neighborhood
kids. Essentially, she was a loner growing up. When she was in
junior high, Jess ventured out of her comfort zone, and joined a
boys club.

*Somehow I was included in that club. We had it in the back
rafters of the parsonage. It was a wonderful clubhouse. We
hung carpets around to make the walls, and we had these
little warmers, little fires that had wax in a container with
a piece of string as the wick. I can't think of anything more
dangerous! But we had wonderful times. There were probably
four or five girls, and the rest were boys.*

She happily hung out with the boys for years, building
airplanes out of balsa wood, and digging tunnels. When she got
to high school, her parents decided to send her to a prep school.

*I was horrified. I remember going in my room, and throwing
myself on my bed and screaming. I didn't want to leave my
friends. I was involved with various young men at that point.
I used to come home from operetta practice through the
woods, so Arthur and I could kiss. I think these little items
were on my mother's mind. All I know was I had nothing to
say about it. That was it.*

*So off I went to the Northampton School for Girls in
Northampton, Massachusetts. And I loved it. I was behind*

in math, because of the differences in the school systems, so I worked with a math teacher, an older woman who loved math. It was so wonderful. And I was not a good student at all. We had these breaks, and we'd meet in this little social room to play music and dance. This was a prep school for just women, so we danced together.

Miss Jane McVey Walker

I remember dancing with this one woman, and we'd always dance together. I loved it. I loved dancing with that woman. She went on to Smith College. I felt very badly when I saw her with a man. She was dating this man! I thought, "How come she's with him?"

I played field hockey there, and I liked that, but I was not a good student. I was just not interested in it. Consequently, I never passed enough tests to get into Smith College.

There was an option, in those days, to go to a tutorial school to get caught up. Jess enrolled in one in Boston, and learned enough to pass the tests and go to Smith College. Even then, Jess didn't stay long enough to graduate. She was distracted by a man.

My family was going to a beach during the summer, at Harwich Port on Cape Cod in Massachusetts. My mother rented an apartment in this exclusive area in the town, and we met different people who lived nearby and down on the beach. That's where I met my husband. A new family was coming into the area, and we were supposed to be good to them. I went down to the beach this day and saw this guy, and I thought, "I don't know him. He must be one of those that we're supposed to be good to," make him feel at home, and so forth. I really liked him. At night, we went to a "rumpus house." In that neighborhood, a garage had been made over into a place where kids could hang out, play records and do whatever at the "rumpus house."

This fellow, Frank, asked me to dance, and that was it. It's funny to think of it now. That was it. Bang. Bang. He was a freshman at Amherst at that time, which was seven miles down the road from Smith College. So I spent a lot of time at Amherst. His grandfather had gone there, his father had gone there, and his brother was there, too. You know, one of those family things.

At the time, I first heard classical music. My family didn't do music. We didn't do anything like that. I read constantly. My father took me to the library, which was at the other end of town. We both read. My mother did, too, but I remember going with my father.

We would listen to the New York Philharmonic on Sunday afternoons. I just nearly died. For example, I heard for the first time the Cesar Franck Symphony and it was too much! I could hardly stand it, it was so beautiful.

There was a series of symphonies being given at Smith College, and Frank took me to those, an opera series. He'd come over in his great car, and we'd go. I remember once he was drunk, and he got there, looking somewhat disheveled, but we went to the symphony.

I learned to smoke cigarettes, and to drink coffee and alcohol. And I may have learned a few other things, as well. I learned that you can make a Tom Collins last all evening. It's sort of like lemonade. And so, to do what the others were doing, I would order a Tom Collins, and make that last the whole time, wherever we were. Then I really learned to drink. Frank also drank.

I left college and we got married when Frank graduated. It was against both families' wishes. They felt I should finish college, but I was not exactly college material.

*My father wanted to give
us a car as a wedding present,
and Frank refused it. He said,
"No. I'll take care of things."
We didn't know anything about
anything. Frank was quite smart
and really a nice person. He
was just going through this "I'll
show my family stuff," trying out
everything. I went happily along
with him. I didn't have a brain
in my head.*

With Frank in 1940

*We had a big wedding in
the Episcopal Church. I had white satin fancy underpants
with a zipper. In those days, having a zipper was vogue. We
knelt in front of the minister, and I knew that the zipper had
given way. But there was a train on the gown, and we did
this lock-step walk. My underpants were around my feet, but
nobody could tell.*

Jess somehow managed to make it out of the church
sanctuary without leaving her panties behind, and she threw
herself into marriage.

*I did the house-wifely things. My husband's sister came and
taught me how to cook. I felt it was my job, you see, to be a
housewife. I can remember giving talks to women, telling
them that being a housewife could be a career. I mean, look,
you're up working twenty-four hours a day. You're a nurse,
you're a doctor, you're a mistress, blah, blah, blah. Gave them
all this pep talk.*

Over the next decade, Jess had several children. They
hadn't planned on having children right away, but it happened.

It seemed like every time one child got old enough to go off to kindergarten, or day care, Jess would be pregnant again.

Less than a decade into her marriage, it started to crumble. Her husband had gone off to war for a couple years, and when he came back Jess found out he'd spent his time away living with a French woman in Casablanca.

I needed some money one day so I called him up at work and said, "I need some money to go buy blah, blah, blah." He said, "Well, my wallet is in the trousers hanging in the closet." So I got the wallet out, and there was a picture of this woman.

For a couple of years, it was pretty grim between us. But we stuck together, because when you have children you don't get divorced. We were clear on that.

Jess and her husband continued to stay together for the sake of the kids, but their life was tumultuous. They made several moves, leaving the city life that they had all known for suburbia, and then leaving suburbia behind for a farm. Neither she nor Frank knew anything about farming, but his thinking was that as long as they loved the outdoors, it would be okay.

With my mother-in-law's help, we purchased this house that had been abandoned, because the family had grown up, and the mother wanted to move into the city. We moved into this house with ten acres to do farm work. My husband continued his job. He was teaching at Boston University, and had to drive in, rain or shine.

We worked very hard. We were there for 15 years, the longest we ever lived anywhere. We had cows, sheep, and pigs, just enough to raise our own food. I had a huge garden. We worked like mad, and we loved it.

The kids grew up. Some of them had already split. They headed for the city to get out of this place. I don't think there was anything wrong with our family. I think they were naturally adventurous. Everyone eventually moved to different places away from Groton.

But while we were there, we dug our own pond. We had a pond with fresh water springs, and we stocked it with trout, and we had a big garden. We raised all these different animals. Frank milked the cow before he left each morning. Farming was something else again.

Jess' mother had suffered her whole adult life with mental illness, and at one point, while living on the farm, Jess thought she was following in her mother's footsteps.

Along the way, I cracked up. It was back when some of the kids had left, while some were still there. We were going away for a weekend, and I knew I had to go and see my Aunt Grace, who was in Cambridge. I felt I had to go see her before we could go on this camping trip. All of a sudden, I thought, "I'm dying. I'm going to die." I went downstairs, and my husband was in his study with the door closed. I said, "Frank, I don't feel well. I feel like I'm dying. I don't feel well at all." He got an ambulance, and whisked me off to the hospital. I couldn't breathe, and I was sure this was it. I was sure something terrible was happening to me.

It turned out nothing terrible was happening. A doctor came around and he said, "Is there anything you really want to talk about?" I said, "I think I drink too much."

I went to see a psychiatrist, a Quaker man. He was part of our Quaker medical group. I started going to see him, and out of all that came that I needed to do something for myself, and not just my family. I needed to think about myself.

I had a book by Mary McCarthy. It had to do with Florence. It's was a big beautiful book. I said to myself, "Very well, I'm going to make something of myself. I'm going to be somebody."

I used to get on my bike and ride two or three miles over a back dirt road. There was another road available, but I rode up the dirt road. There was a big hill there, and I loved to go tearing down that hill on my bike. I would end up in the town of Groton.

The library was open on Monday mornings. I went around to the library with my Mary McCarthy book, and I began to look up every word that I didn't know. Pretty soon, two librarians got kind of interested and asked, "What are you doing?" I explained, and then one morning they said, "Would you like to help with the over due books?" I said, "Yeah, sure." So, subsequently, I became a librarian, and was opening and closing the library on Wednesday nights, and loving it! I loved it. It took me away from my family. It took me out. I was somebody. I really got into it.

Somewhere along the way, Frank had also decided we should all move to France, since he was a romance language teacher. He cleaned out all the money in the children's bank account, and the family headed across the ocean. Jess said, "It was the most insane thing in the world for us to do." Frank didn't stay satisfied in France for long, and next he tried returning to Boston University. They didn't stay there long. He had some ideas he wanted them to use in the English department, and they were not interested.

Declaring that he'd had enough of Boston, the family once again packed everything in a VW microbus van with a canoe on top. Jess, her husband, and the kids that were still living at home, made the move to Oregon, and settled in. As soon as Frank was working and the kids were in school, Jess once again got a job at a local library.

Things in her life continued to fall apart around her. By now, Jess could no longer ignore the pull toward women she was experiencing, and she began to explore.

I don't remember the exact circumstances, but I knew there was a women's bar. I thought, "No way." I hadn't even known what a lesbian was. But I went. I crept into this bar. The end of the bar was close to the road, and I'd slide into a seat there. The rest of the bar was full of women, and I was scared to death somebody would say something to me. But I got friendly with the bartender, so that was a safe place. Nobody ever came and talked to me, or anything. I began to feel safe with them, and that was good.

My instincts have saved my life at various times when I have been desperate. When we first moved to Portland, Oregon, from the east coast, my family all had new jobs, and I didn't. I went out and began to pick fruits and vegetables with the migrant workers. I picked strawberries with them, which was hard. You are on your knees, and you are there at the crack of dawn. I did beans, which were lots of fun, as they were beautiful. I loved working outside.

I would always get home by the time the kids got home, and I was doing what I wanted to do. Then I raked filberts. The way you gather those nuts is a specific way of raking. I thought that was beautiful. The lines of the trees, all lined up; gorgeous. A woman there taught me how to do that. When the nut season ended, she said, "Maybe you want a job in holly?" I said sure. There was a woman who ran a wreath-making business, beginning around Thanksgiving and running up through Christmas. So she hired me. I prepared the holly for the person who made the wreaths. It was just around the corner from where I lived. I loved it.

My son, who was at Reed College, used to come over for Sunday lunch, and bring his friends. Frank and I would cook a great big meal for Tom and his friends. Then he would have the best time introducing his mother as a "stripper." That's what you were called when you rearranged stuff for wreaths, a "stripper."

The other thing that really saved me was a group of people who had started a food co-op, one of the first ones in Portland. I had heard about it. I had the microbus and I had separated from my husband. They wanted to know if I would pick up the milk, which came in half gallon glass containers, was quite heavy, and wouldn't always fit into regular cars. "Would I do that? Would I pick it up and bring it to the store?" Sure. So I did that. And I met these people who were doing that before, all ages, running a cooperative food store.

I always had my own personal friends, women, with many children, and we'd share stuff. I began to notice, one of them would come in and say, "Gee, how's your cold? Are you feeling better?" They cared about each other. This was a real eye opener to me. Wow. This was something else again.

Things were changing rapidly in Jess' life, and she soon found herself taking her youngest child, Murphy, out of school. They headed down to San Francisco where another daughter, Nancy, lived. Jess had the wanderlust, and she, by her own admission, abandoned Murphy. Nancy became Murphy's legal guardian, but Murphy was essentially living on the streets.

Heading south from San Francisco, Jess began living out of her car, driving all over the country, and even down into Central America. All it cost was the gas, and she ate at local markets. Eventually, she ended up working once again at a food co-op, this time as a cook. She had never been a part of the 1960s culture, and was fascinated, feeling she fit in. She'd saved some money from an inheritance, and became involved in a women's collective bookstore, and then entered into a communal living situation.

Some land came up for sale in the Columbia Gorge, 180 acres, up high. One of the people that I had become involved with, a man, knew about this. And I had the money for the down payment. So I went up and looked at that land with

*him. It was cold and snowy, and it was in the Columbia
River Gorge. It's dead end, magic land.*

*I made the down payment, and a group of us lived there.
There were about ten or twelve of us. I had the only car, and
the only watch. We had no electricity, nothing like that. We
cooked with wood. God, it was beautiful up there. We looked
down on the Columbia River. We had a spring, and we ran
fresh water, gravity flow, into a community building. There
were cliffs around. It was magic land. I changed a lot during
that period when I lived there.*

She still had a house in Portland, but was renting it out
while she lived on the Columbia Gorge. At one point, while Jess
was briefly in town, a friend of her daughters' showed up looking
for a place to stay.

*She said, "You know, I'd really like to go up to this land, and
see what you talk about so much." And I said, "Okay." Off
we went to the land, which is maybe an hour and a quarter
from Portland. On the back part of the 180 acres is this little
run-down cabin. We figured we'd sleep there.*

*She'd brought up some dope, and I smoked with her. I
remember that so well. Of course, we then made love, and
touching a woman's body for the first time, I could nearly
die. It was just too much. I was so high for two or three days
I could hardly speak to anybody. That's how that happened.
From then on, various people along the way have hooked up
with me, and lived with me, and traveled with me, and made
love with me.*

*I ended up in Santa Barbara living on a boat for a while.
That was the cheapest way to live, so I bought this boat.
And along came this woman. I had a friend who was taking
art classes, and I dropped in to see how it was doing. It was
a drawing class, the model wasn't coming and the teacher
wasn't there. So this woman said, "Hey, why don't you*

Jess, early 50s

*model?" I said, "Me? Model?
I've never done that." And she
said, "I'll show you. You don't
have to do much."*

*So then I got signed up to
come in the next time the model
wasn't coming, and I was
there the next week. I became
interested in this woman that
had taught me a little bit
about modeling. She was part
of the class, a student. That
was Sarah. I fell in love with
Sarah. I still love Sarah. We
talk on the phone every now and then for a couple of hours.
Remember this? Remember that?*

*I had a telephone, and I ran a modeling business from
the boat. I had become 'the hot model of Santa Barbara.' I
was in my fifties, I didn't have kids, I was a lesbian, and I
didn't model with my legs close together. I just sat around,
and I was really quite good. I modeled at a graduate school, a
university, for the public school systems, adult education, but
mostly for the city college and artists. I ran this business, and
it was great.*

*Sarah wanted me to come and model for a group of
artists at her place, and I said, "Sure." Afterwards she said,
"Would you like to get in the hot tub?" And I said, "Well,
I don't have a bathing suit." And she said, "It's alright, my
mother-in-law has been here. I have a bathing suit that you
can put on." "Well, all right," I responded. By then, everybody
else had gone. I thought this was a little weird, so I put on
the bathing suit and got in the hot tub in her backyard. It
was a nice little suburban house in Santa Barbara. I thought,
"What am I doing getting in this tub with a married*

woman?" *You know, one thing led to another, and I made love to Sarah. I do love Sarah. I just love her. It's that simple.*

That was one of the few times that I recognized myself as myself. I thought my kids would be horrified if they knew I was modeling naked. You know? I was good, and I was good because of me, not because of anything that I had learned in school. It was me. That's one of the first times that I really recognized my worth. I'd never ever felt anything like that.

The upshot of it was I got practically thrown out of the college. I had gotten hot and heavy into going to school by that time, not having done well at Smith College. I was into getting my degree, but I dropped out and cut all my classes because of Sarah's husband. He would bicycle off at quarter past eight in the morning to go to work. I would come in by eight-thirty. In the garage was this old mattress. Sarah used this space as sort of a study and art studio. We'd make love all morning long, and then we'd hear the mailman coming. He would walk up by the garage, so then we'd have to shut up until he delivered the mail. That went on day after day after day. Eventually, she left her husband. He left her. I moved in.

For Jess, her stint as a model helped bring many aspects of her earlier life into perspective.

People asked me, "How was it being married?" And I said it was an absolute zero. I thought of myself as a zero, until I cracked up, and pushed myself out to get a job in the library system. I was a zero. But here, I was me. Very nice. I loved it. And I was good. Whatever art shows of work happened in that area, I would go to them. I knew that I would always be in the first prize. And I was. Over and over, and over. They hadn't had a model like myself, who felt okay about my body. I wasn't hiding anything. And they hadn't had anybody like that. They had just had the usual models. So that was a nice lift for my esteem.

I had various lovers. Sometimes, some lived with me. I learned from some, and they learned from me. We're all friends. I'm friends with all my lovers. Most of my lovers came to me and said, "Hey, let's do it!" And I said, "Sure, let's do it!" Various things would eventually happen, after three or four years, and they'd move on. After Sarah, I tried a couple of affairs with men. No way. I didn't do that.

While she was beginning to understand herself better, Jess still felt she was a prisoner to the prevailing beliefs about age and about women in the workplace.

Back in Santa Barbara I was taking all the classes that I could that had to do with the ocean. I wanted to be a marine biologist. I went to the head of the department, who knew me, and I asked for his advice. He said, "You know, you're really too old. They'll choose other people when they're choosing people for jobs. They'll choose other people who are younger." And I bought it, you know. I bought it. And there weren't very many role models at that time, thirty years or so ago. And I didn't have the confidence to just stay ahead on my own. But I'm thinking they lost a really good researcher.

Jess may not have had the option to begin a new career in marine biology, but fish, and all things related, continued to play a large role in her life anyway. She began to revisit her own passion for art, creating pieces that reflected her fascination with fish in various media, including wood, clay, bone, and sketching, painting, fabric and paper.

Years earlier, when she had lived overlooking the Columbia River Gorge, Jess had noticed the beauty of the wood in the branches they trimmed from the fruit trees, and she began making earrings. When she'd lived in Baja, her lover had been a pottery and clay, teacher and Jess had learned how to work with that medium.

I no longer was lonely when I was playing with those little pieces of fruitwood. Life went on, and I began to feel a certain satisfaction in doing this. People would say, "Are you an artist?" I would look at the ground and I would say, "No, I make a few things with my hands." Now I say, "Yes, I am an artist." And if I should run into somebody like Picasso, I'd say, "Listen, this is what I like about your work. And if I were you, I'd change this. I really don't like this about your work. Would you like to see my work?"

It takes so long for women. It's taken me 20 years to arrive at that point.

Jess continued to honor her drive to learn new things, whenever and wherever she could. Although during her youth she said she was not "college material," Jess enjoyed college at 85.

Today, I like classes a lot, so I'm auditing at San Francisco State, which is available legally in the state of California, if you are a certain age, in any university. This is a law. And so I've arranged it so I can get to college at the end of an afternoon. I'm not very good at driving at night, and I'm afraid of being alone with men around when it's dark. I can park at the end of the afternoon, because the day students have left, and the evening students have not come. I arrange it so I feel safe. I'm never really alone there.

I've learned a lot of little tricks of how to go to the college successfully at my age. I take a lot of international politics, which I'm interested in. And occasionally, I take art classes that are lecture courses. I'm planning to take one this fall, which has to do with the history of African art. It's given by a person who I have had before, who is excellent. So I'm always interested in learning new things.

Jess has had to make a few concessions to accommodate her advancing age and infirmities, but she's been able to do it without giving up learning, which was essential to her.

Working with clay

So how do I live today? First, I write down a lot of things that need to be done, because I've become very forgetful. What's more, I'm mixing up my dates now, which is even worse. I can't remember whether it's Tuesday, or whether what I said I was going to do was on Tuesday or Wednesday. So I keep a lot of things written down. I consult in my mind. "Okay, what is today? What is it I'm expected to do today?" That sort of thing. I try each day to have something that's sort of a carrot at the end of the day. Usually, it's some kind of art, or it might be a book that I haven't had time to read. Often, I'm too tired at the end of a day to accomplish much reading, and I fall asleep.

Now I'm beginning to read in the paper about nano-technology, n-a-n-o. That has to do with using little chips, computer chips which are one millionth of a meter. They are so tiny that the rules of materials don't exist any longer for them, and I'm not sure what that means. To me, they were indicating "here's the future." I'm fascinated. I'm fascinated by the future.

I am trying to set it up so that when I fall apart, more than I am now, it'll be a situation that'll be comfortable. I haven't quite figured that out yet. I have money in the bank, which I've saved, that I've inherited, and I'm not touching. If I have to, I will, but I think of it as being for the kids. I have money that I've saved myself. I've lived really quite frugally since I was separated from my husband. Where I'm living now is "higher on the hog" than I've ever lived. I was so excited. I have a place to put my toothbrush. I've lived in artist's studios and things like that. There is a place to put your toothbrush in the bathroom! I think that's pretty splendid. So I'm pretty safe. I have family, and I have money in the bank, which I can use if I need to. That's pretty good.

We do have family events. It's a very close family, and we have an extended family as well. So we have great family *gatherings. The traffic is wonderful. And I'm part of a group of nine old lesbian women, mostly in their seventies. We have evolved, over the years, into quite a strong group now. We started out with a different name, and now we have become quite a strong support group. The community aspect, I like that a lot. It's important to me to have friends that I can count on in difficult times. I'm not sure how much we depend on each other yet. In little ways, I think we're beginning to. But as we get on in our lives, I expect we'll provide even more support. I'm thinking about this, and that I was a loner.*

So in connection with my daily life, I was talking about having a little something that's an okay thing, and something that's pleasant, as well as all the things I feel I need to do. I don't spend any time on housework. I've already done that one. So I live in lovely clutter, and get on with my life.

That's what keeps me alive today. I'm live and well, more or less, at 85, because I have an interest in these different things that are happening, and I'm interested in the political things in the world, from a humanitarian viewpoint. How can anybody not be interested?

Jess McVey re-established a strong relationship with her children later in life. She died in 2010 at 92 years of age.

Interviewer:
Ida VSW Red.

copyright photo by Cathy Cade, www.CathyCade.com

Eleanor 'Ellie' Schafer

Born January 1917 in Pennsylvania
Interviewed in 2003, at age 86, in Arizona

I'm a people person, and I need to be working with people.

Ellie attended public school in a building that housed all twelve grades. As in most small towns in Pennsylvania, the school and the local churches were the heart of the community. "That's all we had besides the river to swim and play in during the summer." When she wasn't at school, singing in the church choir, or splashing in the Lehigh River, Ellie could usually be found helping her father.

I had an older sister, two years older, and that was it, two girls. I guess I felt that always meant that I had to be my father's boy, so I was the tomboy in the family. At first, my father had a butcher shop, and then a meat market with a grocery store. I was his helper and I had to learn to drive in my senior year in high school in order to make his deliveries.

When I was at home from my first year in college, he put me right back in the job. I was the deliveryman.

One of the good things about my young life there was that my mother was ambitious for us and, when we finished high school, she wanted us to go to college, to get out of the small town. So my sister and I both went to West Chester. It was a small state college outside of Philadelphia. I didn't know what else to do. My mother wanted me to go into nursing, and I didn't know anything about nursing. She thought it would be a good idea to be a nurse, because this was back in the 1930s. You even had to be a nurse to be an airline hostess back then!

West Chester was a very lovely, quiet town in suburban Philadelphia. Many of the sidewalks were laid with brick, it was that kind of town. We only went home at Thanksgiving, Christmas, and Easter. My sister and I didn't go home in between, but I had relatives in Philadelphia that I could visit. My sister and I lived in the dormitory, which was pretty strict. You were in by 8:00 at night, except Saturdays, it would be 10 p.m. When I went there in 1934, there was only one place where you could smoke in the dormitory.

Dorm life was where I had a first experience with other women, what we would now call lesbians. And that was a very light relationship, really, nothing heavy or steady. A lesson or two, when you would visit in Philadelphia with somebody's friend, or something of that sort, but no exposure, actually, to the lesbian and gay thing. This was the 1930s, pre-WW II and the word 'lesbian' was never used.

Although Ellie had some experiences that told her boys weren't the only game in town, she did as she was expected, and dated some. It wasn't serious. "You might be hanging around with girls in the dormitory after 8:00. Before 8:00, you were dating guys."

Despite her mother's pushing her toward nursing, Ellie majored in physical education, with plans to become a teacher. Ellie struggled some in college but her sister helped her. "In fact, one year, when I had to go to summer school, my sister was working down at the Jersey Shore, and she paid my tuition for summer school." When Ellie graduated in 1938, there were no teaching jobs to be had.

It was still Depression years, and few schools had physical education. I know the school I was raised in certainly didn't. So I didn't get a job when I first got out, but I did get a summer job teaching tennis at a YWCA camp in York, Pennsylvania. They had come down to the college to interview people for that job, and it was a good experience.

Ellie in 1938

That opportunity opened up my next fifteen years of professional work. The York YWCA hired me half time in September 1938, to teach swimming and volleyball to women and girls for their 'in town' program. I worked in their camp the next summer, too. I was really glad for that, because I was very hesitant about being capable of being a disciplinarian with school kids. I just didn't like the idea of having to crack the whip. This was a very pleasant, and more relaxed, kind of atmosphere. I really enjoyed teaching adults more than children.

I rented a room, and ate my meals in a cafeteria. So I was able to survive. I don't remember whether my mother sent me any money that year. In those years, you lived on just a little bit. You didn't have a car. You walked to work, and

*you walked home. I only stayed there one year. Then I heard
about a full time job in Buffalo, at the YWCA.*

*One of the advantages of working with the YWCA, was
that they had a national personnel bureau. So I got myself up
to Buffalo, and worked there for a year. I was able, initially,
to stay at a YWCA residence, which was the least expensive
you could get. With a couple of other women that lived there,
we later leased a furnished flat for the remainder of the year.*

*Then, through the national personnel office, I heard
about another full time position in Cleveland. I got into a
pattern that way, following these lake cities, from Buffalo
to Cleveland, and then, after four years in Cleveland, to
Chicago. All of this was with the YWCA. Why I didn't take
one of the jobs in Hawaii that I saw in the papers, I don't
know! I do know—I was timid. But it was pleasant work.*

During Ellie's years in Cleveland, World War II broke out.
She considered going into the service, as her sister did, but felt
she'd already had her fill of dormitory life. With many women
war workers coming into her Y, Ellie felt that she was, in her own
way, doing her part for the war effort.

Ellie eventually tired of working with the YWCA, and
decided she really wanted to go back to graduate school to
get a master's degree in social work. Unfortunately, military
people were coming out of the service and filling those slots.
Discouraged, Ellie retreated to Philadelphia, planning to help
her sister, who had just had a second child. She thought she'd put
the Y behind her, but they tracked her down, and she ended up
working another five-year stint in Philly. One of the extras that Y
offered was medical exams done by students from the Women's
Medical College Hospital nearby.

*I met a young woman who was in her senior year. She was
coming out of medical school, and trying to do an internship.
We became partners. I had had a partner for a while in*

Cleveland, a gal who, when we met, was married. She didn't mean to be married, but her mother had pushed her into it.

Her relationship in Philadelphia led Ellie to her next move. Frances was setting up a medical practice in Bethlehem, Pennsylvania, and Ellie agreed to help her get it started.

I went out there without any job. I suppose my family thought I was crazy. So I did that for a little while, and then I got bored. I'm a people person, and I need to be working with people.

I saw an article in the newspaper that they were going to open an alcoholism information center, and they needed to hire an executive for this. I didn't know a thing about it! But we noted that the president of the board of that agency was an administrator at the hospital where my friend, Frances, was working, and where she had done her internship. So I went and talked to him, and he said, "Sure. You go talk to this man and to that lady. You're a good person for this job." He didn't really know anything about it, but it worked out.

I was hired for the job, and had to begin to learn about alcoholism. I got a scholarship to go to Yale School of Alcohol Studies for four weeks in July, and it was a very good education.

When I started working in alcoholism, I think there were four books to read. Marty Mann* had written a primer on alcoholism. Then Haggard and Jellinek, from the Yale program, had a book they had written. There was also a doctor in New York who had his own book, and a theory that never worked out. That's all there was to learn from, except directly through recovering people, the AA people.

---

*Mann authored the chapter "Women Suffer Too" in the second through fourth editions of the Big Book of AA. In part because of her life's work, alcoholism became seen as less a moral issue and more a health issue.

Ellie's introduction to the field happened to coincide with a huge layoff at Bethlehem Steel, and many of the laid off workers turned to alcohol. It was a board member at Bethlehem, a recovering alcoholic himself, who had met Marty Mann, who encouraged him to open the center where Ellie got her job. He encouraged Ellie to attend AA meetings, too.

So for the first year, that was my education: go to Yale for four weeks, read these books, talk to alcoholics, and go to AA meetings. I did it religiously. From then on, I've educated many other people through the jobs I've held. I always require them to go to AA meetings, and listen. Don't go there to advise recovering persons.

In 1954, very little research had been done on the subject. The field was just accepting the concept of alcoholism as a disease and Ellie's goal was to help individuals change their minds about alcohol.

Ellie liked her work, but she had been plagued with chronic sinus infections since working in Chicago. Doctors had told her, "You need to take those sinuses to Arizona!" Frances, as a young woman doctor, knew it would be hard to find another practice to join. Therefore, they stayed in Bethlehem seven years, before an opportunity arose, and then they headed to Phoenix.

As a result of networking with others familiar with the type of work she'd done in Pennsylvania, Ellie was able to stay in the alcoholism field. She found this an interesting experience. Since there had been no education programs in town, she had to start from scratch. Before long, the county health department was calling her to work with clients, and she was speaking at nursing schools and other agencies. They even started a "school" to educate the area.

That got me started, but we had a lot of things happening. One day, my board came to me and said, "Eleanor, we feel we need a man at the head of the agency to raise money." That was in 1969. I had started the job in 1962. I had opened the agency. I'd done all the groundwork! Boy, was I angry! Also, the year before that, Frances had said she was leaving for health reasons.

I dug in my heels for a couple of months. My life experiences have been that if one door closes, God opens another one. Right then, St. Luke's Hospital in Phoenix had gotten a mental health grant, and they had some federal monies to do psychiatry, and they had to include alcoholism. They were starting a treatment program at St. Luke's with a doctor who had just come in from Michigan, and he asked me to come and work with him. It turned out to be a much better thing for me. I stayed for over two more months at the agency, and then said, "I'm leaving. I've found another job." And that's what I did.

The job at St. Luke's paid $2,000 less a year than she had been making, principally because Ellie had never been officially schooled as an alcoholism therapist. This was her opportunity to get on-the-job training. Along with her other responsibilities of teaching and lecturing, she worked closely with a therapist for a couple of years. When he left, Ellie became the Chief Therapist, as well as taking on a supervisory position.

I trained a lot of social workers and psychologists, as well as family practice doctors from the other hospitals in the city. Finally, when I was 65, I told St. Luke's I would work until I was 70. Then, at 70 I decided I "wanted" to work two days a week.

While I was Chief Therapist, we started a program, a peer group for older alcoholics. We were finding that among the older group there were two different kinds. There were those who had been heavy drinkers and alcoholics for many years. Also, there were some who were what we started calling "late-onset alcoholics." These were those who had been social drinkers for many years, and then, when they retired, drank excessively.

Ellie also found that a significant number of the people she worked with in the group were also being given prescription drugs such as Valium. Sometimes, these prescriptions had been taken for years on end, to help deal with the loss of a spouse and such. Looking at her own life, she felt she had been very fortunate to have escaped such problems.

On an excursion in Hawaii at age 70.

All this time, after Frances left, I was not seeing anybody. I had no one in my life who was also gay, a very celibate kind of life. Then one of the students came along. She was one who got married and had four children, then discovered she was not sure whether she should be married or not. Her husband was good-looking and he'd given her some good-looking children, but she decided she was gay. We had a short relationship. She left me for someone else. Then I had a short experience with another woman.

Ellie had never been someone to hang out at the bars, but has found she connects with other lesbians through church and other community activities. Most of Ellie's friends are younger. She plays golf with a woman who is 41. Ellie was 86 when she was interviewed.

I think one of the things people seem to be fascinated about is that I'm so old, and I'm gay! This became evident to me when meeting some young lesbians at the Mercury basketball games. I still have a seasons tickets and go all the time.

Ellie continues to live in Phoenix, Arizona. When Arden was in Arizona this past year and hosted a luncheon for women who had shared their stories with the OLOHP, Ellie had to decline because, at 92, she was still working at an alcohol and drug detox program. "Maybe next year," she offered!

Interviewer: Arden Eversmeyer

Louise Cason

Born March 1923

Ruth Taylor

Born April 1923

Both born in Florida.
Both interviewed in 2008, at age 85, in Florida.

Louise: *I ran hard enough that Ruthie could catch up with me!*

I grew up in Lakeland, and graduated from Lakeland High School. I had an inkling that I might be gay in high school. I spent the night, one night, with a girlfriend, and I was terribly aware of her body. It sort of scared me. Then I went to college. I didn't know many people there, but the second year Ruth and I took physics together. The electricity! She was a year ahead of me, and it didn't take long for us to find out. As she says, "I ran hard enough that Ruthie could catch up with me."

The next year we roomed together, and we were pretty obvious. It was a women's college, Florida State. So there were more than just the two of us traveling around holding hands. I was also very clear about the fact that I was determined to go to medical school. I had been saying that since I was in high school. I went to Florida State with the avowed determination to get into medical school.

My biochemistry professor was probably the strongest woman in that college, and the smartest, and had gotten her Ph.D. from the University of Chicago, in about 1928. She took a very personal interest in me, too personal; not in a sexual sense, but career ambitions.

It was her feeling that if Ruthie and I continued together, that would jeopardize my career. So, she called me down, with another woman, a house mother, in attendance, and with the Dean's blessing, to give me the word: "You take this job in Texas, which we have arranged for you, and don't tell Ruthie why you're going. You just tell her you have to go. If you do that, we will give you letters of recommendation for medical school."

The message was very strong: If you don't do that, if you go on with Ruthie, that'll end your career. And the condition was that I never tell Ruthie why I was going to Texas. So, I didn't tell Ruthie. I told her that I had to go to Texas, that there was a job there, and so on. Ruthie got a job at Gainesville, at one of the research labs as a chemist. She thought I was gone for good.

So off I go to Texas. I learned a lot, because I could work in the daytime at their medical school doing chemistry in the Physiology Department, and I could go to school at night at the University of Houston. I finished all the credits for my degree, and transferred back to Florida State. I got my degree from Florida State, with a very strong recommendation for medical school. After two and a half years, I was accepted *by the University of Chicago Medical School, which was a triumph, let me tell you.*

After I got there, I was a nervous wreck, going to school all day, and working until 12:00 or 1:00 at night. I had to change schedules, so I worked on the graveyard shift at the Goodyear Synthetic Rubber Corporation, in the Sinclair Oil Refinery. That was a trip! I was the only woman in the plant working from 4:00 p.m. to midnight. But not one time did anybody ever make a pass at me, or make any kind of a remark. When I left, the guys took up a little cash donation and they gave me a couple of hundred dollars. I thought that was quite a triumph. They were just the nicest bunch of guys you could ever imagine.

I had one friend in medical school, a woman that I had known at Florida State. She met me at the train, and then I got into the dorm. The group of women that was in that area of the dorm were all getting master's degree in social work, predominantly psychiatric social work. My roommate was a tall, nice looking woman, a widow, and I became fond of her, which scared the life out of me. All that I could see was getting thrown out of school.

I just about had a nervous breakdown! But, being psychiatric social workers, they sort of understood what was going on, and they got me to a psychiatrist at the medical school who I saw, on and off, for several years. If not for that, I don't think I would have gotten through. That whole experience was turmoil.

The last two years, I lived with a woman, and we were casually involved. She was Roman Catholic, and I think she thought that if anybody touched her, she would probably spend the rest of her life in hell.

After Chicago, Louise headed to North Carolina, to Duke University, to continue her studies and to work. She loved and hated Duke. She hated the racial prejudice that was accepted as an every day way of life. While working at the hospital at Duke, she had a personal experience that made it clear that racism wasn't just pervasive, it was institutionalized. A young blond woman was brought in with lockjaw. Treating her required a private room, kept dark and quiet, as well as an around-the-clock nurse, and a doctor nearby at all times. Then a very young black child was brought into the emergency room, who needed the same treatment. Since the hospital couldn't afford two 24-hour nurses, with doctors in the immediate area in case they were needed, Louise put the young boy in the same room with the white woman, separating them with a screen.

> The professor came in and then he came out and said, "Who did this?" I said "I did." "Move that child to the back of the ward," he ordered. I said, "He won't get any care back there. There's no nurse that's going to be at his bedside." Then I picked up the chart, and I said, "If you want him moved, you write the order. I will not." Well, the guy stomped off the floor, slammed the door, and the two children lived. Neither one of them died because they were two skin colors. But, they did not renew my contract. So there I was with my one year.

Louise turned to a male friend for help. He was someone she found herself drawn to, and she even had a brief affair with him. He put her in touch with his uncle, who was a very famous pediatrician at a Jewish hospital in Brooklyn.

> I didn't know anything about Jews. It was lovely, and I enjoyed it immensely. Dr. Crammer thought I was the "bees knees," and made me chief resident a month later. So I had two years of not only pediatric experience, but supervisory experience. I came out pretty well trained.

Once she'd finished her training, Louise had to decide where she wanted to go next. She'd had enough of Chicago, and wasn't enamored of New York City, either. Both were too big. What she really wanted to do was to return to Florida. But going back to her small home town didn't make sense. Louise had a sister and a brother, both working in the Miami area, and thought she might get some help from them.

At least they could help me a little bit to find a place. I bravely set forth and opened an office alone, and hung out my shingle. I borrowed enough money to get an examining table and some equipment, and hung a shingle out in front of the building. I was ready to conquer the world. It was a little slow, but I made a terrible error.

There was a nurse at the hospital in New York that was nine or ten years older than I, a splendid nurse. She decided that she wanted me physically, and every other way, so I slept with her. So she came to Florida with me, to be my office nurse. It went pretty well for a while. About nine or ten years later, I had enough money to make a down payment on a house. I didn't pick an expensive house. It was an old house, livable, with the most beautiful yard. It was 100 feet wide, and 200 feet deep, and it had nine huge live oak trees. I couldn't resist it. I didn't care what the house looked like, you know. The roof didn't even leak.

Well, we turned it into a livable place. That went on until some women friends, that I had become acquainted with, stopped by one evening.

Dr. Cason, age 58

+ 127 +

One of them boldly went up to Geraldine and said, "Well, don't you all sleep together?" Oh God. Next thing you know, Geraldine moved down stairs. She wouldn't even stay on the second floor with me.

There I was, in 1975. I had the house and it was paid for. My car was paid for. But I had to move my office. I had to get out of the building. I moved over to Coral Gables, and borrowed money from my sister. I was very successful in Gables, and I made up for it.

Her new practice in Coral Gables was well underway, and as Louise was able to get her feet back under her, she started to reach out to find friends once again. She connected with Allegra, a woman about her own age, who was a Ph.D. researcher, and they began to live together. Sleeping on separate floors with Geraldine had made Louise cautious. This time, she made sure they both acknowledged the nature of the relationship before they lived together. "You know what I am. If you don't, you better not move in with me, because I am not going to live alone." The woman moved in, and much to Louise's dismay, it turned out she was a raging alcoholic. But that was okay. Better things were just around the corner.

I'd gotten a bulletin from the chemistry department at Florida State. And whose name was there in it? Ruth Taylor. So, I called, and got her telephone number and address, and I wrote her a letter. "Dear Ruthie. Do you remember me?"

So we started corresponding. I went up to see her a few times. It became very obvious that we loved each other as much as we had in college. She was long divorced by that time. So I gently asked Allegra to take her alcoholic self out of my house. She didn't have much choice, as it was my house.

She left, and Ruthie moved in.

Ruth:

We were very lucky to find each other.

We met in college. We took a physics class together. Then, I discovered that she lived just upstairs in the dormitory where I was living. I was still living with a good friend from Clearwater. Between taking the physics class and living so close, we became closer. I was a year ahead of her. We roomed together. I think we went to summer school one summer. Then we lived together the next year. Everything was fine as far as we knew.

    Then she got called in by the house mother, and they had arranged for someone they knew to help her if she left school. The arrangement was that I would not be told. I knew she was going. And I guess, the finances were important. She'd been working while at the University, while she was at school. And there seems to have been some suggestion to her that if she wanted to go to medical school, that she should do this. But nobody told me that. I found that out years later.

With only the occasional, casual contact between herself and Louise for the next few years, the connection faded. Ruth finished college, got a job as a chemist at a nearby agricultural laboratory, and later taught high school chemistry. Ruth also married, and raised four children. She stayed with her husband while raising the children, but left when the kids were grown.

> *I got a letter from Louise after she'd gotten my address from an alumni mailing. So we got back together. I was about ready to retire by that time. So we worked it out that I'd move in with her.*

It wasn't all smooth and easy, but Ruth and Louise dealt with things as they came up, making the most of their second chance. One hurdle was Ruthie's children. When she explained the situation to one of her daughters, her initial response was, "If Louise is so important, where has she been all these years?"

Louise and Ruth

Louise continued to work after she and Ruthie had found one another once again. She had closed her private practice, and gone to work at Miami Children's Hospital. She was one of three people who ran the hospital. After a few years, she retired altogether, and Ruthie and Louise made one more move in their lives, this time back to Gainesville. There, they settled in together, enjoying occasional travels, and raising Dalmation show dogs.

They still have boxes of books sitting unpacked, but they don't mind. Driving became an issue, so they had to give up the car. They both have some health challenges: Louise's are mostly physical, while Ruthie struggles with her memory. But other things are more important now.

Louise

Ruthie moved in, and we've been together ever since. It will be twenty-five years next summer. We've been, I think, fantastically happy.

Ruthie

I feel like we were very lucky to find each other. We've been entirely compatible. She sometimes thinks, because of her handicaps, that I might be sorry I did this, but I don't feel that way. I feel like we're both very fortunate to have a friendship like this.

Ruth and Louise continue to share their lives in Florida.

Interviewer: Arden Eversmeyer

Canoeing together in their mid 70s

Elaine Weber

Born July 1925 in Pennsylvania
Interviewed in 2008, at age 83, in Florida

I didn't know where to go. I didn't know what to do. I didn't know who to talk to.

Take five brothers, and throw in one girl—a good blueprint for growing up a tomboy if there ever was one. Elaine said her dad might have thought he got a daughter, but what he got was a tomboy. "I loved baseball, football, and any other sport. And my brothers were the first ones who wanted to pick me to be on their side."

Elaine's mother never worked outside the home, but there was no doubt she worked. Her father owned a small laundry during the Depression, so all of the family helped.

In a way, she never left the house. She would do her house-work, do the cooking, and then do what else women were supposed to do. Then, when Dad needed her, she went with him. By that time, the boys were old enough to take care of themselves, to take care of their room and do the cleaning, she told 'em.

Mother was helping my father out, and then she would bring some laundry home to be ironed. That's why I'm very shy of irons! I hate 'em. I did a lot of ironing. She kept me out of school every Friday to iron, and to get them the laundry back to their customers before the weekend. But you know, I was paid a quarter a week, and that was a lot of money. What we didn't have, we didn't miss, and probably didn't need.

Dad and Mom didn't go to church, but they made us go to Bible school, at least until we learned about the Bible, and stuff like that.

We walked everyplace we went. We went down to the swimmin' hole, and we had to walk. But it was healthy, and a fun time. You'd walk to the creek to go swimming in the middle of summer, and by the time you got home, you were so stinkin' hot and wet, you're thinking, "Whoa! We should've stayed there!" But it was a good time.

When I was younger, there were times when we would go on the railroad tracks and pick up any coal that had dropped off the cars, and take it home. If we did it near December, we knew if we were bad, we would get a piece in our stocking.

She attended public schools from kindergarten through twelfth grade, and graduated in 1943, but not without a slight hitch near the end. "I tried to join the service in 1941, or 1942, because of the war." Elaine's older brother was in the Marines, and he convinced her parents not to sign for her. Instead, she stuck it out to finish high school.

I was in the commercial course. I took shorthand and typing. Therefore, rather than go out and make airplanes, like Rosie the Riveter did, my mother insisted that I stay in the office, because that's what I was trained for. Now I say, "Jeez. Was

I stupid!" I was too namby-pamby as far as my mom was concerned. Because Rosie's making hundreds of dollars a week, and here I am making $18 a week in an office.

I just shake my head when I think about it. I thought, "Jeez. What was wrong with me? Why didn't I go do what I really wanted to do?" You didn't rebel against your parents. You did what they asked. And then they said, "Okay. When you graduate from high school, you can have one week off and then get a job." That's what I did. We knew that we didn't disobey our parents.

I went into a place called Bud Field, in a town called Bustletown, Pennsylvania, where they were making trains. That's where I met

Doing what was expected of her

my husband. He was in the accounting office, and I was in the office for filing and clerking, what I was trained for. We would go out in the shop, where all the other workers were, and serve them lunch. We got paid a few bucks on the side for that.

Then I went down into the factory and worked on the line, on a conveyer belt, in a place where they made Philco radios and TVs. I made a little bit more money there, and lots of womenfolk friends, because men were still in the war, and the women took over all the jobs. I lost my job because I got pregnant.

In those days, if you were pregnant you were allowed to work three months, and then you had to quit. Elaine tried to find more work once she'd had her son, but couldn't, so she stayed home with the baby, and soon was pregnant again. When her second boy was three years old, her mother-in-law came to stay, and take care of the boys so she could get a job.

I enjoyed working. It got me out of the house, and it got me to be my own self. At that point, my husband started working for the state of New Jersey, and things got a little heavy then. He got tangled up with another woman. My kids were getting older, and there was no way I was going to divorce him!

As the battle raged over the potential divorce, and custody of the boys, something else unexpected happened: Elaine came to the realization that she was a lesbian.

During the course of his playing around, I got friendly with a woman, and that's when I experienced my true lesbianism. That's when it came to light. I always thought of myself as having a 'sleeping dragon' of some sort. It was way back in my mind.

My marriage was not an abusive marriage at all. We did go places. We went on vacations, and stuff like that. We even built a cabin up in the Poconos. Put a hammer in my hand, or even a paintbrush, and the tomboy thing comes out! Apparently my husband enjoyed it, because he liked the help. We got along rather well.

Although she managed to live peacefully with her husband, she knew something wasn't right. Elaine was in her mid-40s when she met this woman.

And, of course, I picked a married woman. Of course, I was married, too, so I didn't think it mattered at all. Six or eight months of foolin' around, and she didn't reciprocate. I did all the work! She wasn't gay. She was just enjoying what the hell was going on! After that, we moved. My husband retired, we moved down to Florida, and that was the end of that relationship.

But I always knew it was there. I always knew. Even through high school. I was athletically inclined, and I was approached right after I graduated by four women in our hometown. They asked me if I wanted to go on the road and play baseball. At that point, I thought, "What am I going to live on?" And I think my mother and father sort of got news that these ladies were butches, you know, dykes. "No. You're not going anywhere. You're staying home, and you're going to work, and you're going to do what everybody else is gonna do: like your girlfriends that have boyfriends, you're gonna get married, have kids, and grandchildren." God forbid you don't have grandchildren! So I just did what came naturally, that's all. Very complacent, very obedient. I thought, "Okay, I guess this is what I'm designed for."

I've been asked many, many times by lesbians and my close friends, "If he cheated on you, why didn't you divorce him? You could have gotten out of it." Well, in the first place I had two children, and those children come first. And I didn't know what was gonna happen to 'em if I divorced him. He wanted the kids. The only thing that kept him from leaving me was that his girlfriend was married and had a couple of kids, and he knew that she would never get her kids. Her husband would take the kids, and that would be the end of it. She wouldn't leave her husband, so it all settled down.

It all settled down, and they stayed together. Elaine was determined that her kids were going to college, and her husband was going to pay for it. She stayed in the marriage for 51 years. When she finally 'came out' in her late 70s, and told a friend who had known her for years, the friend said, "Well, you sure kept it under wraps, didn't you!" Elaine answered, "I didn't think I had the guts to come out." She had thought about it along the way. Other than her one affair, Elaine never had another relationship with a woman during her marriage. It was a huge step.

> *I would get a crush on somebody, but nothing would ever come of it. I was in a situation where I was looking for my security blanket. I had vows. "For better or for worse. 'Til death do us part."*
>
> *I don't know when it came out, but there was a movie on TV, on Lifetime, called* An Unexpected Love. *I happened to watch it, and I thought, "Oh, my God. This is where I would love to be." If that wasn't bad enough, then they hit me with the L Word!*
>
> *That just started it. My husband passed away in 2000, and it was at least two years later that I'd seen the movie, and the L Word. I didn't know where to go. I didn't know what to do. I didn't know who to talk to.*

For lack of a better idea, in her late 70s, Elaine boldly asked a woman, who worked for a lawn care company, if she was a lesbian. The worker graciously agreed to talk with her. Desperation made her quite the risk-taker.

> *I was going through a grocery store, and I saw these two gals together. I was in front of them as I went through the cashier, and they came in behind me. When I got my groceries, I just stood in the aisle and waited for the first one to come through. I don't know why I didn't get belted in the head or some- thing, for asking questions like that! She came through and I said to her, "Is that your partner behind you?" She said, "Yes, it is." And I said, "Okay. I want to talk to you. I'm coming out. I'm just a newbie. I mean, I know all about women. I know what I want to do with 'em, but I don't know how to contact them. How to find them."*

Gwen and her partner came over to me, and we exchanged email addresses and phone numbers. Eventually, I wound up in the MCC church, talking to the minister. I talked to him for over an hour and a half, expressing my feelings, and all about this kind of stuff that was going on. That's how I really got started.

Elaine found a place online where she could correspond with other women who were fans of the *L Word*, and found a woman who offered to help her. She told Elaine about Silver Threads, an annual event for lesbian singles and couples, age 50 and older, held in St. Petersburg, Florida.

So I did that. I signed up and went down, not knowing anyone. Not knowing a soul. But I thought, well, not to brag about myself or anything, but I've been told my personality comes out, so I went down and I met so many people. But I was anxious. It was a whole new environment. When I went to the dances, and I saw the partners dancing together, I got so aggravated, all jealous. I got the feeling, "Why the hell can't I find somebody?"

She wasn't one to stand by the sidelines for long though, and Elaine did make several very good friends at Silver Threads. Life was much better for her. Having lots of close women friends meant she would need to talk to her family. Elaine ran into a problem with one of her sons, a situation that was all the more difficult because he was still living with her.

When I told him, I said, "Your mother's traveling with the gay community. I'm a lesbian." And he said, "No. You're too old to be a lesbian in the first place, and, in the second place, you're not pretty enough!" I told some of my friends that, and they said, "I don't even know your son, and I don't like him!"

But I said to him, "Deal with it, if you don't like my lifestyle. I didn't like your lifestyle the whole time you were coming up. I didn't like yours, but I put up with it. If you can't deal with it, the front door is out there, and I'll even help you pack."

"I intend to bring people to the house. I don't need you to be nasty to them, or to be sarcastic, or anything like that," I said. "If that happens, and I find out about it, 9-1-1 is a nice, easy number."

Although things aren't smooth and easy, she and her son worked things out well enough to co-exist peacefully. "I come and go as I please. I tell him, 'I'll see you in a couple of weeks,' or 'I'll see you in a day.' It doesn't stop me from moving."

I was lying in bed one night, and I was reading the Golden Threads publication that came through the mail. I happened to see a little piece of article, an advertisement, about women coming out late in life, signed with an email. I just thought, "Okay, I'll do it. Just for the heck of it, to see what happens."

Elaine, flanked by authors Ann Bannon and Radclyffe, in 2005

So I emailed them and got hold of a young fella. He said, "Jennifer and Bea want to talk to you personally, on the phone." I thought, "Oh, lordy. What did I do? Am I opening up 'Pandora's Box?' Maybe I shouldn't have, with all this interviewing, and stuff like that."

The two documentarians were going to be in Florida, and asked if they could come interview Elaine in person. They arrived with cameras and video equipment. Once they were done, Elaine offered to drive them to catch a flight out of town. Instead of going out of the nearest airport, she talked them into going over to Tampa. After dropping them off, Elaine would then go visit her brother, who lived there. Instead, her brother became part of the interview, too.

Elaine had come out to her brother while driving to a family reunion. She commented on his still wearing his wedding ring, despite his wife being dead. She challenged him to take it off, and put it in a drawer, so he could meet other women. His response was, "Well, where's yours?" Elaine had given her ring to her granddaughter. He asked if she was looking for another man. "No. As a matter of fact, I'm looking for a woman."

He sat and looked out the window for a while, before turning back to her. When she said it even more plainly, telling him she was gay, he said, "Well, hell, I knew you were a lesbian when you were seventeen."

"Well, why in the world didn't you tell me?" I asked. He said, "I figured you'd figure it out." But it took me a long time. So he said, "Well, just don't get hurt. I hope you don't get hurt. It's your lifestyle. If that's what you want, you go ahead."

Other than her youngest son, her family has been supportive. When Elaine called to tell her oldest granddaughter, her response was "You go, Nanna!" Elaine thinks it's easier for the generation that has grown up with classmates who are out.

I have a ribbon, my rainbow ribbon, that I put on the trunk of my car. And a little rainbow doggie in my window. Some
friends say, "You're flaunting it too much," even though they are gay. And I say, "I intend to try to do something about it. I'm looking to make myself a name. If I can help anybody come out, and feel comfortable with themselves, why not?"

With granddaughter in 2000

Friends had told Elaine about a magazine called *Curve.* Although she'd never seen it, she'd heard that there weren't enough articles in it about older women. When a friend passed her name along to the *Curve* staff, and they contacted her for an interview, she jumped at the chance. Now, after having done so many interviews, her granddaughter brags to everyone who'll listen, introducing Elaine as though she's a celebrity, which she obviously is in her granddaughter's eyes.

The documentary I was in, Out Late, was shown in Spain, and all over the U.S., even in Tampa. But, frankly, it's come to the point where sometimes I think, "Your story is getting a little old now!"

At my age, I'm not looking for anybody that wants to get married, or anything like that, you know. But I would like a companion on my arm. I would like the love of a woman. I want to be happy for the rest of my life, whatever is left for me.

Now, I feel the warmth, the love, and the greetings, and everything else from <u>all</u> the gay community.

Elaine continues to thrive in Florida.

Interviewer: Arden Eversmeyer

Out on the town in 2007, at age 82

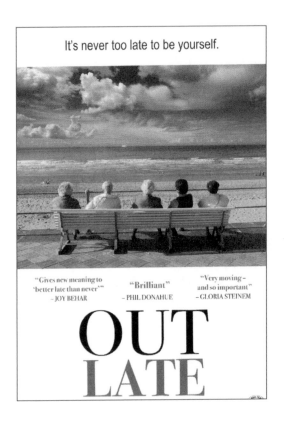

Elaine is prominently featured in the documentary *Out Late*, released in the United States in November 2011. This graphic is from the cover. *Out Late*, ASIN: B005CQJS82, http://www.foreverfilmsinc.com/

Pat
Durham

Born July 1926 in Missouri
Interviewed in 2001, at age 74, in California

My God, everything I really enjoy involves being with women.

The Depression was hard on everyone, no matter what their profession. When Pat was born, her father was studying to be an archeologist at a small college in rural northern Missouri, and there certainly wasn't much work for him in that field. So, off the family went to southern California, where job prospects weren't any better, but there were family members who pushed him to learn a more marketable skill.

Los Angeles is where I grew up. It was a pretty ordinary childhood; we were a middle class family. We moved around a fair amount. My father was a doctor, an osteopath. He didn't really want to do that, but his family wanted him to. He lived for outdoor stuff. Later in his life, when he gave up osteopathy, he went into forestry, mining quicksilver and stuff like that! He never was a very successful doctor, and he never had a lot of money.

Pat grew up with two brothers, both older than she. Like most children, she had a love-hate relationship with them. She hated them for taking her bike apart, to turn it into a tandem bike with one of their bicycles, that she didn't even get to ride! She loved them when they all snuck out into the back yard one day, when her parents were out for the evening, and set up a tent, intending to stay there for the night. "My parents came home and there was nobody in the house. They were absolutely frantic, and called the police. It never occurred to them to look in the back yard."

Being outdoors featured strongly in Pat's early years, too. Each winter, the family would all pile into their Olds 98, which always made Pat carsick, and head into the nearby mountains to toboggan. In the spring, they'd go look out over the San Joaquin Valley, where you could see nothing but lupine, poppies, and Indian paintbrush plants in bloom.

My grandparents lived in Reedley, in the Fresno valley, and had 110 acres of grapes up there. One of the many things I remember well is that all of the grandchildren would spend the whole summer there. The seven of us cousins used to have a great time. I learned about irrigation. I always took a pony to ride. It was, all in all, a good childhood. The one unbreakable rule was that we couldn't fight. But I hated it when my parents fought.

I went to a special elementary school for 4th, 5th, and 6th grades. It was marvelous! We hardly ever sat in the classroom. We built a great big hot air balloon. The school had an outside incinerator, and the janitor would go up the ladder, and fill up the balloons with hot air, and let them up in the neighborhood. I never learned to spell all that year! I remember taking spelling tests and missing 17 out of

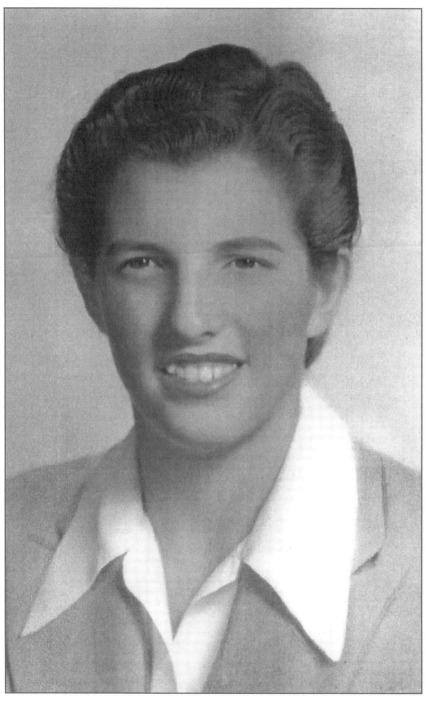

At age 18

20. Nobody ever did anything about it. It was a really fun school. I loved it.

Life at home wasn't as much fun. Pat's parents continued to fight, and finally divorced. Her mother then had what was termed a "mental breakdown," and spent all of Pat's high school years in an institution. Her dad moved to Stanford and set up a practice, taking Pat with him.

We lived in the basement of his office on Main Street, and it was pitch black, with no daylight and no kitchen. We ate out three meals a day. It was more or less okay. I just spent a lot of time on overnights with friends. I was straight. My friends were very straight young women, too. I was into athletics, and decided early on that I wanted to be a Physical Education teacher. I had tunnel vision until I became one.

My high school graduation was one of the most terrible experiences of my life. My mother had been in a mental institution for about four years. My older brother had finally managed to get her out. She and my dad hated each other at this point. One of the conditions of her getting out was that she would never come to see me.

The next to the last day of school, I got a call to the office. I hadn't seen her for three or four years. At the time, when someone went into a mental institution, you were asked not to write or contact them for at least six months. I hadn't had any contact in a long, long time.

I didn't know what to do. There she was. We were all getting yearbooks signed, and my mother hated it. It was really obvious to her that I didn't want her there. I didn't know what to do with her. I couldn't take her home, and she had no place to stay. I asked her if she wanted to stay over at my grandmother's. Finally, I called my dad. He said, "We'll come and pick her up and take her to a motel." So my father wouldn't come to my graduation because my mother was

Wedding to Louie at age 23

there. I hated having her there. It was just terrible. Neither one of us ever got over that. We just never talked about it.

In a twist of fate, Pat ended up having to live with her mother when she was in college. "I didn't have any money. She had room for me. I survived." It was strange, but it gave Pat a chance to learn about her mother. She'd never known that her mother had seven brothers, or that her maternal grandfather had been a judge. Pat had never once heard from them as grandparents, had never received a card, gift, phone call or anything from them.

Fulfilling her burning desire, Pat went to UCLA for four years and majored in physical education, graduating in 1948. She got a job right out of school teaching in Hemet, a small town in the San Jacinto Valley. She didn't stay for long.

I taught there a year and met Louie Durham, who was to become my husband. I stayed another year, then we married and moved to Los Angeles. He was a Methodist minister. I taught for two semesters at UCLA. He thought I was crazy, because I was teaching skiing in a class I was taking. The person who was supposed to teach it never showed up. I knew nothing about skiing. I used to ski, but half the time on my butt! I demonstrated skiing once, and went down the whole way on my tailbone, so I never demonstrated anything again. But I had a good time teaching there. They paid well.

Pat had never dated before, either in high school or college. Louie was her first. As Pat put it, "falling in love with a minister was a weird thing to do." She hadn't been raised in any church, and had no experiences or examples from which to draw. Luckily, Louie wasn't a traditional minister, so she didn't have to play the traditional minister's wife role. Pregnancy interrupted Pat's teaching career and, after having two children, she and Louie moved to Nashville.

Nashville was a trip! We were there when all the student protests and sit-ins started, the civil rights movement. The church thought we were there to integrate them, and they were really angry. There were some African-American ministers working for the Board of Education, and we put together programs for the white youth to talk to African-Americans. It was amazing. This was the first time they had ever met a black person who wasn't a garbage collector, or a maid. The youth were amazed that they were able to have intelligent conversations with them. That was why the adults thought we were trying to integrate the church.

Pat and her family both witnessed and participated in a shift in thinking in Nashville. People did sit-ins at lunch counters and boycotted department stores. It was quite an awakening for them all. They didn't stay in Tennessee long; soon they moved back to California, this time to San Francisco. That was another culture shock. "I had no idea there were so many families without a father, and with two or three kids at home." Pat was torn when her children would ask to play with friends after school, and she found out there wasn't an adult at home. Her new life presented Pat with all sorts of enlightening experiences, since homosexuality had not been a part of their family's ministry until they moved there.

My eyes were opened. I saw what the world was all about. The first "out" lesbians I ever knew were Phyllis Lyon and Del Martin. It was fascinating to me. One of the first things I did was to create the Council on Religion and the Homosexual. We had one of the first meetings in my house. I was a little nervous. I thought all the neighbors would know. I don't know what I was expecting. I was in the kitchen doing the wifely things, and then I went to the meeting. By the time I got in there, all the introductions had been made. It was all men. I was trying to decide who was gay and who was straight, and I couldn't do it. That just blew another stereotype. It was just fascinating to me that I couldn't tell.

I didn't know the word "lesbian" for a long time. When I was a young woman in UCLA in the P.E. department, when I look back I'm sure three-fourths of them were lesbians, but I didn't know that. I mean, the parties they had were all women parties. One day the Director of the Women's Record P.E. Department, and one of the most liked teachers, just disappeared. They were gone. I don't know if everyone else knew what I did. They appeared to be straight.

The head of the Men's Team Department was a member of the church Louie was in. He didn't know about me going to UCLA and knowing the women, so he was telling Louie that the two women turned out to be lesbians, and they were just removed. Even though I didn't know anything about being a lesbian, or gay, or homosexual, I thought that was a really terrible thing to have happen, because they were really good teachers. As far as I knew, no one had done any harm, or harmed me. That was my first real awareness about this group of people that were really being discriminated against.

Even with this going on in Pat's life, she still had no reason to wonder about herself. She was happily married, and felt she had found a good man, a man who was talented in the area of sexuality, someone who cared about her as much as about his own pleasure.

During this era, something Pat remembers called the "National Sex Club" came into existence. It was a group that believed people needed visual images of sexual encounters. Pat and her husband watched a lot of the films.

I knew that I got much more turned on with films of two women than I did of a man and two women, or two men. Unbelievable. Louie and I moved into trying to have an open relationship, an alternative style of living.

Pat and her husband became part of a regular group that decided to try living together. When they couldn't find a house they could afford, Louie talked the church they were involved in into buying a huge, 12 bedroom house, and leasing it to them. To make it work, they had to bring other people into the mix, people who, it turned out, didn't have the same interests as the original four. "They thought it would never happen. They thought we just talked a lot."

Louie and Pat lived in the huge house for the next fifteen years, with various family members and other couples coming and going. The women loved it, sharing household and child-rearing responsibilities. It wasn't quite as easy for the men, who had to take their share of tasks they had always had done for them in the earlier, more traditional living situations.

Their family also expanded, as they took in a foster child, adopted a son, and had Jim, a nephew of Louie's, living with them. One night, when Louie was out of town, Jim asked to talk to Pat. He said he'd been living a lie, denying he was gay when his family asked, and he wanted Pat to talk to them for him. "I was upset that he'd lied the whole time. He went to every bathhouse and place you could have gay sex, and actually died of AIDS."

As her own children grew, Pat also became involved in volunteer work with the PTA, YMCA, League of Women

Voters and so on, which put her out in the world, working with a variety of people. She also started to become a bit restless.

> *We were in the communal house. It was in the early 70s. We had decided we'd try this "open marriage" stuff, which was interesting. Finding other women was easy for Louie. "If he can find them, how can I find a man?" I thought. I had never dated. I didn't know anything about it.*
>
> *It was painful for me. I thought maybe I could accept it, until there were nights I knew he was with somebody else. At this point in my life, sex was more like recreation. I needed reassurance that I was a sexual being. I had some really good times, I have to say. I never considered having a relationship as this was all "fun and games." At any rate, after that, we separated.*

Pat tried hard, but her marriage came apart after 26 years. When Louie became involved with another woman who was important to him, Pat even was willing to try a three-way relationship, but it didn't work. When Pat left, and spent the summer with this same woman, Louie was outraged. She and Pat ended up being friends, and that woman ended up staying with Louie.

It was clear Pat and Louie couldn't live together any longer, but neither of them wanted to get a divorce. It had gotten to the point where she "couldn't ask him what time it was without having a fight." They separated. Louie left the house and Pat remained. Even though she was making very little money, and lived frugally, Louie made even less, and wasn't all that careful with his spending of the money in their joint account.

It was while they were separated, but not yet divorced, that Pat became fully aware of her lesbian feelings. "I believe I was very heterosexual when we separated." She was getting by running a small home business, and found out that the Women's Center in San Francisco had gotten a grant for a program for older women. They were hiring four women over forty to work with this new program, and Pat was interested. However, she couldn't risk giving up the security of her own business, even if it didn't make much money. Her exposure to the Women's Center got Pat thinking.

> It was just a revelation: not that I was a lesbian, but that the things that I most valued in life, other than my marriage, were the things that I didn't do, like work in adoptions, and work with the Girl Scouts. The list just went on and on as Pat realized, "My God. Everything I really enjoy involves being with women."

Pat knew she needed to find out if there was any chance to have a life with women. To do so, she knew she was going to have to take a risk.

> I decided if I was ever going to change, I better get damn well busy and do it. So I came back, and called up the Women's Center and, as it happened, the job had not been listed at every place it was supposed to be, and they had to reopen applications. I got the job, and sold my business. Everyone on the staff, everyone that was hired besides me, was a lesbian.

Before long, Pat's curiosity got the best of her, and she arranged to spend the night with a friend to find out one way or the other. Pat was so nervous, she had to get stoned. "We had a delightful time."

Eventually, Pat realized she couldn't go on subsidizing Louie's trips with other women, and they filed for divorce.

> It was a friendly divorce. We used the same lawyer, and we divided up the property. But I was surprised when the final divorce decree came in the mail. It had an emotional impact, though I wasn't sorry that it happened. I was really surprised that it made any difference to me at all, one way or the other.

In her job at the Women's Center, Pat worked with a program called OPTIONS For Women Over Age Forty. Part of that job was fundraising, and the struggle to raise funds to support the program wore on her spirit.

We needed to have a fairy godmother drop a few hundred thousand dollars on us. I had to quit or find a way to renew my energy. The first option seemed impossible; the second, I really didn't want to do. The third seemed the only feasible alternative.

Renewing my energy took the form of a three-month leave of absence. I took off with a woman friend, a cat, a used pop-up tent trailer, and headed for the out-of-doors.

The two women only had their first stop, Yosemite, planned. From there, they allowed themselves to wander, staying in each place as long as it felt right, and cutting themselves off from the outside world.

The trip was magical in many ways: watching the full moon rise over the sculpted columns of Bryce Canyon, feeling the effort of salmon leaping the falls of a rushing creek, seeing the wonder of cactus in full, vibrant bloom, experiencing the surprise and joy in finding a beautiful agate among ordinary beach rocks, marveling in the majesty of a soaring eagle.

Special, too, was getting in touch with those physical activities I enjoyed in my younger years: chopping wood, building fires, riding my bike, flying a kite, whittling, and wading in the surf.

What most surprised me about the trip, was that I never got bored. I had thought that perhaps three months was too long to just 'take off.' What proved to be true was that it wasn't nearly long enough. I seemed to have an infinite capacity to take in the star-filled skies, to walk the beaches, and to just be.

With Magge in 1992

Pat was with her first lover for years and, although it was a "hugely romantic episode," it wasn't an easy relationship. Barb was bipolar. Memories of what Pat went through with her mother's illness made it especially difficult, but they stayed together for 14 years before calling it quits.

It was hard to tell my kids because I didn't know what they would think. My daughter was a big feminist, so I finally told her. She had this big grin and said, "That's wonderful, Mom. As long as you're happy, that's fine." They've all been that way.

The next woman in Pat's life was Magge, a woman 18 years her junior. Magge was actually one of Pat's bosses when she worked with GLOE, Gay and Lesbian Outreach for Elders, for several years. Pat and Magge were officially "domestic partners" after registering as such in San Francisco in 1992. They left California for a while, but weather and Magge's medical needs brought them back to San Francisco before long. Magge was diagnosed with lupus, became extremely ill and died at age 54.

Regrouping, Pat found another passion in working with elder LGBT people. In one of her volunteer positions, Pat was instrumental in creating a program that honored old lesbians who had made significant contributions to the community.

Wow! Old women, lesbians: we are, indeed, offering a great deal to the community at large. You could almost see women change as they realized they had done important work.

The program Pat was working with is called the Pat Bond Award. Pat Bond was an entertainer, an impersonator, who had given a great deal to the local community. When Pat Bond became ill, and didn't have money for her care, a few of her friends raised funds to pay her medical bills. She died before all the money was used, so that became the seed money for the award program. The Old Dyke Award goes to a lesbian who hasn't been previously acknowledged to any great extent.

Even though most everyone thought that the City of San Francisco was gay and lesbian friendly and sensitive to their needs, Pat found out that wasn't really so once she accepted the mayor's appointment to serve on the Commission on Aging Advisory Council.

I was the first "out" lesbian commissioner! The Commission had a two-inch thick manual about all their programs. I went through the whole damn thing, and I think lesbians and gays were mentioned in there twice. They had lists of all the services they offered. Even though GLOE had been funded by them for a number of years, they were never listed by the Commission.

Discouraged, but not dissuaded, Pat dug in her heels and challenged the people who needed to be challenged. She got LGBT organizations and services included on the lists. She found it very hard to work with the other members on the commission, many of whom were closeted gay men. One of the fights she took on was a move to get the options of gay and lesbian onto the intake forms people filled out when seeking aging services. "Gays and lesbians did not feel welcome in many places. Although there were lots of us, one way to find out was to begin counting us."

She wasn't sure she made a big difference in her work for the city, but Pat certainly gave it her best. What it made crystal clear to her was that politics were not her cup of tea. She resigned the commission, but continued to fight through other venues, and earned several recognitions for her efforts. In fact, in 1996 Pat was given the Pat Bond Award by the Board of Supervisors of the City of San Francisco. Then, in 1997 she received a certificate from the city honoring her for her work on behalf of the Commission on Aging.

Pat didn't sit back, didn't go along, and was rather proud whenever she heard them say, "Darn! Here she comes again."

Pat Durham died in 2005, leaving behind her wonderful partner, Rosemary Hathaway.

Interviewer: Arden Eversmeyer

Arden Eversmeyer
and
Charlotte Avery

Arden Eversmeyer

Born April 1931 in Wisconsin
Interviewed in 1990 and 1998,
at ages 59 and 67, Texas

What do you think lesbians do when they turn 50, self-destruct?

I was a depression kid, the first born child, the eldest of two girls. My education was in what was called a demonstration school. It was associated with a teacher's college. They had one class for each grade, with a master's level teacher who had student teachers assigned to her. We had an excellent education there. When we came into the Texas school system in 1943, my sister jumped a full grade, and I jumped one semester. I was not allowed to jump a full year because I had not had a Texas history class.

I was a tomboy, and a Daddy's girl. He was a warm and very gentle, nurturing man. Mom was extremely brilliant, a perfectionist, and a controlling person. When I didn't fall into the traditional, little girl type interests, I had a sister eleven months behind me, who filled the bill. That was good.

It took the pressure off me. So most of my nurturing, while I was growing up came from my father.

I liked to play the boy's games. I usually beat them at all of them. I always had all their marbles in my bucket. I could skate, and I could hit the ball as well as most of the boys, so I was just one of them.

My sister was playing with dolls, learning to cook, and doing all the traditional things that girls are supposed to learn as they grow up. She fit the mold, which was wonderful, because Mother had someone to work with. She didn't hassle me too much, other than when I ruined my clothes.

My dad told me one time, "We will provide for you the best equipment within our means. But, the first time you exhibit that you cannot be a young lady and play that sport, we'll take the equipment away." I knew I could do all the things that were important to me as long as I didn't turn into a roughneck. I could do the sports, and still be an acceptable girl, and not have to do all that other girl stuff.

As the country worked its way out of the Depression, it entered into World War II, and everything was rationed. Life didn't revolve around a television yet, but radio was important. Arden got an allowance, and clearly remembers spending it to buy a can of black olives each week.

I got my olives, and a peanut butter, lettuce and mayonnaise sandwich, and sat in front of the radio. I had a whole series of programs I listened to, including The Shadow *and* One Man's Family. *The family might come in, and I might offer them an olive, but I had bought them with my own money, and they were mine. The sandwich was on homemade bread. I didn't taste store-bought bread until I was eleven or twelve. Both of my parents were wonderful cooks.*

I got my physical growth very young, and there were two or three years when I was a full head taller than my classmates. I was almost my full height of 5' 9", before I was twelve. I got teased, and I got belligerent. "Don't talk to me that way or I'll punch you out!" As I got older, I did become a bit of a bully. I was chubby and my nickname was 'Tubby.' Children do not give nice nicknames to each other. I just got to where I could make them mind their manners. I got to where I hurt children who hurt me.

If I couldn't be an A student like my sister was, then I could do something else. There was a need to do something well for approval. I was okay the way I was for my dad; but, I never quite measured up for my mom. Whatever I did, I could have done better, whether my grades, or I could have been more 'lady-like.'

Arden's family had made their move to Texas when she was twelve, and it was life-changing. They got there in the summer, and the neighborhood kids took to teasing Arden and her sister because they talked differently. It was a teacher that made life the most difficult for Arden.

The Texas history teacher was near retirement. She shamed and mocked me the entire semester. I didn't know the state bird, I didn't know the state flower, I didn't know where the capitol was, and I didn't know all the things the other kids had grown up with. It got to the point that she would ask me a question and pick on me no matter who had their hand up. I was so terrified of this woman!

At 16 years of age

She made life Hell for me! Hell! Within a few months, I went from being an extroverted bully, an outgoing girl, to a complete and total introvert.

Arden didn't have many friends in high school, and being a teenager was confusing. She clearly remembers falling for a female teacher.

I was madly, completely, totally, helplessly in love with my junior high gym teacher. I know she was a lesbian. I have no doubts of it. She was kind and gentle. And she was a mother substitute. I had a consuming feeling for her. She didn't encourage me. She didn't reject me. She was my first overwhelming emotional experience.

It wasn't until she was in graduate school that Arden learned that she was dyslexic. She could read, but had trouble storing the information. The disability had made high school especially difficult, but she learned to cope academically. The high school counselor even advised Arden not to pursue college, since it was clear she would not succeed. Try as she might, Arden was a C student in school, which was a disappointment to her mother, who had graduated cum laude with a double major. Her father's philosophy was that if a grade represented her very best effort, then she should be proud, whatever the grade was.

With high school behind her, Arden needed to make a decision as to what came next. Acknowledging that there were few women going into medicine and law, with limited areas in which they could practice, Arden felt her choices of "an acceptable profession" were very limited. "When I went to college, there were three things a woman could do: you could be a secretary, a nurse, or a teacher. That was it."

Once away at college, she was awed by the powerful women she met, faculty and students, and it wasn't long before she had her first sexual experience and it was with a woman. She had dated men in high school and when she first started college. She was even engaged twice, but it didn't feel right.

> *I was trying to acknowledge my true self. In what I was trying to do, marry a man, that was wrong. It was more than not wanting to marry the guy. I had always been uneasy. I could never stand for a boy to put his hands on me. I never wanted to sit in the backseat of a car and neck. I always got pissed if the boy thought I owed him something because I went out on a date with him.*
>
> *I'd always had a best friend, one that I spent more time with than any other. It was comfortable and it was mutual.*
>
> *In retrospect, I can identify one or two women in high school who were lesbians but, at that point in time, they were dating, too. All during that time, I can never remember hearing anything about a homosexual lifestyle. I don't remember anyone making fun of a "queer," during that time.*
>
> *I tried. I did all the right moves with men, but nothing took. I never had any solid reason why. It just didn't feel right.*
>
> *I was a freshman, and I came out to myself with a senior. Freshmen weren't supposed to fraternize with seniors, but on the P.E. teams we were co-mingled. It was the first coming out for both of us. She wasn't experienced, but she was aware.*

The fact that there were lots of lesbians at Texas State College for Women (TSCW) comforted Arden.

> *It was wonderful to realize that I wasn't the only one in the world, that there wasn't something wrong with me. We had friends like us. We were accepted. But it was very difficult, and secrecy was a must. You had to be so careful. We had purges back in those days. Kids would leave campus on weekends, and on Monday, when everyone should be there, we'd discover all these people who should be there, were not.*

It didn't take documentation or proof. All it took was somebody that said somebody was "queer." There would be whole groups that would disappear, as many as 50 one weekend my freshman year. You had to be careful. It puts you underground. It was said that every dorm had a person who was watching, gathering information. This was in 1949 and 1950.

Arden continued her relationship with that senior throughout that year, and had what she characterized as "a profound experience that forever influenced my life."

During her freshman year, Arden had also connected with a woman that everyone seemed to know, and everyone was talking about. Her name was Tre.* She had just arrived after riding her Schwinn bicycle to TSCW in Denton, Texas, from Greenwich Village, in New York! Tre was known for hand-making custom fitted sandals for students, so Arden ordered a pair. "They were pure leather, and there was no way they were going to wear out. But, looking for a reason to go back, I decided that what I needed was another style." When Arden picked up her second pair, she stayed for the afternoon.

We were just visiting. Of course, here I was a freshman, newly out to myself as a lesbian, with this awesome person. I ended up sitting on one bed, while she sat on the other. How I feel today about myself comes directly from that one day visit in that room with that person. She told me that the way I am is the way I am because God put me here. It has nothing to do with anything anybody did to me. It is simply who I am. She gave me a sense of inner peace that day that I have carried all my life. Tre was only at TSCW that

---

*In 1984, Arden saw an article in People magazine that profiled Tre as heading an all-woman construction company in California. She reconnected with her in 1987, and later had the opportunity to gather her herstory, which is included in A Gift of Age. (see letter on pg. 371) *summer. I was lucky enough for this person to pass through my life when I first discovered a name for my sexuality. I never felt bad about who I was, but I was at peace about the whole thing after that afternoon with Tre.*

Since there were almost no other resources, books, or anything else to help her with what she was experiencing, Arden considers herself very lucky to have found Tre, and a few other supportive people. "I read my first lesbian book after college. It was the classic, The Well of Loneliness, which everyone needs to read, but not use as a model."

She now felt comfortable with who she was, yet Arden struggled to used the word 'lesbian.'

It was not used that much. The term used was 'gay.' Today, 'lesbian' is used more, and I think that's okay, too. Except, the word 'lesbian' has been used by society in such a punishing way. There is so much internalized homophobia about it. Learning to love the word, and to adopt it, takes some work.

In college, at 18

At the end of that first school year, Arden's first love went off to take a teaching position. They saw each other a few times, but the relationship faded away. There were a couple of other relationships in college, but nothing that was lasting.

As she neared graduation, Arden's father advised her to take the best job offered to her, but not in the Dallas area, where her mother would expect her to live at home. Immediately after college, Arden took additional training to become one of the first women certified to teach Driver Education in Texas. This led to a position establishing a program, and teaching driver education in a school in a small, affluent town hundreds of miles away, in West Texas. This was an impressive job for someone fresh out of school. There, Arden was the youngest teacher in the school district, and the superintendent affectionately addressed her by the name "Daughter."

It was a marvelous experience, but it was so lonely. There were no identifiable gays or lesbians out there. Also, there were no middle class people outside of the teachers there.

It was not even "respectable" to go to the roller rink. I went one night, and the next day the Chief of Police came out to my school. He patiently explained that the skating rink was no place for a school teacher to be. I even had a police escort to the basketball games. They would pick me up in their cars at my house, just so I would have something to do. There were two movie houses in town. I could go there. There were a lot of young couples, but not a lot of single people. It really was an experience in isolation.

One year in west Texas was enough for Arden. She put applications in to teach in Houston, where she got a position teaching physical education and health at a high school. New to the city, Arden stayed with a friend who played on a softball team, and went to games with her. Softball was big, with state and national leagues drawing thousands of spectators to tournaments. Teams were essentially made up of lesbians, with a few straight women in the mix. Softball provided an important place for lesbians to connect. It was there that Arden met her first long-term partner, Tommie.

Women's softball, back then, was fast pitch. We are talking about fine athletics! Tommie was eight years older than me. She was awesome, a legend in her time, and that made it difficult for her and for us. We started living together in the fall of 1952. We lived in an apartment until my father died in 1955.

Then it was expected, assumed in American culture, that a single daughter would become the caretaker of her widowed mother. Supposedly a single female had no responsibilities to keep her from it. My mother came, and the assumption was that I was going to move in with her. Tommie and I had been together for three years.

Looking back, there is no question that my parents knew about me then. My father had a long discussion with Tommie before he died. He asked her to take care of me.

I told my mother that I would come live with her if Tommie could come as well. We put our furniture in storage, and moved into my mother's house. She became more and more dependent. She wouldn't go anywhere without us, and she was only 48 years old at the time.

Tommie and Arden stayed with Arden's mother for a year before they went in search of their own home. They had been looking at homes before Arden's father died, and needed to look again. Arden's mother was bitter and unhappy, but they pursued moving out anyway.

At the time, women couldn't qualify for a mortgage unless they had 50% of the house value for a down payment. We could not qualify for a conventional mortgage. Women also couldn't qualify for a Homestead Exemption, that only a man could have.

What we did was to find a G.I. equity house, bought the equity from a man, and assumed his payments. The house cost $12,400, and we had a 4% loan. A woman couldn't even have a charge account in her own name in those days! And married women had fewer rights than single women!

Their new neighbors seemed to accept them right away. In fact, the wives would often point to Arden and Tommie's yard, and say, "If those two women can keep their yard as neat as that, then you can get out there and do it!" Tommie was like the Pied Piper, and all the neighborhood kids loved her.

As a teacher in 1978

Other lesbians may have hung out in the bars, but Arden and her friends didn't. "We knew there were bars, and never went to them. Back in those years queer bars were raided." Most of the bars were men's bars, but they did hear of one that was for women called 'The Natchez Lounge'. The bar scene was not safe. If Arden and her friends had been in a bar when it was raided, they knew, without a doubt, that they would have never recovered professionally. Instead, Arden and Tommie were part of their own friendship group, with five other women couples who would get together, both to socialize and help with each other's homes. Home projects ran the gamut from painting to roofing to carpentry to plumbing to tree-trimming. For the friendship group, it was a way to learn, was fun, and saved everyone money. It wasn't all home projects though, as the group did a lot of camping and fishing together, also.

On Arden and Tommie's thirtieth anniversary, Tommie was diagnosed with cancer. Arden had taken an early retirement, and they were able to spend most of their time together during Tommie's illness. Their friendship group was always with them, staying with Arden, both at home and at the hospital. "They had to deal with their own separation from

Tommie, but they were there for me. No human had better or more loving support than I had."

Amazingly, given the times and the fact that they were in conservative Texas, both the hospital and the doctors treated Arden and Tommie as they would any other couple. They had taken all the steps they could: having wills drawn up, living wills, and durable powers of attorney. They were also lucky that no one in Tommie's family tried to step in and take over.

The day before she died, Tommie had an especially restless, combative day. The therapist she had been seeing, to deal with her impending death, took Arden for a walk and explained the situation to her. "What you're seeing in there is not her fear of dying, but her fear, or reluctance, to leave you. I want you to go back in there and talk to her. I want you to give her your permission to die. Tell her that you will be fine."

> I hope I'll never have to do this again in my lifetime. I went back in there. I stood there and I talked and talked. She opened her eyes. I told her I was going to be fine. It was okay. I asked her if she understood what I was saying. She closed her eyes. She was quiet.

The following day, a parade of people came to say their goodbyes, with Tommie comforting each of them. Later that night, she died.

> We had a good life. Like anybody who makes a life together, two women, two men, or a man and a woman, it doesn't matter. There are good times, and hard times. We had all of that. Nothing is ever perfect. We truly loved one another. We cared about one another. It was a warm, gentle 33 years of my life.

Tommie had been a bookkeeper, and had worked for the same company for almost 40 years at the time she died. They knew about her relationship with Arden, and, although it had never been discussed, Arden was always welcome around the office, and was treated as the widow after Tommie's death.

In the thirty-three years Tommie and Arden had been together, neither of them had ever really been out. For self-preservation, Arden, and most of her friends, believed they had to live extremely closeted lives.

There are thousands of lesbians over 55 years of age in Houston, but it is a very invisible population. We came out to ourselves in the years when you would be put in a mental hospital and treated for homosexuality, or jailed, or purged from college. There is no doubt that, if I had ever come out, I would have lost my job, and I would have never had another job in education. Pure survival dictated that you lead a double life. You had your true you, your pure self, that very invisible life. Then you had the life that our culture says you must live.

All of the women in my friendship circle felt the same way. These women are still in my life. Some of them have been in relationships for 48 to 50 years, and they are still closeted. And you become more and more isolated as you get older, because your contacts diminish.

In Arden and Tommie's own lives, and among their circle of friends, there had always been roles that could basically be described as 'butch' and 'femme.'

There was a very definite acceptable code of conduct and behavior that was assigned. I came out of that kind of environment. It wasn't that Tommie wore men's clothes, she didn't. She was feminine. But there were things that I would not have thought about doing when the two of us were out in public. I didn't drive, and I never paid the bill at a restaurant. She took care of the money when we were out, and also the family money. I had input, but she took care of the finances. I was the saving person. We had skills that complemented each other.

After she died, and I wanted to have a cup of coffee with a friend, if that friend was single and 'butch,' I could not pick up the phone and call her. I could not initiate it. It's just an understood thing. There is no set of rules, but there are behaviors that are acceptable, and some are not. About a year later, some members of my friendship group thought it was time for me to get out and start to do things. They offered to chaperone me to various events. The 'butch' laughed and said to me, "We need to protect you from all those big, bad 'butches' out there." I went, not because I felt that I needed them along, but because I felt isolated.

A year or so after Tommie's death, Arden began to venture out a bit more. She started by becoming a docent at the zoo. Then she found OWL, the Older Women's League, an activist group of mostly straight individuals, working to better the condition of old women. It took several years, grieving and growing, years Arden recognizes as one of the most exciting and productive times of her life.

Taking those first few steps helped, but Arden was still restless. Then she found a "place of serenity" at a local New Age shop, a place she could go to sit and meditate. There she met a young woman in her early twenties, who introduced Arden to a women's community she didn't even know existed. Arden wondered how it could possibly be that none of her friendship group ever knew there were hundreds, even thousands, of lesbians in Houston. The little bit her group knew about feminism had come from books that they'd read, then put in the incinerator, so they wouldn't be caught with them. For Arden, it was like entering a whole new world.

Arden laughingly remembers her first act of activism. She encountered young lesbians that were shocked to meet her, and to realize that there were old lesbians. Arden would ask, "What do you think lesbians do when they turn fifty? Self-destruct?"

Once Arden knew there was more out there waiting for her, there was no going back. Turning to books, to find out if there was a place for old lesbians in the greater lesbian community, Arden read about SAGE, Senior Action in a Gay Environment, in New York, and GLOE, Gay and Lesbian Outreach to Elders, in San Francisco. What she didn't find was anything for old lesbians in her own area.

The wheels began turning, and Arden started thinking about how to form a group to meet her needs in Houston. She took off on a research adventure to California, where, in addition to reconnecting with Tre, she met some powerful women, including Margaret Cruikshank, Phyllis Lyon, and Matile Poor Rothschilde.

> *I made the comment to Matile that I had this nagging feeling that this thing I wanted to do, to set up a support group for older lesbians, might be self-serving. We'd had a long visit and she knew something of my background. She said, "Oh, I don't think so. I think what I am hearing is the birth of a social conscience." It was a startling thing to hear. I said, "If, indeed, that is what it is, isn't it bad that it came so late?" Matile answered, "It's not so late. It's at the right time in your life."*
>
> *That trip to California was one of the biggest turning points of my life. Immediately, back in Houston, I put together a team of people involved in various aspects of gerontology. I was the only person over 50, and the group had to spend some time and effort consciousness-raising around age, so that it wasn't the young people telling the old people what they should do, or what was best for them.*

Out of this exploration came LOAF, the acronym originally for Lesbians Over Age Fifty-five, an age that was later lowered to fifty. LOAF took off, quickly gaining more than a hundred members. Having come out of the California model, LOAF was, naturally, an unstructured organization working by consensus. As a group, LOAF was willing to acknowledge that straight women have it rough as they age, too. But they knew older lesbians are even more isolated at this crucial point of their lives.

At the same time Arden was shepherding LOAF through its infancy, and reveling in all the new found connections she was making, she was saddened to realize that her relationships with her own decades-old friendship group had been altered. "I had become a scary phenomenon to them because my needs changed. They still love me. But relationships with them have changed." Over time, those relationships were rebuilt, but with Arden now out about her sexuality in the larger community, an element of caution was added. They had not followed her out of the closet.

Having stepped out of the closet socially, Arden now felt a need to officially come out to her mother. Her mother had been in therapy for a few months, and was hinting around. Being the dutiful daughter, Arden checked with the therapist first, who told her "Why don't you and your mother get off this merry-go-round." Arden told her mother, and her mother just sat there. Finally she said "I've suspected as much for about four months." "Four months! I'm 55 years old at the time and I've been in a relationship for 33 years. Mother had often lived in our home. She had been coming to this awareness for only about four months!"

Even after coming out to her family, so many friends, and even acquaintances, Arden sometimes found it hard.

I would not deny it if someone came to me and asked me, depending on the circumstances. The five years after Tommie died had been such a growth period for me. Our society discounts old people, especially old women. They are of absolutely no value, unless as a caretaker. In the eyes of the

larger society, our power is taken from us when we can't be
sexually attractive, or an appendage to a male, or we cannot
reproduce. As long as a woman can be competitive sexually,
she has some value.

Arden often sees this same dynamic playing itself out
within the lesbian community, with young lesbians discounting
the old lesbians. "I was so angry that I was 54, a widow, and my
life was over." Arden is very philosophical about what she would
like to see in the future. Her thoughts aren't just a wish list, but a
list of things she is actively working toward.

I would like to see old women feel good about being old. I
would like to see old women take back their power. I would
like to see the women of LOAF work on the terrible issues
of their internalized homophobia, and deal with the issues of
being an old lesbian, and deal with the word 'lesbian.' It's been
so stigmatized. I would like to see the women of our lifestyle
deal with their own spiritual loss. There is so much stuff about
sin and homosexuality. I would like to see women realize that
the punishment we feel has been created by men. All our laws
have been made by men. All our churches have been created
by men. All the things that make us feel less than we are are
the result of those things. I would have them be comfortable
with being women, being lesbian and, being old.

Arden may have led a full life by the time she was 60, but it
was far from over. The next chapter began when, at a meeting of
LOAF, Arden met Charlotte, the next love of her life.

What is wonderful in Charlotte's and my relationship is
that together we have been finding this activist path. Our
sensibilities tend to be along the same lines. The primary
attraction between Charlotte and me is on a spiritual level.
The spiritual aspect was never present in all the years I was
with Tommie.

It's wonderful to have this. Not to discount other times of my life, but this period has involved more change in a faster period of time. Charlotte and I have done more in three years than lots of people do in their lifetime.

Arden in Charlotte in 1995

Early in their relationship, Arden and Charlotte traveled to Austin to view the AIDS quilt, and that weekend just happened to coincide with a march, when 30,000 people marched on the capital.

That was our first experience in something like that. We never got over it. If you ever get involved in something like that, it forever changes how you feel about things, and what you're willing to do. That was quite a weekend for us.

Much of Arden's free time for the next several years revolved around helping take care of her mother, but she didn't let it consume her. A friend had introduced her to a fledgling national organization that worked to improve the lives of old lesbians, called OLOC, Old Lesbians Organizing for Change.

We went to a steering committee meeting the first weekend in December 1990, in San Antonio, Texas, and sat around a table with about 15 of the most powerful, charismatic, old women I have ever been exposed to. I sat next to Barbara Macdonald for the whole weekend and was so absolutely awestruck that I almost couldn't talk.

Arden and Charlotte began serving on the Steering Committee of OLOC, and in 1997 Arden accepted the role of co-director. Arden's circle of friends grew to include women from all over the country. In their work with OLOC, Charlotte and Arden traveled to Atlanta, Georgia, and participated in the 1991 National Lesbian Conference. That was an incredible experience. They also were involved in the 1993 March on Washington. OLOC had called in a few favors, and their contingent was the first walking group behind the dignitaries. Their chant as they marched was, "Two, Four, Six, Eight. How do you know your grandma's straight?"

Arden also participated in the planning and execution of several national OLOC conferences called 'Gatherings.' One of the challenges there was to get the women attending to use the word 'old.' As a group, they try to counteract some of society's obsession with youth. They also started a campaign against ageist birthday cards that depict old women as senile and non-sexual.

Most of Arden's friends, old and new, were around her age, and Arden became concerned as some of the women died, and their stories disappeared with them. Personally, she had given a lengthy interview about her life to a student in 1990, which was updated in 1998. After looking around and failing to find anyone else working to preserve the stories of her contemporaries, Arden took it upon herself to learn a bit about the process, and began interviewing old lesbians in the Houston area.

In 2001, Arden took a big step in her work with what was to become known as the "Old Lesbian Oral Herstory Project," when she and Charlotte drove to California on a trip dedicated to collecting more interviews. This was the first time she'd gone beyond focusing on gathering stories from her own geographic area. Later that same year, they took another interviewing trip, this time to Colorado.

In March of 2001, her project, and excerpts from four stories, were the cover story in the Houston gay publication, *OutSmart*. This was the first major recognition for the herstory project. Shortly thereafter, when the University of Houston dedicated a week during Women's Month to lesbians, they provided grant money to create a visual display of the Project. After it was displayed at the University, it was given to Arden. "That display is part of my workshop presentation today." That same summer, Arden also received an award from the Uncommon Legacy Foundation for her work in the community, and she continued her leadership in LOAF, the organization she founded more than a decade earlier.

What was already a busy year suddenly got even busier when a routine pre-op physical for cataract surgery revealed tumors in both of Arden's breasts. When all the tests were completed, all the tumors were found to be malignant. Accepted as a patient at MD Anderson Cancer Institute in Houston, Arden, and Charlotte, began another long journey together.

From the very first day, Charlotte and I were out to every medical person involved in my care. It was great not to have to watch pronouns, and to be unconditionally accepted.

Treatment consisted of four rounds of chemotherapy to shrink the tumors. As soon as she recovered from the chemo, there was surgery to remove both breasts, followed by another round of chemo. This was then followed by dozens of radiation treatments, and years of drug therapy. Each step along the way had its own set of side effects, but as soon as the worst of the ordeal was over, Charlotte and Arden headed to the Davis Mountains, in west Texas.

This had always been a favorite spot for both of us. Friends met us there, including one who was an ordained minister. We found a spot in the mountains where we had our commitment ceremony. It was not something we had talked much about until my journey with cancer.

Arden did her best not to let this monumental happening in her life keep her from doing everything else she was able to do. She continued to travel for OLOC meetings, despite having to argue with airport security in order to get all of her medical supplies through. Neither did it keep Charlotte and Arden from cheering on their beloved women's pro basketball team, the Comets, or from attending other social events.

> I had a wonderful caregiver, Charlotte, who did all kinds of nursing chores. She told me up front that she didn't do barf, so we never had to deal with that.

The Herstory project continued to grow under Arden's loving care and devotion, and OLOC finally asked if they could adopt it. This would provide some funding, as well as publicity for the project. Arden agreed, with one proviso: she would retain control of it, and would continue as its guiding force, as long as she was able. OLOC's growing connections within the total community of lesbians made finding potential interviewees for the project an easier task.

This period of Arden and Charlotte's lives, filled with family demands and health challenges, made traveling very far, or being gone very long difficult. They started on a quest to visit every county courthouse in Texas. This was no small feat, since there are 254 of them! But it helped them, to take short trips away that let them focus on themselves and their relationship. By the time they completed their courthouse project, health and family restrictions had eased, and they set their sights on visiting a series of huge carved sculptures, made from whole tree boles. The sculptures, called 'Whispering Giants,' are located throughout the country, and each depicts a Native American from that region. Together, Arden and Charlotte have located and visited dozens of these, and are still on the trail of others.

All the while, the Old Lesbian Oral Herstory Project continued to grow, and Arden felt it was time to step down from the OLOC Steering Committee. The national office for OLOC had also moved, and that gave Arden more time for her

At home in 2007, working on Herstories

other work. "We got a new motor home and started planning trips to combine meetings, interviews and play time." In 2004 alone, they made trips and did interviews in Arizona, California, and Michigan. The next year, they went to Florida, where their trip ended abruptly, as Arden took a misstep and shattered her wrist. It would take more than a broken wrist to slow her down, though, as she spent untold hours helping to organize a national event for OLOC in Houston that fall.

The year 2006 was just as busy as ever, as Arden and Charlotte attended the National Women's Music Festival, collected interviews all over the country, went on a cruise to Alaska, and hosted a Ph.D. student working on a dissertation subject related to the Herstory Project. Arden also gave two workshops on the herstories, one at a gathering of old lesbians in Vancouver, British Columbia, and another for Shell Oil. "That was the first time I was not 'speaking to the choir,' and the program was well received."

Instead of slowing down, Arden and the OLOHP seem to be gathering steam. Now all the stories are being backed up, scanned, and copies are being kept in a second location. Arden continues to travel, gathering and sharing, along the way.

> *Our trips continue, planned far in advance to combine play and oral herstory interviews. Referrals for interviews continue to come in. The sense of urgency never leaves, as this generation of amazing women disappear. It's important that these women become a documented part of our history.*
>
> *It's a wonderful time of life.*

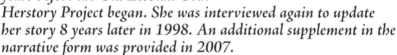

Arden continues to live in Texas. Interviewer: Marguerite Shelton

Arden was first interviewed in 1990, years before the Old Lesbian Oral Herstory Project began. She was interviewed again to update her story 8 years later in 1998. An additional supplement in the narrative form was provided in 2007.

If Arden runs into a friend she hasn't seen in a while, the subject will soon turn to the Herstory Project and she will happily update them with the growing number of completed herstories.

Charlotte Avery

Born February 1930 in Texas
Interviewed in 2000, at age 70, in Texas

He cried, and I cried, and then
I went to the softball game.

My father and mother married when they were real young,
on my mother's seventeenth birthday. They followed the
crops. My daddy would do carpenter work and work in the
fields, and my mother would pick cotton, cook for the field
hands, and stuff like that. They traveled in a covered wagon
from north Texas to south Texas. This was probably in about
1914 or 1915.

Charlotte's family ended up staying in south Texas when
her father got a job at the Sinclair Refinery, but he was a drinker
and quickly got fired, ending up back doing carpenter work. His
drinking was an ongoing problem that affected the whole family.

I don't have any memory of my life from the time I was
born until I was about six years old. I guess it was just too

traumatic, so I just blocked it out. But I remember having a little wagon when I was young, and I'd pull it up to the store, about five blocks away, to get a block of ice. I'd cover it with tow sacks to keep it from melting. Sometimes Momma would send me to the store to get a loaf of bread, and I'd eat two or three slices before I got back home.

We lived right behind the grammar school where I went to school. It was a two-story building. All the grades went to that school. At the end of the sidewalk there was this little old shell and sand place, and I used to play there with the doodle bugs. I'd stay down there, or go over to the school and shoot marbles, just anything to be out of the house. There was always a bunch of chaos, anger, and stuff when my daddy was home. That's all I remember of weekends: he was drunk, raising Cain, and cussin' Momma.

I remember him having an old Model T, and he came home drunk and ran into the side of the house. Our house had those clapboards that ran up and down. He knocked those boards off, and we'd get out there the next day and nail them on, or stuff the cracks with newspaper.

We had screen windows, and a wood stove. We didn't have indoor plumbing until we moved. There were two adults and seven children living in a two room house. When I was twelve years

Charlotte at 3 years old

old, we moved about five blocks from where we were living, into a four-room house. Then we had indoor plumbing. I used to saw logs with a cross-cut saw, and then split the logs for firewood. I had to dig holes in the back yard to bury garbage. That's how I cut the big toe off my left foot, with a "sharpshooter."

Growing up during the 1930s, with an alcoholic father who kept the family stirred up all the time, was difficult. Charlotte's mother offered some balance, and stability, for a while. However, that wouldn't last.

My mother was beautiful. She used to iron for the neighbors to make money, because Daddy never gave her any. He'd buy all the groceries. If there was any money left on Friday when he got paid, he'd buy the groceries and bring them home. But a lot of times he drank all the money up, and there'd be no groceries. So she started taking in ironing. She'd make up pastry, and bread and stuff, and take it to our neighbors.

I remember during World War II, when my oldest brother was in the Navy, Momma kept our nephew, my brother's boy, and they paid her a few bucks for doing that. She never did have any money of her own until my daddy started getting Social Security, and the social worker told her that half of that money was hers. So she made Daddy give her her half, and she'd spend it on all the things she wanted to eat, like fruits and vegetables. Daddy only liked potatoes and beans, and things like that. Momma could buy anything she wanted then.

If it was around Christmas time, she'd get a washcloth, or something, and wrap it up and give it to her kids for Christmas. She was always buying something for somebody else, and never did spend any money on herself. She had a hard life.

The hardships of life took their toll on Charlotte's mother, and after a while she sank into depression and tried to commit suicide. Charlotte and her sister, Mary, began taking turns going to school when their mother was depressed, afraid of what might happen if no one was there. That began to take a toll on Charlotte's education.

> I was supposed to graduate in 1948, but I was going to school every other day. I failed my typing. It wasn't that I couldn't have done the typing, it was just that I didn't like it to begin with, and didn't see the point in it. So I went back to summer school in 1950 and got my diploma. I addressed a thousand envelopes for the school district tax election to get my typing credit! The teachers all knew what our situation was at home, and took a lot into consideration.

Church played an interesting role in Charlotte's tumultuous upbringing, too. While it offered a refuge for her and her siblings in some respects, it also added to her inner turmoil.

> Me and my momma and the kids, Mary and Bob, went to the Methodist church when we were living in that little two room house. We'd walk down the lane. There was a pasture to the south of us, and there was a barbed wire fence. We'd walk along that barbed wire fence down to First Street, where the church was. But the women made fun of my momma because she didn't have real pretty clothes to go to church in. We always had homemade clothes, or second hand clothes. You know how people are: if you don't have a lot of money, or look right, what they considered "look right," they made fun of you.

In Charlotte's memories, her father didn't really participate with the family very much, and when he did, everyone wished he hadn't.

He didn't do anything but go to work, get paid, and get drunk. Once or twice I remember him splitting some logs in the back yard for the stove, but I split a helluva lot more logs than he did. When he wasn't drinking, he was just sitting in the rocker reading. When he was drinking, he'd always want us kids to come sit on his lap, and he'd tell us how much he loved us. Then he'd get mad about something, and you never knew whether he loved you or whether he hated you.

Getting out of the home and working while she was in high school gave Charlotte a break from the demands and stresses of home life.

When I was in high school in Houston, there was a little confectionery store across the street that sold candy, gum, fruit pies and soda water. I'd go there and work before school, during the lunch hour, and after school. I was probably 14 or 15 years old then.

The last three years of high school I worked at the theater as a cashier. My sister, Mary, worked behind the candy and popcorn counter. Sometimes I'd work behind the candy counter, too. I remember in 1948, when I was working behind the candy counter one night popping popcorn, a man, probably about 18 or 19, came in to the movie theater. He was all wet 'cause it was raining outside, and stood at the door, looking at me, and I was looking at him.

We started dating and, in fact, became engaged. During that time, I also started going to softball games. Joan played softball, and we played on the team together. I didn't play very long as I wasn't too good. They were having a women's fast pitch softball tournament at Memorial Park, and I wanted to go. So about a week before I was supposed to be married, I broke the engagement.

I told him I just felt like I was making a mistake. He cried, and I cried, and then I went to the softball game. So

I guess that's when I probably came out to myself. I realized that if I got married to him, I would be making a mistake.

Looking back at her years in high school, Charlotte wondered why she hadn't figured it out earlier. "I always had a couple of girlfriends in school. I'd have the best looking girlfriends, even better looking than the football players had. Even at 13 to 15 years old, I'd have a special friend at school, and we'd walk back and forth to school together." When a friend would come back to school and say she wasn't allowed to spend time with Charlotte any longer, she was hurt and confused.

Nobody ever said that I was a homosexual, or a lesbian, or said anything to my face. It was just real hurtful. Nobody talked about anything at home. They knew what was going on, and everybody kept everything a damn secret.

Finishing high school, and realizing there weren't many decent jobs available to women, Charlotte and a friend, Joyce, both decided to join the Air Force.

Just out of high school, 1949

We went to join the Air Force, and they gave us papers to have my parents sign, since I was under 21. We were supposed to go back up the next day get our physical exams. Joyce came over the next morning and said, "Well, are you ready to go?" And I said, "No, I can't go." "Why not?" she asked. "Well, Momma won't sign my paper," I said. "You son of a bitch!" she replied. So she went off to the Air Force, and I stayed home.

Charlotte did find a good job, and went to work for Western Electric, where she stayed for the next 33 years. Western Electric was the service center for Southwestern Bell, and Charlotte started out working in the shop. That solved her job problem but she still needed a social life. One of the few places you could go to find other lesbians in the 1950s and 1960s was the gay bars.

> *I would go to the bar and have a couple of beers, just to be with people. A friend of mine nicknamed me 'Bump,' because I just never had too much to say. You could talk to me and I'd say something, but I never would strike up a conversation on my own. I'd go to the bar just to be with people.*

The other place Charlotte was able to find other women like herself was at the softball games. Texas was the focus of a very active women's softball system.

> *There were a lot of women there. Lorreta, my girlfriend, played softball and lived way up in Dallas. I went with her for awhile. We would run up a million dollar phone bill. She was a nurse, and worked nights. Sometimes she'd call me two or three times a night. Long distance relationships just don't work well, though.*
>
> *Then in the early 1950s, there was this girl at the ball game, and I asked somebody who it was. "Oh, that's Arden. That's Tommie's girlfriend."*

Charlotte knew of, and respected, Tommie, so she didn't approach Arden. She certainly didn't know that her life and Arden's would become entwined decades later. Throughout her 20s, Charlotte's social life continued to revolve around going to softball games, and spending time with a few of her running buddies. Just that and work.

> *I went to Western Electric in August of 1950, and I stayed there 33 years. I worked in the shop. Western Electric*

was the service center for Southwestern Bell, before the
Bell companies split up in 1983. We repaired all kinds
of telephone equipment. Then I worked in the Teletype
Department for about ten years. I really liked that. I like to
take things apart, put new parts in machines, put them back
together, and then test them. I really enjoyed that. Then they
invented the transistor, and everything changed. When I
retired in 1983, I was working on circuit boards, repairing
and checking them.

About 1980, after all that affirmative action stuff, they
were supposed to offer supervisor jobs to the women. So,
naturally, they offered me one. I was a smart aleck. I'd seen
all these supervisors that didn't know their butt from a hole
in the ground, and you knew how they got to be supervisor.
You'd go ask them a question, and they'd just give you a book
and say, "Here, read this and it'll tell you what to do." So
they asked me if I wanted to be a supervisor, and I told them,
"No, my morals are too high."

At work in 1961, dressed for the annual "Go Texan Day" celebration

I never went to college. All the training I had with work was on-the-job training. One time, they sent me to Columbus, Ohio, for an electronics course. I used to feel kind of inferior to people who had been to college and had lots of degrees and stuff. But I've discovered that some of those people didn't have any common sense, so I don't think I did too badly with my high school education.

Back in 1950, I started off making 92¢ an hour, and when I retired I was making $13.85 an hour. I was paid the same as the men because we were all in a union.

During her working years, Charlotte identified as a gay woman, since she had yet to hear the word 'lesbian.' Even though she knew she was different, Charlotte didn't have any word for it. "I just knew that I enjoyed being with women." Eventually, she thought of herself as 'gay.' "Homosexual doesn't sound good, but if you're gay, that sounded okay."

During that time, Charlotte was, for the most part, a loner. She did have a few relationships, including one long, significant one. Charlotte and Sharon got together in 1971, and stayed together for the next nine years.

All during that time, Sharon drank on a daily basis. She had a problem with alcohol, and just like any other kind of relationship, I guess I was attracted to what I was familiar with. I had been raised in an alcoholic household. I always had the feeling that if I was good to her, if I bought her nice clothes, if we had nice vacations, or whatever, there was always something I could do to make her quit drinking. Well, that didn't work.

In 1980, her employer told Sharon she could either go into treatment, and get help for her alcoholism, or she would lose her job. She was in the hospital for 28 days, and they had what they called a 'family week.' Sharon's parents lived in California, and she didn't want them to know anything about it anyway. I got involved in Al-Anon's 12-Step program, and that 'family week' really changed my life.

I finally discovered that I wasn't responsible for her drinking, nor could I do anything about it. The only thing I had control over was myself and my behavior. I discovered that my behavior was just like the behavior of my dad, who was an alcoholic. I wasn't alcoholic myself, but I had all the characteristics.

I was a rescuer. I was the one in the family that they always brought all their problems to, because they knew that I'd fix it. The only way I ever got a feeling of self-worth was by doing stuff like that.

I was devastated when Sharon left. I stayed alone for about eight years. Sometimes I'd go to two or three Al-Anon meetings a day. I worked at the Al-Anon Intergroup Office for two years after I retired, answering the phone and talking to people wanting to know where a meeting was.

I had my older sister go to Al-Anon for one of her boys who was having a problem with alcohol. She went for awhile, but then she decided it wasn't for her. Everything was always a big secret in her family, and they never talked about any-thing. It got to be too painful for her, so she just quit going. But it helped me a lot to learn about the disease, and how it affected the family. It answered a lot of questions about why my father was the way he was. Both of my brothers, my dad, and one sister were alcoholic, and my mother was manic-depressive. When I got involved in Al-Anon, I quit rescuing my family.

Having lost Sharon, and not wanting to put herself out there again, Charlotte spent much of her time alone for the next few years. But in 1987, several years after she retired, Charlotte's life as a loner changed. That's when she crossed paths once again with Arden, the woman she'd noticed at a softball game decades earlier. Arden's first partner, Tommie, had died several years before, and once she began to recover from her loss, Arden started a social organization for older lesbians in Houston called LOAF, Lesbians Over Age Fifty.

Charlotte went on a camping trip with some of the women from LOAF, and fell head over heels. Neither Charlotte nor Arden were looking to start a new relationship, but they didn't seem to have much choice in the matter. Before long, they were inseparable. Together, they learned about the larger lesbian community, not just in Houston, but across the United States.

Life changed drastically for Charlotte when she came out. A famous Texas football coach, Bum Phillips, was often quoted as saying his team wasn't going to knock on the door, they were "gonna kick the door in." According to Charlotte, she didn't just come out, she kicked the door off the closet. She and Arden dove head first into community activism, and never looked back.

> Twice, I've marched on the state capitol in Austin, Texas. I got involved in PFLAG, because Arden came out to her mother, and we started taking her mother to PFLAG. Then we both started going, and Arden went to Al-Anon with me, too. Then we got involved in OLOC, Old Lesbians Organizing for Change. You have to be 60 to belong. We were both on the steering committee for that, and that's been real interesting.
>
> We went to the National Lesbian Conference in Atlanta, Georgia, as a part of OLOC. On the marquee at the civic center was, "Welcome Old Lesbians." Boy, that was a thrill. I can't remember how many were there, something like 5,000. Everywhere you'd go, all you'd see was lesbians. If you walked down the street, all you'd see would be lesbians. Everybody treated us well. That was empowering.
>
> In Washington, D.C., we were in the front of the parade at the March on Washington. We had special seating down

by the stage, and that was really a sight. There were a million people there. Of course, they discounted it, and said there was only about 400,000, but they always do that. There's no way they're going to acknowledge that there could be a million gays or lesbians in Washington, D.C.

Her family probably always knew, on some level, that Charlotte was a lesbian, but it was never spoken about, never named. When Charlotte was in her late 60s, she decided ignoring the truth had gone on too long, and on National Coming Out Day, she sent them all a letter. (letter on page 194)

I sent letters to all of my family, and came out to them. I told them I wasn't doing this for them, I was doing this for myself. I was just tired of keeping everything a secret. I have a feeling they were ashamed of me. I told them that I had always been a lesbian, and that I was a child of God and I would not discuss the Bible with anybody. I had one response from my sister's son, who is probably a gay man, but who has never been allowed to be who he is. I hand-delivered the letter to my niece, Judy, and she just wadded it up and threw it in the garbage. A couple of them accepted it, and don't have a problem with me being a lesbian. But one sister is so homophobic it makes my blood boil sometimes.

Life never did slow down for Charlotte. She knows she has to have met at least 400 or 500 lesbians through LOAF. They've been going long enough that she's now lost several good friends over the years. "Betty Rudnick was one of my favorites. She was my fishing buddy," Charlotte recalled.

I'm 70 years old, and the thing that makes me the most uncomfortable about being 70 is that my little pride gets hurt when I can't do the things I used to do. I can't work out in the yard and dig, get up on ladders and do a lot of stuff.

Another of the many interests that keep Charlotte busy is her involvement in a group for young gay and lesbian kids in their area.

Arden and I, mostly Arden, are going to mentor these two young lesbians. They're really neat. One of them has some medical problems that she is going to have surgery for, and she's not able to work. I can imagine how she must feel, having to depend on her partner for financial stuff right now. I have always had problems asking for anything I needed. I wouldn't ask anybody for anything. I'm so independent.

Charlotte lives on her pension from Western Electric, but she worries about how she could have been better about planning for her future.

I would probably be in real good shape, but after my daddy got sick with cancer in the late 1950s (he died in '63), when he got so he couldn't work any more, I helped my mother and daddy financially a lot. And I've always taken vacations

Arden and Charlotte's commitment ceremony in the hills of West Texas.

*every year. I spent a lot of money on mother and daddy,
buying things for them, especially Momma, things that she
never did have. So, I'm saving money now, for the first time.*

*I wish I'd met Miss Arden in 1950, but I didn't. I went
to the Methodist Church, the First Methodist Church in
downtown Houston, for over 30 years. After Sharon left,
I stopped going to church. I began to be aware of how the
church felt about homosexuals, so I quit going altogether.
But when Arden and I got together, she was going to Unity
Church, and I started going, too. I felt like I'd come home.
I never could understand all the hate that comes out of the
fundamentalists as far as homosexuals are concerned. That's
not what Jesus teaches. It's just like when I was a little kid,
and we lived in this little town, Galena Park. Probably
wasn't 200 people there, but everybody knew my father was
an alcoholic, and they made fun of us kids, and my momma.
I don't much care for hypocrites.*

*Well, I tell you what: since I retired, back in 1983, and
got involved in activist work, they've been the happiest years
of my life.*

*Charlotte's continues to live in
Houston, with her 'Sugar,' Arden.
Together, they have crisscrossed
the United States over and over,
gathering the stories of lesbians 70
and older.*

Interviewer: Arden Eversmeyer

Lucille 'Lucy' Frey

Born August 1932 in Missouri
Interviewed at age 74 in Missouri

We have to believe or we won't do anything.

I was actually born in a barn. When people said to me later, "Whatsa matter, you born in a barn?" I'd say, "Yep." School was about three miles away, through a cow pasture that had a really mean bull in it, across a few creeks, and through the woods. But when my siblings went to school, I wanted to go, too. I'd stand and watch for them to come home, and ask them what they learned that day. Pretty soon I was saying, "Mom, could I go to school, too?"

That was the start of Lucy's life-long love affair with learning. She was born and raised in a rural, undeveloped area of the Ozark Mountains in Missouri, during the Depression. Her parents and two siblings were actually living in a barn that belonged to her blacksmith grandfather. Her parents were both "hardscrabble farmers," and like many families in that era, scraped out a living however they could. Her dad carried the mail, and worked with the WPA building stone schoolhouses, and her mom raised and canned most of their own food.

My dad said he would have liked to be the one to get to stay home and take care of everything, because he wasn't that sociable. But there was no way a woman could earn a living for a family out in that world.

Lucy gives her dad credit for development of her tenacity and interest in what was going on outside her rural surroundings. He had quit school in the eighth grade, when he tired of being whipped. "I think that he probably said, 'Are you sure about that?' to the teacher, and the teacher beat him for it." In Lucy's eyes, her dad was one of the most intelligent men she had ever known.

My folks would have company because my mother was sociable. The women would stay in the kitchen after dinner, and the men would gather in the living room. I could only take so much of hearing how to can green beans and diaper babies, so I would go tuck myself under my dad's arm and listen to the men talk about whether the New Deal was working or not, or what was going on in Europe, and things like that.

One day they turned their attention to how they were raising their kids. One man said, "Well, I want my kids to be in at night by 11:00." The next one said, "I require my kids to be home by 10:00." I eagerly waited to see what my dad said. When they finished, he said, "I think I expect my children to act like they've got some sense of their own." That really laid a heavy burden on me. When I went to high school, the kids thought I was a drag, because on every occasion I was trying to figure out "How would I act if I had some sense of my own?"

Lucy's family was part of the local Baptist community, where there were plenty of restrictions on behavior. Basically, "If it's fun, it's sinful. So don't do it!" Luckily, her parents didn't attend regularly, and didn't adhere to that dictum very closely.

If I went to church, it was because it was a social thing to do, and not a religious thing. I did not find religion in churches. Any spirituality I have, I found sitting out under a tree and communicating with nature.

I went to one-room country schools through the eighth grade. Nobody in my family had ever gone to high school, but I told my dad, "I am going to high school. I don't know how. I would rather stay home to do it, but if there's no way I can stay home, I'll run away and do it."

I went to Plato High School for ninth grade by wading four creeks, and catching a bus and riding eleven miles, which wasn't too bad. Tiny little school. I loved it. At the end of the school year, the superintendent came and talked to my dad. He said, "The school board has decided they can't afford to send the bus that far after your daughter, but it's important that your daughter go to school. You've gotta figure out how to do that."

Dad explored the possibilities and arranged for me to go to Houston High School. I had to walk three miles to catch the bus, and it was up over a hill. There were no creeks, but there was a graveyard, with lots of ghosts and some haunted houses. Then I caught the school bus and rode 33 miles to Houston High School.

The wolves chased me home one night, the last three miles. The bus was late that night, and it was dark. When I was walking through the woods, I heard the wolves. They got closer, and as I crossed one valley they came up behind. One found my trail and they started following me. I said later, "It was too dark for me to see the trail, so I just made a new one!" When I got home and told my dad, he said, "You can't do that anymore. It's too dangerous." So he arranged with a store owner in Upton for me to get room and board there for working in the store until I graduated.

High school came to an end in 1949, with Lucy graduating as the valedictorian of her class. With that behind her, she then had to decide what came next. Options for a young woman in 1949 were few and far between. She'd helped raise her siblings, and knew she "didn't need to go out and do that!"

The choices for women in those days, if you didn't want to just get married and have a batch of kids, were to be a teacher, a nurse, or a secretary. In our part of the country, there weren't any nurses or secretaries, so teaching was it. This wonderful old, tobacco-chewing friend of my dad's was president of the school board at Long Valley School. He loaned me $250 so I could go to college that summer and teach in the fall. I went into teaching as a way for me to go to college.

23 years old

Lucy began teaching in the school where she had attended grades four through eight, at Long Valley School. Feeling that teachers shouldn't stay long in one-room school, she only taught there two years before moving on to a nearby school.

That was a school that was really kind of wild. Kids were known for running off their teachers. Sometimes, the teachers didn't even last a full year. However, I was a good softball player. So were some of those 'mean' boys that ran off the teachers. But because I could out-throw them, they had lots of respect for me. And if their younger siblings misbehaved in school, those boys straightened 'em out!

Since I was already teaching, I only went to college during summers and stayed ahead of the requirements. It took me eight years to get my bachelor's degree. My major was education. I still loved school, so I continued going every summer, and finally got a master's degree in English literature from the University of Missouri at Columbia.

Never staying at one Missouri school for long, Lucy taught several other places, with various levels of success and satisfaction. At one point, when she was about to change schools again, Lucy explored becoming an airline stewardess. She loved to travel, but she wasn't even considered, because "they didn't let stewardesses wear glasses back in those days," and she was near-sighted. Even though she did go on to teach for three more years, this time in Sullivan, Missouri, the idea of traveling had gotten into her system.

I got this yearning to travel, to see the world. In 1956, I sent out letters to every place on the map of North America that looked interesting and asked, "Do you need a teacher?" Tequcigalpa, Honduras, wanted to hire me at an American school there. Anchorage, Alaska, was so eager to get me that they sent me a contract in February of 1957, and hired me just on the strength of what I had written. They hired me sight unseen.

So in 1957, I loaded up my 1956 Chevrolet and drove to Alaska. My kid brother, Paul, had just graduated from high school, and didn't know what he wanted to do with his life.

He said, "I'm goin' with you," so we drove to Alaska together. I slept in the front seat, and he slept in the back seat. We didn't even have a good map. We took the north fork of every road we came to, and it eventually got us there.

Despite initial plans to only stay a few years, Lucy went on to teach and live in Alaska for the next 37 years, retiring from the Anchorage School District in 1975. Not all those years were in the classroom, however.

The last five years, I was the Social Studies Coordinator for the whole district. Most people don't know it, but the Anchorage School District is one of the largest districts in America. So it was a pretty challenging job. I was called upon, as a Social Studies expert, to consult with other school districts in other places.

That experience set Lucy on a slightly different path; upon retiring, she formed an educational consultant firm. She remained based in Alaska, but this new phase of her career took her to the Bristol Bay, in the southwest corner of the state. While the local folks were interested in what she had to say about social studies, the major industry in the area was often brought into any discussion.

Teaching in Alaska, age 43

Any time there was a lull in the conversation out there, people would talk about fishing. The Bristol Bay area is one of the major fishing areas in the world. I learned that to do commercial fishing, you had to have a permit. Those permits are issued to keep the area from being over-fished. One day I said, "If any of these permits ever come up for sale, I might be interested. Let me know."

It wasn't long before the opportunity arose to get a shore-fishing permit, and Lucy had to make a decision. The permit cost was $25,000. She knew she couldn't afford it, but wondered if she could get together a group of friends to buy it collectively. After successfully pulling together five partners and getting the permit, two other permits became available. She repeated the process until a group of 15 partners was formed. These groups fished the three permits along the mouth of the Kvichak River. There was, however, one rather significant problem: none of them had any experience fishing commercially.

I kept asking people, "How do you do this?" I got so many different answers that I realized there is no one way; you just make it up as you go. So we went out there and, as one of our teachers said, 'We probably had more college degrees than had ever before congregated along Bristol Bay!' We had a lot of fun. The first year there was a fish run like, as the Natives said, "Almost like the old days." They said, "In the old days, you could walk across the river on the backs of the fish."

One day, we glanced out and somebody said, "Look at that!" As far as the eye could see, there were fish leaping, heading back to their spawning grounds. There were so many fish that year, that we paid for our permits. Of course, there were other years when there were hardly any fish.

There were good years, and there were bad years. I'm glad I did it, because of all the wonderful experiences we had. It wasn't like anything else I'll ever experience. I did it for five years. If you did other things, it got so that six weeks in the summer took too big a chunk out of the other things that you wanted to do.

One of the "other things" taking much of Lucy's attention, was her partnership with another woman in the ownership of the Alaska Women's Bookstore. It was through this woman that Lucy realized that she wasn't very aware of women's history and literature. To rectify that situation, she set out to learn more, and acquired a Ph.D. in the subject. According to Lucy, "I would still be going to school if there was a way to do it."

The bookstore didn't make money, and eventually was passed on to others. Lucy had hoped someone else could make a go of it, as it was a major political center where women could distribute information and gather together. When it finally closed after seven years, it saddened her.

When the economy of Alaska began to struggle, and people were abandoning homes in Anchorage, Lucy kept encouraging women she knew to buy houses, while they were cheap. It happened so often that the realtor she was sending them to suggested that Lucy get a real estate license so she could get a commission. That led to another career, which kept her busy for a few more years.

Eventually, she ended up back in Missouri, close to where she'd been raised. At first, she worked selling real estate for a local office, but found the politics and ultra-patriotic attitudes were too much for her. Tensions came to a head when Lucy wrote a letter to the editor, stating that she preferred her tax money to be spent helping people, instead of dropping bombs. She was fired from her job. She could have started her own office, since she was a broker, but she'd had enough.

Being back in Missouri was also very challenging for her as a feminist, and as a lesbian.

By the time I was in fifth grade, I knew that it wasn't that good lookin' boy that I was attracted to; it was the eighth grade girl who played the guitar so well. I just knew that I wasn't destined to be some guy's wife. I didn't have the

Camping near Telkeetna, Alaska

language for my feelings until the women's movement of the 1970's gave me the language. Then I knew who I was, and that I was okay.

That's why they don't let us talk about it now. Because if more women glimpsed that as an opportunity, would they ever shack up with that guy that they're having to put up with now? I don't think so. I think this whole anti-gay thing has to do with the political subjugation of women. Those straight men don't want to put up with gay men who won't participate in keeping women under their thumbs! That's what their whole system is set up on, the religion, the economy, and all of it.

We still don't have equality, and I'm agitating. While I lived in Alaska, we passed a state Equal Rights Amendment. When I last visited Alaska, I asked how we get another *study on the status of women going, because things had kind of stalled out, and there was no leadership. I had a chunk of money, and donated it to the University for feminist research. Two other women donated money, also. We figured that surely the University was smart enough to make an 8% return a year, and could give $1,000 a year as an incentive toward some feminist research. Well, after I left, they failed to do that for a number of years. I started agitating from down here in Missouri, and told them if they weren't going to use the money for what we donated it for, I wanted my money back. Of course that scared 'em.*

Lucy left the funds there, making sure it was used the way she intended. Some women wanted to do another study on the status of women, and to revive the women's movement there.

It's more likely to happen in Alaska than it is here, because women are so scared here to speak out. Missouri does not have an equal rights amendment, and women are making 77¢ to the male dollar nationally. Why can't it be the same? I think we ought to kick the hell out of the system, and see that we get equality. I'd like to be equal under the U.S. Constitution in my lifetime.

Asked if she thought equal rights and equal status for women was possible, Lucy said, "We have to believe, or we won't do anything."

We ought to agitate! We sat around in the 1970s when the civil rights movement was going on, and the women's movement was learning how to do it. We would ask ourselves, "Can the Martin Luther Kings get anywhere without the Malcolm Xs?" Martin Luther King looked like somebody the patriarchy could work with, while Malcolm X was taking hostages and burning buildings.

In the women's movement, we didn't have anybody burning buildings and taking hostages. When Reagan got elected, and it was obvious that the ERA was dead, we sat around in Anchorage and said, "What shall we do? We can't just let it go down without a whimper." But everything we thought of to do, we couldn't do. Everything we thought of, somebody would say, "But somebody could get hurt." Women aren't willing to let anybody get hurt. So we're defeated by the best of our intentions.

When I went to the peace conference in Dallas recently, they pushed us with, "What can you do, when you go home, that will forward the cause of peace?" All I could think of that I could do here, I already have done. I marched against the war with a group in Springfield. I marched for peace with a group in Camdenton. But there is no group in this county to march with. Since I can get into trouble by writing letters to the editor, that's what I said I would do, and I have done that since I got here.

Lucy was surprised and pleased to see that her county actually voted blue (democratic) in the recent election. It also voted for stem cell research, and was taking other progressive steps forward.

I've been told by some people that they watch to see what signs are in my yard before they make up their minds about which candidate to support. Somebody told the editor of the paper, I heard, that the only reason they keep taking his dull paper is that every now and then there's an intelligent letter to the editor. I think that has made a little bit of difference, but not enough. I'm kind of stymied in my own community, about what else to do to make a difference.

Finding like-minded people, much less like-minded women, in Missouri has been hard. Lucy attended the local Democratic meetings, but found they don't really do much of anything.

I try, but it's hard to find a group. The activists in Alaska were women. I was even registered in Alaska as a Republican. We had open primaries, so it didn't matter how you were registered. I never changed my registration, because I liked knowing what the enemy was up to. The Republican Party has shifted so drastically in the last 40 years, I keep asking my friends, "Whatever happened to the Republican Party of Abraham Lincoln and Susan B. Anthony?"

It's hard to find activist groups here. I've tried the League of Women Voters in Springfield. The Alaska League was pretty active. When I suggested to the Business and Professional Women's group, over at Buffalo, that we should invite the candidates, and see which ones favored equality for women, before we decided how to vote, the president looked at me and said, "I think you're in the wrong club."

I went to the Feminist Hullabaloo that was held in Sante Fe, New Mexico, in 2007, where I enjoyed seeing a lot of old friends again, thrilled that we were just having a meeting. I was disappointed that we didn't come out of that with a plan of action. I've comforted myself since then by remembering that before the feminist activist movement began in the 1970s, from the late 1960s on, there had to be a lot of consciousness-raising groups. So I consider the Feminist Hullabaloo as just a consciousness-raising event, and I think maybe some activism may grow out of it.

I've attended state NOW meetings. I've said to them, "Okay, abortion rights are important. But they are not our reason for existence." We need to concentrate on the bigger picture of women's rights, and then abortion will be put in its place, and will take care of itself.

I asked old Delbert Scott, who is our state legislator, if he was going to support women's rights, because I deserve to be equal. He said, "Oh, women have enough rights." "Are you kidding?" I said. "Yeah, if you give them any more rights, they'll probably get more abortions." He tells me, a 70+ year old woman, that! Both sides really stress that too much. I loved the days when we marched with signs that said, "Stop all abortions. Don't sleep with men." We were radical!

Lucy has always been who she is, never trying to hide it, but not just sitting around and talking about it, either. She picks up the trash on a 3/4 mile stretch of Highway 316, and wonders if some of the locals might throw things out in that area intentionally, because she's the one who'll clean it up. "If I were a pretty, little, heterosexual woman, maybe they'd be out there helping me." Lucy wonders if being an old lesbian is the reason, but knows there isn't any way to prove it. "They wouldn't be logical enough to talk to about it, even if I tried."

Despite resistance from some locals, Lucy makes an effort to stay involved in her community, but, at times, they do try her patience. One civic project involved planting a small public space near the fire department. Unsure about the identity of a plant that was thriving, Lucy asked the state garden coordinator to find out what it was.

She had identified it as something called "the tall thistle," that the painted lady butterflies use as a host plant. So here we are, a little local garden group watching that plant grow and Bob came out and chopped it down. I said, "Bob. Why did you do it?" He answered, "Thistles are against the law." He just fluttered all over the place. Of course, musk thistles are declared to be a noxious weed, but not painted lady thistles. And even if it had been a musk thistle, nobody's harvesting hay at the fire department grounds, so it wouldn't have mattered anyway. But in the wake of that, when I went down to his house to ask him why he had cut it down, Bob and his wife threw me out of the house, and said, "Get out of here, you ol' lesbian. Don't come back again."

*He tends to be rude to everyone, but he's nastier to me,
I think, than he is to most. Before that event, he had told
me that they had moved from North Carolina. He said that
he once had a gay son who was killed in a shootout, and
the police never pursued it. By the hatred on that man's face
when he was telling the story, I have a feeling I know who
killed his son.*

Lucy tends to be torn about living in her area of Missouri,
but she tries to make the most of it, contributing to the local
parks and helping in other ways. She keeps two lists: one
with reasons to leave, another with reasons to stay. When she
reconnected with many of her Alaskan friends, while in Santa
Fe at the feminist event, they all agreed that they missed having
the conversations they had there. "We miss the people's ability
to talk substance." She and her friends are toying with the idea
of moving near each other. "Everybody's life is at a stage where I
don't know if that'll ever happen, or not."

"I'm open to about anything."

Lucy Frey continues to live in Missouri

Interviewer: Arden Eversmeyer

Delores 'Dee' Austin

Born March 1936 in Ohio
Interviewed at 65, in January 2001 in Arizona

Learning to be who I am.

Dee was an avid and gifted reader very early in life. She'd been born in a town so small that the schools didn't have a kindergarten, but her family moved to nearby Dayton, Ohio, in time for her to start school. Her interest in reading was almost always nurtured. However, it was a wonder that her passion for reading ever survived the second grade.

> *The teacher would have reading groups, and she would ask us to read a certain page, to look for an answer, or something. But I could read faster than the rest of the kids. So, I'd read page five, then I'm ready to go on, so I'd read on to page six and seven. She took a ruler and cracked my hands for not staying on the page she thought I was supposed to stay on. So I adapted!*

Five-year-old Dee shows off her big trike

Fortunately, not all of her experiences with teachers were so traumatic. A few years later, when she was in the sixth grade, Dee was subjected to hateful taunts, and this teacher's response made a lasting impression on her.

A girl in my class called me a "nigger" out on the playground. I came back in and told the teacher. She doesn't know this, and I don't know where the woman is now, but I credit Miss Moore with my attitude of knowing that there are some whites you don't want to be bothered with, and then there are some that are very nice, and you're glad to have as friends. Because what she did was to sit everybody down and chewed up the girl, talking about "You don't do this." The whole time, I sat there. For a kid who's gotten somebody else in trouble, and you're sitting there feeling so good that they're getting it! Well!

The teacher could have treated it in all different manners, but not her. I still have that picture in my head, of that sixth grade class, and Miss Moore, and the girl who called me the name. She's the only kid in the class whose name I remember!

That incident was basically the only trouble she ever had. Dee never felt excluded from anything by the color of her skin during her school years. Their family moved quite a bit, so she went to several schools. She lived in communities that were all predominantly white. More often than not, she and her siblings were the only black children in the school, which also made each of them the only black child in their respective classes. Even though those circumstances often can be a recipe for disaster, Dee felt that she fit in, and she enjoyed her early school experiences.

We had morning announcements on the PA system, and I gave them for quite some time. I forget how many years. And we had a bookstore where we could buy notebook paper, pencils and all those little kinds of things. I was in charge of the bookstore for several years. That's where I learned what a gross was! We ordered paper by the gross.

I had a lot of support. There was an English teacher who supervised the bookstore. Her name was Miss Edna Surrarrer, and she knew that I loved poetry. She gave me a book of poetry when I graduated from junior high school in 1951, and I still have it.

Dee was the oldest of four, with two sisters, three and five years younger than she, and a brother, seven years younger. Even with siblings and other kids in the neighborhood, Dee still spent most of her time alone.

I usually read. I didn't want to play with them. I was not a kid who played a whole lot. In fact, on one occasion, when we were living in Euclid, it was a nice day and I'd been sitting in the house reading. The other three were outside playing, and mother said, "Delores Ann." Now, when she said my whole name, that meant business. "Delores Ann, put that book down and go outside and play." "But I'm right at this…," I protested. "Put the book down and go outside and play!" she insisted. After a few more "buts," she made me go out, and she locked the screen door so I couldn't get back in!

I can remember there was a newscast sponsored by Marshall Drug Store in Cleveland. Because I wasn't playing with them, my sister would make paper airplanes, and when the announcer would say "Marshall's News Ace Zooms Into Your Home," she would zoom the paper airplanes at me, because I was reading.

It was just that I was different.

Love of reading followed Dee to her grandparents' farm, where she often spent weeks at a time during the summer. Her grandfather farmed, and her grandmother did some day work for a couple of doctors in town. The doctors would give her books to take home, because everyone knew Dee loved to read. While there one summer, Dee got into the stash of books stored in the china cabinet.

> There was a hammock out in the front yard, and I'd get in the hammock and read.
>
> The sister next to me in age would follow Grandpa all over the farm. The only time I'd get out there in those fields is when he made me. I wasn't gonna be doing any gardening on my own. That's not my thing. So, I would read. I saw this book The Well of Loneliness, and I said, "Oh, that sounds interesting."
>
> I was ten or twelve, and I remember it. Lying there in that hammock, reading this book, I knew exactly what I was reading. I knew enough not to tell my mother what I was reading. I knew enough not to ask my grandmother where she got the book. I know she didn't read it, or it would not have been there!
>
> From the time I was born, I was called an 'old soul.' So, I understood the book. Later, I wondered whether or not I understood about 'being different' because I was always the only black person in classes. Then I decided, "No, I don't think so."

Although she couldn't relate to some of the story, Dee knew it spoke to a part of her, and she never forgot the book. It wasn't until she was in high school that she understood more fully what being a lesbian meant. She dated some boys, but wasn't interested in guys like her friends were, and that didn't bother Dee. But it did bother her mother.

> There was one time when I remember having a conversation with my mother. There was some kind of dance that was gonna be at school. All the girls could ask the boys. It

couldn't have been a Sadie Hawkins dance, because that's in February. But whatever it was, I had asked this guy to go. He had said, "No," or else he had said he'd call me back, and when he did, he said, "No." I was pretty upset. I told my mother I was going to be a bachelorette the rest of my life, have my own place, and do my own thing. Mother cried. And my mother was a very quiet, and very gentle woman.

I said, "Okay. I won't do that. I'll get married some time." I have a feeling that she knew that I was different, and the tears might have been for the difficulty she thought I might have.

Dee had wondered about herself when she read *The Well of Loneliness*, but her first physical experience with another woman waited until she was in college.

I had a roommate. She was scared of storms, and we got in bed together and did some petting around. I think she was a lesbian, but she came from a rather fundamentalist Baptist background, and she was ashamed of what she had done. I didn't feel any shame. It felt good. It was just a little playing around, and I probably would have played around some more, and gotten into it a little heavier. But she wouldn't do that. I was too nice a person.

So nothing more came of it, and Dee left that part of her for awhile. Dee "did what everybody else did" in the 1950s: When she neared graduation from college with a teaching degree, she got married.

Dee speculates that she probably married early, because she felt she didn't have any family. She had lost both her parents very early in her life. Her father died when she was still in high school, and she lost her mother to cancer as she was just starting college. She and her three siblings had all gone to live with other relatives. Dee's aunt and uncle technically became her guardians, but she never felt welcome with them. Once she was in college, they never invited her to any of the family gatherings. "I think it was because they thought I was different. I have a feeling they thought I was a lesbian, although they would never say it."

Since her aunt and uncle were her guardians, Dee was expected to spend any time she had during school breaks with them, but it was just too hard for her.

> I couldn't wait until I was 21, and I didn't have to stay with them. That last Christmas, I arranged to stay with a friend of mine. She and her mother lived together. We arranged how much I would pay her, and contribute toward food. She really didn't want me to pay her a lot of money. She knew what my situation was.
>
> It was such different treatment. During the summers, I would come home to my aunt and uncle's after working a late shift, and the food from dinner had all been put away in little Tupperware containers in the refrigerator. I would have to go figure out what I wanted, and warm it up. When I was at my friend's home, I would say, "I'm working until seven, and by the time I get the bus it will be about 8:00 when I get home." She would put a serving of potatoes, some meat, and some of this and that on a plate, cover it up, and put it in the warmer. So, when I got home, there was a warm dish of food for me. Huge difference.

Dee continued to be excluded from family events, even after she was married. It was one of the most hurtful things she ever had to deal with. Trying to make the most of it, Dee took all the shifts at the phone company no one else wanted during holidays. By putting that together with money from Social Security and scholarships, working the holiday shifts enabled her to finish college with her teaching degree, without any support from her aunt and uncle.

Five years into her marriage and her career as an elementary school teacher, Dee had a child, Lionel. Shortly thereafter, she went back to school again, this time to get her master's degree. Dee specialized in reading.

What I wanted to do was to work with kids in college, not in a developmental mode. I was a strong believer in the fact that you don't read a book on electronics the same way you read a book on sociology. Some of the women teachers in the reading program didn't have that same belief. I had to be kind of clever, and work around things. They had a reading lab at the school, where you could learn speed reading and that kind of thing. When I finished my course work, they hired me. That took me out of the public schools, and into teaching college.

Dee began teaching at the same college she'd attended, the same college where her husband was serving as the Assistant Dean of Men.

He'd been recruited for that position. When I went to talk to my Dean, it was before there were salary scales. The Dean offered me an amount that was a lot less than I wanted. I tried to get more, but he said, "No. Your husband is working." I thought, "That's not fair!" I found out later that another colleague, a black woman who was head of her household, who did not have a master's degree completed, was getting paid more than I, because of her family position.
Fortunately, that dean left. There was a woman who replaced him. I can still see her. She was just filling in while they did a search for a permanent dean. The college dealt with the money for salaries at that time by giving her X amount of dollars, and she could allocate that however she wanted to. She could divide that amongst the faculty as she saw fit. The woman sat down and noticed the existing women's salaries compared to the men's salaries. I got a big

chunk, a big raise that year. She told me, "I saw that the women were not getting the money that the men were, and I decided I had a chance to do something about it. And I did."

Almost two decades later, Dee and her family moved to California, looking for a new start. A small part of a book Dee had been reading had started her thinking about her relationship with her husband. There was a line in the book that said when one partner had a need to love, and the other one is selfish and wants love, that's the perfect dance. It went on to say, if either one of those people change and become aware of those feelings, then the dance steps change, and it won't work any longer. "At that point, I knew my husband had been fooling around, and, as I became more feminist, and more into who I was as a woman, the dance changed." Dee felt leaving her husband would be a sin, since she had taken vows in church. She turned to a minister to get some guidance.

I told him about what was going on in the marriage, and then my feelings about this commitment that I had made in church, "until death, do we part." He said, "Whoever said that one of these sins is greater than the other?" And he talked about how, in the very early church, there was this hierarchy of sins, and that it was developed for money. So one day, in one of our sessions, he said, "Do you love him?" I thought, "Nobody has ever asked me that question." He asked me near the end of the session, and said, "We'll talk about this next time." When I came back, I said, "No. I don't." I told my husband it was over. Now I wanted to spend time learning to be who I am.

Dee felt liberated, not just from her marriage, but in many ways. She spent more time involved in poetry, photography, and travel. "It was like I had this freedom to be myself." Dee also felt empowered, and soon tackled finishing her Ph.D. dissertation.

"I had started the Ph.D. program before we were separated, and my ex was a little upset about that. He had an Ed.D. and I had actually written his dissertation. I am a good writer." In fact, when Dee got her degree, her brother congratulated her on her second doctorate! "He knew that I had done a lot of the work on my ex-husband's dissertation. In one way, it had been helpful. It was like practice."

Living by herself during the fifteen years after the divorce, Dee learned more about spirituality, and continued in her life-long affair with reading. Growing up with strong family ties in the AME (African Methodist Episcopal) church, Dee always tried to find a church wherever she went. Going to a Lutheran church that was close to her home, she was amazed to find former members of several other denominations.

> *When I was at the University of Cincinnati getting my master's degree is when the feminist movement was coming along, and I was ready for it. I moved from identifying myself as being religious, to being spiritual.*

Best of all, the church had a husband and wife ministerial team, and Dee liked seeing a woman in the pulpit. Ever after, Dee only participated in churches that had women in positions of leadership.

Dee was now 60, had her Ph.D., and a successful career as a college professor. She had reached a time in life when most people would have settled into a comfortable set of knowns, with

Dr. Delores Austin

most of their major life milestones behind them. However, Dee's life was about to change drastically.

The confluence of two totally unrelated events led 60-year-old Dee to come out as a lesbian. The weekend after the horrific bombing in Oklahoma City, Dee wrote an editorial for the newspaper about how the bombing had affected her, and what she thought about the country. That same weekend, she learned her adopted uncle was dying. Dee clearly remembers the thoughts that ran through her mind as she stood in her driveway, after having spent the day with friends.

I had friends with me earlier, and now I'm here alone. And I don't want to be alone any longer. I needed to talk to somebody, to continue to talk about the bombing, and my uncle, or to lie together and share pillow talk.

She knew she didn't want the pillow talk to be with a man, and so she made the decision, she had to come out.

Dee made a lunch engagement with a colleague that she was almost 100% sure was a lesbian. "I told her, and she said, 'I always thought you were!' Then she added, 'You need community.'" Encouraged, Dee repeated the exercise, calling an already out lesbian she knew from a women's group.

"I guess you wonder what I wanted to talk to you about?" Grinning, the friend answered, "I have an idea, but you have to say it." Immediately upon hearing Dee's admission, the friend said, "I knew that's what you wanted to tell me. I've wondered for years when you were going to come out. I was so certain, that I started to bring some books along."

With the help of her friends, Dee was introduced to the lesbian community, and, not surprisingly, found many women she already knew from other parts of her life.

Coming out at age 60 was the beginning. Finding women her own age was hard. As it happens, friends introduced her to friends, and eventually Dee met someone special.

*In the middle of a conversation with Betty, out of the blue
she asked me if I had ever met her friend, Jane. I said, "No."
So we kept talking, and she stopped again and said, "Do you
mind if I give Jane your phone number?" I thought to myself,
"Nothing ventured, nothing gained." She took the number
down and left.*

*I did not expect to hear from her friend, Jane, anytime
soon, because Betty was going out of town. But the next day,
at about 5:15, after the rates went down, the phone rang,
and she introduced herself. I started laughing. I just laughed
and laughed, then I apologized to the woman. "I'm sorry, but
Betty sure didn't waste any time, did she?" I said.*

Jane and Dee lived over a hundred miles apart, but agreed
to meet for lunch in a couple of weeks. "We met for lunch, and
spent the next six hours together."

*We ate lunch, then drove over on the other side of the high-
way and walked along the beach. As we were walking, I
looked down at my feet and saw a shell. It was a half shell,
and you could see where the muscles had been attached that
enabled it to open and shut. One half was dark, and one was
light. You could see this line, which connected the two sides,
and the shell was in perfect shape. I picked it up and we
looked at it, and I said, "I think that it's telling us something."*

*We talked and talked. I shocked her when I told her
I had never been with a woman before. We both said that
we really weren't interested in immediately getting into a
relationship living together with someone.*

For the next year, Dee and Jane built their relationship
slowly, living far apart, traveling back and forth. "I was 60 at the
time that this happened. We finally decided that this schedule
was too much for two old ladies! We began not remembering
where our clothes were."

While coming out to her friends had gone fairly smoothly, coming out to her family wasn't quite as easy. Some reluctantly accepted her declaration, while others were not so kind. Coming out to her son, Lionel, was much easier, and he seemed understanding.

I wanted to tell Lionel before I got involved with anybody. I met Jane in September, and I was going to visit him in October, so I was semi-involved. I was sitting in his kitchen, and I said to him, "Do you ever wonder why I spend more time around women than around men?" He said, "No." I thought, "This it not going to be an easy conversation." So I went ahead, and I told him. And then I said, "Is there anything you want to ask me? Any questions?" He said, "No." I asked, "Does it surprise you?" "No. If you were married, that would surprise me. But since you're not, that doesn't surprise me." And that was it.

As accepting as he was, Lionel still had a thing or two to learn. Whenever he and his wife would call to chat with Dee, it was Lionel's wife who would ask about Jane. Noticing the pattern, Dee sent her daughter-in-law a note.

I told her how much I appreciated the fact that when she called, she always asked about Jane. You know, if we were a heterosexual couple, people would ask how's my husband? And most people don't do that now.

Lionel's wife must have shared the note with him, because ever after, when he would call Dee, he would ask, "How's Jane?" or "Tell Jane I said, 'Hi.'" And Jane loves him. "She keeps telling me that he's a keeper." Jane had been out to her own kids for a long time, and they love Dee, too.

Dee continues to have a good relationship with her son. He has a good job, and has helped her out with a computer, a digital camera, and so on.

He's a good kid. Not just because he gives me things. There are so many people who don't even know where their children are, and the children don't pay any attention to their parents. They don't offer any help. Lionel has not ever been stingy. He said to me, "Mother, I would not be where I am if it weren't for you." That's his feeling about it, so that's good. My son is the one that donated his kidney when I needed a transplant. I have my son's kidney.

There are gifts we are all given that most of us seldom recognize, but sometimes, health concerns make a person a bit more introspective than usual.

When I was a child, once a year, at church, they would have family Sunday. Our family had been asked to read this prayer jointly at a particular time in the service. So we were sitting in the living room at home, and we were reading it. We were reading it in such a monotonous tone that I made a comment. "It doesn't really sound good reading it this way." Daddy turned to me and said, "You think you can do it better?" I said, "Yes." "All right. Read it your way." And I read it my way, and he said, "Yes. That does sound a little bit better." I then guided us in practicing how to read it. That's the way we did it.

Dee knows she was lucky to feel, at an early age, even as a child, that her opinion was welcomed. She knew she had to be respectful, but also knew that she was allowed to disagree. It was a lesson she feels helped her to shape her whole life.

When it came time to explore their options as to where to live in retirement, Dee and Jane began visiting the Pueblo, a women's community in Arizona. Dee remembers crying every time they had to drive back to California. "I just fell in love with it, and with the community."

Spirituality continued to be a driving force throughout Dee's life, and when the husband-wife ministerial team she had loved left the Lutheran church she'd been attending, she joined the First Congregational Church in Santa Barbara, California.

Jane went to the church's Women's National Conference with me the first year that we were together, and it nearly blew her mind. I was doing a presentation at a workshop on the history of women as healers. She wanted to go. Jane had been working Saturdays and Sundays, and hadn't been going to church much. She was fed up with the Catholic church. I thought, "I'm not going to push her to go to these various worship services while we're there." As it turned out, I wanted to stay in the room and rest, but she was always saying, "Let's go to this one" and "Let's go to that one!"

Jane and Dee in 2000

Jane was just blown away. There were women who were preaching. There were openly lesbian women who were preaching. Now she's become a church member as well. My spiritual journey has been a very important part of my life.

Dee and Jane have been in Arizona for several years now and visitors to their home often notice, and comment on, the unique shell, half dark and half light, that is mounted, framed, and proudly displayed in their home.

Dee continues to live her life to the fullest with Jane in Arizona.

Interviewer: Arden Eversmeyer

Bessie Morris

Born July 1924
in Kentucky

Joan Meyers

Born December 1934
in Pennsylvania

Interviewed at ages 81 and 71, in 2005 in Texas

Bessie: *We thought we were the only two.*

*Mamma didn't work outside the home. She worked before
she got married, but Daddy said that he would take care
of everybody. They had everything but a white picket fence
around the house. In fact, Daddy often said the only thing he
wanted running around his house was a white picket fence!*

*Mamma decided she wanted to work at one time, and
Daddy said she couldn't. If she did, he would quit his job. She
went ahead and got a job and went to work, and he quit his*

job. In half a day's time, she was home. She could not stand being away from the kids. After that, she always worked at home. A big family takes a lot of work, lot of ironing, washing, and house cleaning to do. And I mean it was <u>all</u> done.

Bessie was born in Louisville, Kentucky, and was raised with five brothers and a sister. She was number six. Her family moved around quite a bit early on, but eventually settled in Texas.

We didn't have time for church. Mamma was busy taking care of the kids. She didn't send us much, even when we were small. The boys actually went more than I did. She was a very strict mother. When she said to do something we had better do it. She didn't mind using that old razor strap if we didn't mind her.

After we moved to South Houston, Texas, Daddy worked at Shell Oil for a lot of years. The interurban ran from Houston to Galveston. He got a job at the Humble Oil and Refining Company in Houston. He worked there for years in the seismograph department.

One of my brothers was going to Pasadena High School, and the teacher gave a math problem the class couldn't work. My brother said, "I may not be able to work it, but my daddy can." The teacher said, "If your daddy works that problem, tell him to come see me, and I will give him a job." He worked the problem, and went to see the teacher. As a result, he taught machine shop at Pasadena High School for several years, until the war was over. Then he went to work as a supervisor at the Texas City Refining Company in Texas City. He worked down there until he got sick, and he couldn't work any more. Mom stayed home and worked all that time.

When I graduated from high school, I went back for an extra year. I was not old enough to get a job. Back then you had to be eighteen. I graduated at age sixteen, and turned seventeen in July. So I had to go back to school for an extra

Bessie in 1952

year. I used to always say I wanted to go into the Marines, but my daddy wouldn't let me go. He said that was not a place for girls. He said I couldn't do anything like that.

Then I went to work for Meador Brothers Grocery in South Houston. I later worked for a builder for about four months. I finally went to work for the Department of Defense. Then I worked at the VA hospital as a payroll clerk for about a year. When the Department of Defense called me back, I decided to go, because they paid me a higher salary.

I worked for the AFEES, the Armed Forces Examining and Entrance Station. It was government work, so I quit the VA and went back to AFEES. I stayed with them until they had an opening in customs, and then transferred to the Intercontinental Airport. I went to work as a mail clerk, handling all the incoming mail. The companies had different brokers, and they handled the shipments for companies. The companies would broker to handle all their paperwork for inbound and outbound shipments. The brokers picked up paperwork from customs, then went to the airline to pick up their shipments. I worked there until 1986, when I retired.

Bessie met her first girlfriend, Ann, in 1943. But she'd had feelings for a girl earlier, someone from school.

She used to write me letters all the time, and wanted to come spend the night. She wanted to hug and kiss me. I didn't know much other than I was taught, that women didn't do things like that. Then I met Ann in 1943, and I was with her for twelve years. Then this other girl I met just came in and took over bossing me, and I couldn't get rid of her. She hung around from 1955 to 1961.

Maybe I went to the bars a couple of times, once by myself. I didn't know anybody. I used to drink a lot back then, and I was afraid of getting caught in a raid.

I had straight friends, because my girlfriend was working for Goodyear. We just never had a big group of friends. We would play softball. She formed a softball team in 1949, and that is when we started playing ball. Most of the girls that were on the team were gay, but we thought we were the only two like that. We wouldn't dare let anybody know. But then, that is when I really discovered there were others like me.

I didn't have a name for it, though I often wondered. From four years old, I always wanted to play hide-and-seek and kick-the-can with the boys. My sister used to ask Mama to make me play dolls with her. I never wanted to play dolls.

Bessie, in the center of the bottom row,
posing with her softball team in the early 1950s

Softball began to be an important part of Bessie's life. As a left-handed pitcher, she stood out in the crowd, and she was really good at it. Bessie played seriously from 1949 to 1955, and then took a break. A friend talked her back into the game, and she played for the Rebels for another 11 years, hanging up her bat and glove in 1971. That was a long time to play women's softball at that level, and, as time went on, Bessie ended up having both knees and shoulders replaced.

But the wear and tear on her body wasn't the only reason to quit playing. As she neared the end of her pitching career, Bessie met Joan. When they moved in together, they built a house quite a distance away from where the softball action took place. Traveling back and forth for practices and games became time consuming. Balancing that with her career and a new relationship helped her make the decision to call it quits. Deciding to put her energies elsewhere paid off.

On the 22nd of this month, Joan and I will have been together 43 years. That's a pretty long time for her to crack the whip over me. We have had our ups and downs.

Joan: *We're Still Working On It*

Born in the coal mining area of Pennsylvania, Joan had what she remembers as an idyllic childhood, filled with fun, lots of swimming, and going wherever she wanted to go. It wasn't unusual for families to send their children to work at this time, but Joan's mother didn't believe in that. She let Joan and her siblings enjoy their childhood.

Before I was born, my dad used to work in a coal mine. When he was a little guy, he jumped out of the window at school because the teacher hit him. So he just left. My grandmother said, "If you aren't going to school, you're going to work." He was so short his lunch pail dragged on the ground, but he worked the coal mines many years.

My mother wanted our family to move out of the coal regions because there are sink holes, and she was afraid the kids would get swallowed up. My Mom said she was afraid my two brothers and one sister would get hurt. My sister was twelve years older than me, and my brothers were fourteen and fifteen years older, big difference in our ages. So the family moved to Stony Creek, and my dad went to work for Carpenter Steel. He worked there until he retired. My mother was a housewife while I was young. She had worked for Hershey, but that was when my brothers and sisters were very little. She loved it. She said Mr. Hershey was the nicest person you ever wanted to meet, and that the plant was so clean, you could eat off the floor.

When I was little, my sister took me everywhere she went. I often said to her, "Sis, did those people mind you dragging this little brat along with you?" She said they never said a word. She got married at seventeen, and she still carried me everywhere.

My mother had a nervous breakdown when I was growing up, so Sis and Paul took care of me. We went on vacations together, and we all went to church together. After my mother got better from her breakdown, we all went to church together, too.

Joan attended public schools and, after graduating from Mt. Penn High School, she went to a small, nearby university in the Poconos mountains. She graduated from there with a major in health and physical education, and a minor in social studies, and immediately found a job teaching. After just one year teaching health in a nearby Hershey school, Joan decided it was time to be a bit more adventurous, and she took a job in Texas. During the summer between high school and college, Joan had spent the summer in Texas, and loved it.

On the surface, Joan's life was still idyllic, but that wasn't to last. There were a few bumps in the road. Not long after she moved to Texas, Joan met Bessie. It quickly became clear to Joan that she had no choice but to rethink how she saw her life going. She'd had some earlier experiences with women that had left her overly cautious. Some of those experiences were very early in life.

I always knew there was something wrong with me. All the friends that I had, there were six or eight of us, used to run around together. Then all of a sudden they wanted to go to dances, and dance with boys, and I didn't want to do any of those things. I knew something was wrong. When I was about eight or ten, there was a little girl that lived down the street from me with her grandmother. I don't know why, but she and I were just close from the time we got up in the morning until we went to bed. We used to play "Army" and all that sort of stuff, and when she moved away with her mother, I was crushed. Her name was Joann Keller. I cried for days. I was all by myself.

So then when I got to college, I met all new friends. The physical education department was all gay, you know. I knew I was at the right place. For some reason, that year they decided they did not want any gay people in their physical education department. They started clamping down. I guess I was a sophomore then, and three of my best friends got kicked out. I was walking the straight and narrow. I knew my daddy was putting out money for my education that he could use for something else, and I wanted to take advantage of it.

Joan at 23

Joan had one brief affair in college, but the woman decided to get married, and Joan put it behind her. When she met Bessie, that was different. Bessie was Joan's first real relationship.

When we got together, we both said to each other, "Are you sure? Because I don't want a fly-by-night relationship. If you don't want a lifetime commitment, then let's just move on." We decided we wanted to spend our lives together, and that was it. We're still working on it.

Moving to Texas had been a big move for a small-town girl, but once she hit Texas, her wanderlust was quenched, and she spent the next 30+ years teaching at the same school. Along the way, Joan also went back to school, gaining a master's degree from Sam Houston University.

I went out there and taught health, physical education and social studies. I also taught some Texas and U.S. history. I liked the school and stayed there the whole time. But we did have a little problem.

Somebody told the school that I had a friend named Bessie Morris, and she was not a nice person. I said, "She has always been nice around me, and that's all I've got to say. She's my friend, and will stay my friend." They said that I had been there so long, and that they knew me. The person that had called, had called two school board members, the principal of the junior high, the superintendent of schools, and a couple of other people in the community. The address they gave for themselves was a vacant lot. The school personnel said they were not going to do anything about it. They just wanted me to be aware of the situation.

Bessie said she had an idea about who called, but I don't know. I was very fortunate that they believed in me. I was always on time at my job, and I did what I was supposed to do. I never caused any trouble. I helped the students, and I wasn't there to hold a stick over them. When they needed a hug, they got one. I felt that might be the only hug they were going to get that day.

Bessie and Joan:

Life in a rural, small town atmosphere has imposed some limitations. Bessie says, "Some friends may suspect I'm a lesbian, but I am not out to them." Asked if she has any gay members in her family, Bessie answers quickly, "Not to my knowledge. If there are, they are in the closet, like me." Joan has never come out to her family either, but she's sure they know on some level.

I am sure they know, because they call her Aunt Bessie. They are grown and have kids of their own, but they still call us "Aunt." My sister says, "I love y'all, and make sure to tell Bessie that I love her." They consider that if one of us is going to do something, the other is, too. And they love Bessie.

I am the only gay person in my family. I wouldn't wish it on anybody, because it's hard not letting anybody know. I guess if some people knew it, they wouldn't want to bother with you. It's not easy living a lie.

I love the church I go to. I love the people. They are friendly, but would they turn their back on me if they knew?

Probably so, just like two people we play cards with would probably do. I don't know. I don't think my family would, because they take both of us as one.

I wish we knew some other people.

After both had retired, Joan and Bessie began to feel more free to be out in their community, and participated in the Houston Pride Parade. Bessie died in October 2011. Joan continues to live in Willis, Texas.

Interviewer: Arden Eversmeyer

Bessie, age 79, and Joan, age 69, visit the Grand Caymans

In 2005, Bessie was invited to throw out
the first pitch in a softball tournament.

Gloria Stancich

Born June 1935 in Ohio
Interviewed in 2006 at age 71 in Washington

I'm a great one for coalition building.

When my parents were married, my mother said she didn't know where babies came from. She had no preparation, sex education, or whatever. So she was very young, age 16 when she married, and 17 when my brother was born.

I was born in Akron, Ohio, at home. The cord was wrapped around my neck when I was born, so I wasn't breathing. I was actually blue. The doctor, who was our family doctor, did mouth-to-mouth resuscitation on me. I'm not sure if that's what made me left-handed and right-brained or not, but if it is, I'm grateful. But those were my auspicious beginnings. I was born at 8:45 in the morning, and I weighed eight and three-quarter pounds.

Gloria had two brothers, but one had died soon after birth in a horrible incident. He'd been born at home, as were his siblings, and was taken to the hospital later for circumcision.

When the doctor failed to clamp the incision, and left him alone, the baby bled to death. That left Gloria to grow up with Bob, who was 12 years her senior. Bob married early, and had a daughter that became Gloria's playmate.

Gloria's father grew up working in the coal mines in the southern areas of Ohio. Mining was a common way to make a living until the coal played out and workers fled north to Akron, which was then the hub for all the rubber companies. Once he moved to Akron, Gloria's father met his future wife at her family's boarding house, where he had found lodgings.

> *My father had been taken out of school at the age of eight, as were most boys whose parents worked in the coal mines, and they were taken to work in the mines. Small burros and small boys were what went into the coal mines to pull the coal out after it had been dynamited. The boys loaded the carts, and the burros pulled the carts up to the surface. So he was a coal miner for many years. Later, he went to work for the railroad and, after the Depression, at one of the rubber companies.*
>
> *After they got married, my mother worked at a company called The Hooven Company, as a typist. My mother was a flapper. She sowed her oats after she got married. My maternal grandmother raised my brother Bob for the first few years, while mother got some living under her belt. She had beautiful, long, dark wavy hair that she cut short. She had it bobbed. This was in the twenties, of course.*

School came relatively easy to Gloria. She didn't get to go to kindergarten because she would have had to walk too far. As it was, when she began first grade, she had to walk a mile to the nearest school bus stop.

> *I was a very shy kid, which a lot of people can't possibly imagine. My mother decided I should go to dancing school.*

Gloria at 4 years old

There were lots of dancing schools in Akron. So I started dancing when I was four. I continued to take lessons and by the time I was ten or eleven, I was taking weekly lessons in tap, ballet, acrobatic, baton, voice, piano, drama and ballroom. Then there was swimming on Saturdays at the Y. I had each of those lessons once every week. So I was very busy while I was also getting my education during those years.

When I was seven or eight, I started dancing in what we call key clubs now, for the Eagles, Elks, and Moose. They would have kids come in from dance schools and provide their Saturday night entertainment. We would each get five bucks for doing this. So I started dancing in front of an audience when I was very young.

I had what I think was a comfortable, easy time in elementary school. I got good grades, had lots of friends, but not many extracurricular school activities, because I was off to one kind of lesson or another after school. I liked to learn, and was curious about how things worked, and where ideas came from. I had a crush on my gym teacher, Miss Biondi.

When I was a freshman in high school, my dance studio formed a group of ten or twelve of us who joined with other performers, and we spent the summers performing at county fairs. We were the grandstand show at the county fairs. We

*would go and work for three or four days at a fair, and then
we would all pile into a converted school bus or converted
limousine, and ride to the next city or township fair. We
worked all over Ohio, Michigan, Pennsylvania, New York,
and Indiana. I spent my summers, all four years that I was
in high school, on the road with this troupe. We also worked
with magicians and trained seals. By the time I was 16,
I was also working professionally in nightclubs during the
winter, although it was not legal. I didn't look 16, I guess. So
I was also earning some money at that point.*

*Even though we moved into a different school district
just before I started high school, I was able to go to the
same school as my friends, Garfield High in Akron, Ohio.
I made above average grades and was in the National Honor
Society. I nearly flunked algebra and aced geometry. Foreign
languages came easy, and I took four years of Spanish.*

*I was in love with the Spanish teacher, Juliet Parenti,
who had a brother named Romeo! I also took two years
of French. I hung out with a good group of young women,
one of whom became my lover during our sophomore year,
until graduation. She and I used to double date often, and
switched guys at one point.*

*Our group was referred to, affectionately, by one of our
teachers as the 'Gang Green.' We had lots of slumber parties,
often at my house. One night, after school was out at the end
of our junior year, we had a bonfire in the driveway, and
burned our chemistry manuals. Another time, we decided to
walk the mile or so up to the Rubber Bowl, an open sports
arena near the Goodyear blimp hangar, and the Derby
Downs. That's where the international Soap Box Derby is
held each year. We walked up in our pajamas and blankets
to watch the sunrise, then had to walk back in the daylight
with traffic whizzing around us! We had our last slumber
party the night of our graduation, June 11, 1953.*

College wasn't something talked about when Gloria was growing up. As far as she knew, she would only have a few options when it came to a profession. She could either go into nursing, teaching, or be a secretary, and at one point, Gloria's mom started encouraging her to go into teaching.

By then, it was quite clear that I was probably not going to get married. I was under a lot of pressure to be a traditional mother and housewife, but I had discovered my lesbianism long before that. I was a little child when I realized I was women-identified.

I considered going to college, and actually made plans for that after high school. I had auditioned for a dance group that was going to be working at a club in Canada, and I arranged to join them for the summer. This was the summer of 1953. The night of my graduation, I said good-bye to my lover, who was going off to another college, and had a slumber party at my house for my high school gang. The next morning, I got on the train for Ottawa, Canada.

It was on my 18th birthday that I left to join this dance group in Ottawa. Actually, we were in Hull, Quebec, which is just across the river from Ottawa. I worked there several months that summer, and decided that I didn't want to go home and go to college. I was just having way too much fun.

Opting not to go back home broke my mother's heart, which really surprised me. She had not only supported my dancing career, but also encouraged it. She wasn't exactly a backstage mother, but she certainly enjoyed it. My dad used to drive me in the most horrible winter weather. If we couldn't drive, he would go on the train with me to Youngstown, or Pittsburgh, or somewhere else that I had to get to. They were very supportive. So I was surprised that my mom was as upset as she was about my not coming back home.

Promotional photograph of 17 year old Gloria in 1952

I stayed with the dance group, and they went from Hull to Montreal to Washington, D.C., and then to Chicago. We were working supper clubs. There were four of us, and we were working with a woman who was a contortionist, seven feet tall and skinny as a rail, with long limbs that she could wind everywhere. It was incredible to watch her. Not a very handsome woman, but fascinating to watch contort. And then we'd dance behind her.

We were in Chicago at the Moulin Rouge, a club underneath the Brass Rail, in the Chicago Loop. I was getting ready to go home for Christmas, and the boss said, "You're not going home, you're working for Christmas." And I said, "I don't think so. I've never been away from home for Christmas. I have to go home for Christmas." And he said, "Well, if you go home, don't come back." So I did, and I didn't.

Even though she hadn't thought it was in her future, when she got back home Gloria started college at Kent State University. She managed to stick it out for one quarter before she couldn't stand it any longer. From her perspective, the students were such children. After all, she'd had all of these exciting, worldly experiences!

I left college and went back to Chicago, where I was working with a guy. He and I were going to have a dance act together. I took $200 out of my savings, promising my mother that I would have that money back in the bank by the end of the summer, or I would come back and go to school. We practiced, and practiced, and practiced, but Don wasn't too interested in getting on the road. I finally got a job as a policy typist at One West Wacker Drive, with Liberty Mutual Insurance Company. I was living in a small hotel on the north end, and shared a bathroom with a prostitute. I was taking the subway, but then realized I was going to have to save even more money. So I was walking back and forth from the near North End to my job, and eating one candy bar a day to save enough money so that I could repay that $200, because I wasn't gonna go back home.

Don was a terrific dancer, and we had some tremendous routines put together, but he was just not ever going to get anything booked on the road. So I auditioned for another group in Chicago, The Sullivan Dancers, and went back to work with four girls. We were called 'girls' then. Now I would have to say we were 'women.'

We went to Detroit. We were working at Killarney Castle, across the river in Windsor, Ontario, Canada, and staying in Detroit. I met lots and lots of show business people that came through there at that time, including Sally Rand, Simmy Bow, Henny Youngman, ventriloquist Jimmy Nelson (Nestlé makes the very best Chaw-clut), and his dummies. We used to stay up. Our last show was done at 2:00 in the morning, and we'd all go out for breakfast, go home and sleep for a few hours, and then head for the beach or wherever, then be back at the club by 8:00 at night. And that was the pattern. We were doing two or three shows a night.

Drinking at the bar was part of the job. We were to sit at the bar. Most of the girls drank what were called B drinks, which were watered down. I always thought that was cheating, so I drank real stuff. It was probably not a good idea. All this was before my 21st birthday.

At any rate, we were in Detroit, and there was a club in Chicago that wanted us to come back and work there. They wanted to bill us as the 'Blonde Bombshells.' I was a redhead by then, and had been a redhead for quite awhile. My father had always wanted a redhead. The baby that died was a redhead. Neither Bob nor I had red hair. When I left high school, I dyed my hair red. So I was a redhead. These people in Chicago wanted us to be blondes. I balked again. I was threatened with being fired again. I had learned my lesson *about people in Chicago, so I said, "Okay, I'll bleach my hair blonde." It turned pink for several months, before they could get it blonde.*

We did end up in Chicago, in this club that never had any customers, and I couldn't figure out why it didn't. We did two shows a night, and we'd have maybe three or four people there. But it was always a sea of white tablecloths in the supper club. We went from there to another club in Milwaukee. As I realized there was a connection between the one in Chicago and the club in Milwaukee, I finally figured out that it was run by the Mafia. The club in Chicago was just a front for whatever else they were doing there. How I survived some of those days, I'll never know, but I had a great time. And there were always guys around to do my bidding. Everybody wanted to date a showgirl, so I had lots of guys hanging around.

Traveling back and forth between the major cities in the region began to wear on Gloria, and she decided to go back to Kent State and give college another try. She wasn't giving up performing, only limiting it to weekends, and not traveling too far. Now that she was again near her mother, questions kicked into high gear: "When are you going to get married?" and "When am I going to have grand-children?" Fighting her mother, and finding her relationships with women fleeting, Gloria began to seriously date a man she had met at one of the clubs where she was dancing.

I met Tony, and he was a real smooth talker. He was a lot of things that my mother disapproved of. He was 13 years older than me. He was Catholic. He was a recovering alcoholic. He was divorced. So what a perfect way to get back at my mother, right? Marry a man that she didn't approve of. You know, cutting off your nose to spite your face! But anyway, he was, as I said, a smooth talker.

"Purple dress and red hair! What was I thinking?"
Gloria, on her 20th birthday

We were dating, and he was seeing to it that we were working the same clubs at the same time so that we could keep up the dating. Then he decided to quit his job. We were doing club dates on weekends and he began working at the Veterans Administration in Cleveland, Ohio. He was three years clean and sober, and he decided to go back to Tacoma, Washington to visit his parents. We agreed that I would finish my whatever-I-was-doing, I was probably in school, and go out on the train.

When I got there, he met me at the station and took me to the Washington Apartments building in Tacoma. His clothes were in the closet. I said, "No, no... no, no, no! We're not living together." Reluctantly, he took his clothes, and got somewhere else to stay. A day or two later, he took me to meet his parents. They were elderly, it seemed to me then, in their 60s. Maybe his dad was 70. I just fell in love with his mom.

He had told them that we were already married. And I guess he was smart to have done that. If he really wanted me to marry him, that did it. I called my mom, and she just hit the ceiling. She didn't want anything to do with it. So I donned my best black dress and a black coat, and we went off to the Congregational Church.

I got married in black. I did indeed. I have some pictures somewhere. His mom was just ecstatic, but then we had to go to Ohio to prove that I wasn't already pregnant. My mother was quite sure that the only reason I would get married was because I had to. I was a virgin when I got married, as far *as any male penetration was concerned. She would never have believed that either, I don't think. But it was true.*

Her mother calmed down a bit once she saw that Gloria's stomach was still quite flat, and threw a wedding reception for the couple. They only stayed in Ohio for a short time before returning to Tacoma to live. There weren't as many venues for Gloria and Tony to perform in the area, but they did get a few gigs. By then, they had worked up a duo act. Tony was a comedian, and did impressions. His stage name was Tony Karloff, a name he'd assumed after once working as actor Boris Karloff's movie stand in. Gloria still danced, but did some comedy patter with Tony as well.

Tony's mother became seriously ill, and for a long while Gloria did her best to help care for her. She'd had emergency surgery, and then developed serious complications that left her essentially bedridden. Helping care for her involved lots of lifting. Tony had a bad back, and Gloria was now pregnant, so they had no options but to put Tony's mother in a nursing facility.

When I discovered I was pregnant, the doctor asked me if my husband and I wanted this child. I was incensed. Thinking back on that, that it was 1957, I had no idea what he would have said if I had said 'no.' If he would have offered an abortion or adoption, I have no idea. But I've often puzzled about that. At any rate, Tony's mother died in September, when I was not quite three months pregnant. So she did not live to see her only grandchild.

We stayed to take care of 'the old man,' which is what Tony called his father. In December, it became clear that we weren't going to have much support here, as far as the baby was concerned, so we decided to go back to Akron for the birth. We went back to Ohio, and I arranged for some help to come in for Tony's dad. He had more or less given up after his wife had died. He just kind of let himself go downhill. I frankly think he had cancer, but it was never diagnosed. He died in January, about three weeks after we left. Tony went back to Tacoma to settle the estate.

Tony was working sporadically. I was not working, of course, because I was pregnant. I gave birth to Chris on March 2, 1958, at the hospital in Akron, Ohio. He was born almost a month early. I had a very short labor. My water broke on Sunday morning. Tony had worked the night before at a night club, and didn't get home until three or four in the morning. When I got up, I shook him and said, "My water broke." He said, "Go get your dad to fix it." We were living in an apartment behind my parents, over a three-car garage. He thought I meant the water pipes were broken. I went down and told my mother, and went to the hospital.

The baby hadn't dropped yet, so they kept me at the hospital. The doctor said, "You're not going to deliver 'til tomorrow, probably." She promptly left town to go visit her brother somewhere 50 or 60 miles away. I was in the third stage of labor before I told anybody, because the doctor had said I wasn't going to have the baby today. I figured these pains were just normal pains. I nearly delivered without a doctor. They called the sheriff, who stopped the doctor on the highway, and the state patrol got her back.

I remember her high heels clicking. I could hear her coming down the hall behind me, when they finally knocked me out. The baby came into the world with a big knot on his head, a hematoma, from battering against my pelvic area, because they kept slamming my legs down on the table to keep him from being born until the doctor got there.

The next thing I remember, after the mask coming down, was that they were telling me that Christopher Paul was here. And I said, "I want to hold him." They said, "We took him in to circumcise him." I started to scream. He was fine, and

*they brought him back. I had agreed to circumcision, but was
in this fog from anesthesia.*

*They brought him back to me in his little isolette, and
they wheeled me down the hall with the isolette behind me.
As we passed, Tony was sitting in the little waiting room
watching Bonanza, because it was Sunday night. I remember
saying to him, very caustically, "There's your son."*

Chris was born in March of 1958, and Gloria went back
to school that summer, to Akron University. Since she didn't
have enough to do caring for herself, a newborn, a household, a
husband, and going to school, Gloria went back to performing
with Tony. One holdover from World War II was that you could
still earn a teaching certificate with just two years of college, so
that's what Gloria did.

With her teaching certificate, and 2 ½ years of college
to her credit, the family moved back to Washington, and
Gloria enrolled at the University of Puget Sound to work on a
bachelor's degree. Once again, she and Tony were performing
at local clubs whenever they could. Money was tight, and Tony
began to work a scheme, sending checks back and forth between
banks in Washington and Ohio. Of course, that caught up to
him before long, and they ended up being hauled into court.

*I think it was about $5,000 at that point, but he didn't
have any obvious means of paying it back. So I agreed that
I would take care of it. On my word, that I would pay it off,
they allowed me to do it over a period of time. That was kind
of the last straw in our marriage.*

*We were working a New Year's Eve club date at the
Officers Club at Fort Lewis near Tacoma, and then we were
going to Seattle, to another military base, to do a show the
same night. We were doing two shows within a very short
period of time. Tony didn't drive often, but for some reason
he was driving that night. I didn't drink then. I had quit*

drinking on my 21st birthday, and did not drink the entire time I was married to Tony because he was sober. Anyway, he was driving, and I asked him, as we were driving toward Seattle, "What are your intentions for the money that we're making tonight?" He just went berserk, and was driving erratically. I said, "You need to pull over so that I can drive." He finally did that. We were on the freeway, and before I took the wheel, I told him that that was the last straw. The next day I called an attorney.

The marriage was eventually dissolved, but at that time there was a residency requirement to obtain a divorce in the state of Washington. Gloria and Tony had not been living back there long enough. Before making it clear to Tony that completing the residency requirement was what was going on, Gloria made arrangements to get Chris away to a safe place. She was sure Tony would take Chris and run, with no idea of what to do next.

Separating was a messy process that dragged on and on. The good thing was that Tony wasn't drinking, but neither was he supporting Gloria and Chris while they waited for the divorce. To make ends meet, Chris went into a day nursery, and Gloria began substitute teaching, so she could pay the rent and continue her college work. In July 1961, the divorce was final, and Gloria had received her bachelor's degree.

I taught first grade for a year in Tacoma. I had a mentor, a professor at the University of Puget Sound in the history department, who was a writer and a very charismatic woman. I'd fallen madly in love with her. Her husband and youngest daughter lived here in town as well. She was mentoring me, as far as the school was concerned, and also teasing me along. But that never came to be anything. She insisted I should go to graduate school. That had never entered my little middle class mind. I said, "I don't have the money to go to graduate school, this is ridiculous. I'm lucky to have gotten this far." She said, "Well, tell your parents." She was from a very wealthy family in Chicago, and had no idea what it was like to be either poor or less well off. My parents were both working, but that wasn't the issue. The issue was, what in hell do you need a master's degree for, you know?

She called my parents, and talked to my mother. My mother, I don't know if she hung up on her or not, but my mentor got the message. She just couldn't believe that my parents wouldn't pay my way through school. So during that year that I was teaching first grade, I saved enough money to go to graduate school.

I looked around for a college that offered a program that I thought I'd be satisfied with, and chose San Francisco State College. They had a humanities program. Even though I knew that that program was not going to really help me, as far as my career was concerned, it promised some more information and guidance about the spirituality that I was still seeking. Indeed, that was true. The Humanities Master of Arts degree focused on interdisciplinary studies, exploring the connections among the various manifestations of human beings over the history of our evolution through the fields of sociology, anthropology, economics, spirituality, politics, art, and much more.

I packed up everything in our car, and Chris and I headed down to Grants Pass, Oregon, and over to the coast. We stopped to visit with some friends, and got into San Francisco. We temporarily got a hotel room, while I looked for a place for us to stay. I found a little tiny one and a half room apartment behind one of the attached houses out on the west side of San Francisco. You entered the apartment through the garage of the house. There was a family living there: a fireman with his wife and four children, the oldest of whom was Chris's age, which was four at that time.

I marched into San Francisco State College to see my graduate advisor, and told him I needed to be finished in a year, because that's all the money I had. He laughed at me. I did it in a year and a half. It took me a little longer than I wanted, but a half a year less than what he had said it was going to take.

With master's degree in hand, Gloria moved down to southern California, and took a temporary job as a typist, then substitute taught French until the new school year started and she could get a teaching job. That fall, she was hired full-time in San Marino School District, and spent the next three years there.

I taught French there for three years, until I woke up and said, "This is not where you want to spend your life, or what you want to spend it doing." So the day after I received my letter of tenure, I turned in my resignation. I was full of splendid gestures my entire life, it seems! And it was there, when I was living in Claremont and working in San Marino, that I had what was the beginning of my ongoing lesbian relationships. It had taken me that long to get back to where I was in high school, as far as my sexuality was concerned.

Gloria, along with Chris and her partner, Tina, moved back up to Washington state. The plan was that she would get a teaching position at the local community college. Although three positions were open for which Gloria felt she was qualified, the department heads were not as enamored of her interdisciplinary degree as she was. Regrouping once again, Gloria spent the next year painting houses, before taking a temporary job with the Washington State Department of Social and Health Services. This was a "temporary" job that lasted the rest of her working career. She started as a case worker, but once they recognized her master's degree, she was able to move up.

I became a supervisor for several years, then I went to Olympia, to department headquarters, and was program manager for a marvelous program called the 'Homemaker Program.' Staffed by state employees, mostly women, they went into homes of families who were in crisis. They took care of the kids, so that they didn't have to go into foster care, while the crisis was resolved. I thought that was a very wonderful and useful way to spend my life, so I built and supervised this program all over the state of Washington. My work was to do that, and to go from office to office around the state. I did that for many years. Then, later, I came back down the career ladder a ways so I could work close to home.

A new career was just one of several significant changes in Gloria's life. She'd always felt a strong affinity to the earth, so when she next moved, it was to a relatively isolated piece of land, sheltered by magnificent trees, teeming with wildlife, and overlooking a bay of Puget Sound. It was the perfect place for Gloria, and was great for Chris.

When Chris was 12, and they were playing out in the yard, Gloria noticed something was wrong with his left foot. An orthopedist determined that Chris was exhibiting mild symptoms of cerebral palsy, that he must have had since birth, and recommended surgery. It was a long and painful process, and by the time Chris was walking without a cast again, Gloria noticed the same thing was happening with his right foot. Neurologists found the problems were actually being caused by a tumor on his spinal cord. The tumor was also impacting his kidneys and bladder, so Gloria and Chris entered several years of delicate surgeries, with extensive recovery periods. One good thing to come out of the enforced inactivity was that Chris discovered a passion, and a talent, for writing.

When she'd divorced and started this new life, Gloria had also started drinking on a regular basis. Drinking became the norm until 1980, when a very odd set of circumstances redirected her life once again.

> *I had been a closet member of the National Organization for Women for years, and one night in 1980, in my usual drunken stupor, I was sitting at my kitchen table near the phone, waiting for my married lover to call me, as I did most every night. I was getting drunker by the moment. The phone rang, and somebody was calling me from NOW, asking me to do something for the organization that I said yes to. The next morning I could not remember what it was that I had agreed to do. All I knew was that it was NOW. I had not been a member of the local organization, because I didn't want to be active, but the national office had given the names of members that lived in the local areas to the local chapters, and that's how they had my name. So I had to go to this meeting, at the YWCA in Tacoma, to find out what it was I had said yes to.*
>
> *It turned out that I had agreed to running as a delegate to their national conference in San Antonio that year. I thought to myself, "This is really strange, because I am not active. Why would they want me to be a delegate?" They had the election while I was at that meeting, and I won this election. Then they told me what I needed to know: why they let me go was that you had to pay your own way.*
>
> *I had that summer decided that I was probably going to commit suicide. When I got this phone call, and found out that I had this obligation to take care of in September, I decided I had to do that first. I went to see a counselor, and talked to her a little bit. She said, "I don't do suicides." I said, "Well, I've got this conference I've got to go to first, so we'll talk when I get back."*
>
> *I decided that I wouldn't drink while I was on this trip. I was rooming with a woman who drank, and I went to the*

liquor store for her. But the whole time I was in San Antonio, I didn't touch a drop of liquor. I was so amazed at what was going on at this national conference. Ellie Smeal was in her third term as the president of NOW. According to the rules, she could not run again. She was stumping for a suspension of the rules, so she could run again as president in order to see us through this period, the time period for ratification of the Equal Rights Amendment.

There was a major battle that went on on the floor of the meeting. There was a group of lesbians that had flown down from Alaska on the plane that I was on. They already had me hyped up about this whole issue. Then there were all of the Ellie Smeal followers. She is one charismatic woman. And so we had all of these factions operating. I'm sitting there, and my head is spinning. I haven't the vaguest idea what to do, or what to say. But I learned enough so that when I got on the plane (and I did get drunk on the plane coming home, because I'd done my job), I decided that maybe there was something else I could do with my life.

Gloria researched what help was available for her through her job, told her boss, and entered a three week in-patient treatment program, which worked. Still energized about all she'd learned in San Antonio, Gloria became extremely active in NOW, serving as the state vice president for a while, as well as sitting on their national disability rights committee. When the deadlines neared for passage of the Equal Rights Amendment, Gloria took time off from work and traveled to Oklahoma, to work as a field organizer. Even though the ERA didn't pass, activism had become an integral part of Gloria's life.

I've been on the boards of a dozen different organizations focused on sexual minority issues, and equality efforts. One is the now inactive Sound Coalition, which was an attempt to really coalesce the various groups around the South Puget

Sound area. It's never been very successful, but I'm a great one for coalition building. I say that word, and people start crawling under tables, but that's what I think we need to do.

I went with a couple of friends from Tacoma Lesbian Concern, a local social group which I've been very active in, to the National Lesbian Conference in Atlanta in 1991. There were thousands, we said ten thousand, lesbians at that conference, from all over the world. It was just incredible.

I saw OLOC, and saw the banners and the T-shirts. I went by the table, and there were the white T-shirts with the purple writing on them. I was just fascinated. In 1991, I was 56, and hadn't come of age yet for OLOC. Barbara Macdonald was speaking, and it was in a closed workshop, in a small room of the conference hotel. Shevy Healey was standing at the door, and I tried to get past Shevy to come in. She said, "Are you a member?" I said, "No, but I'd like to be." "How old are you?" she asked. I said, "Well, I'm 56." "Can't come in," Shevy replied. I said, "Well, I want to hear Barbara Macdonald. I've read her book Look Me In the Eye." Shevy replied, "You cannot come in."

Shevy wouldn't let me in! Finally she left, and wandered off somewhere, so I snuck in and sat in the back, and tried to look as old as I could. I bought a T-shirt, damn it, that ought to get me in! At any rate, that was my introduction to OLOC. I joined, as a supporter, in 1991, and became a full-fledged member when I finally turned 60, in 1995. Shevy and I became fast friends. We visited together, both in Arizona and up here, when she and Ruth Silver came up for summers on Discovery Bay, at the north edge of the Olympic Peninsula. I've learned so much from Shevy's writings and discussions with her. I like to think that we are kindred spirits. She was a bold, articulate, outspoken, and intelligent lesbian/feminist. I miss her.

Life may have been looking up for Gloria, who was now sober and engaged in a variety of social causes, but in a cruel twist of fate she also was having to accept that her lungs were in horrible condition. Gloria lives with histoplasmosis, caused by exposure to a soil-born fungus common in the area of Ohio where she was raised. The fungus stayed dormant for years, but once it became active, it has slowly stolen her ability to breathe very easily.

Gloria has also found her own spirituality during this part of her life. She was raised going to church camps, tent revivals, and singing in the choir, bouncing from church to church, but never quite happy with any of them. While Gloria was doing her graduate studies, she spent quite a bit of time searching for something that fit what she was feeling and thinking. She'd already checked out Catholicism and Judaism, and went on to try out Taoism and Buddhism. Nothing fit until she realized it was a mistake for her to look for something "ready-made." Gloria found her spirituality was earth-centered and here-and-now, not otherworldly. Although Paganism isn't quite the right term for what she practices, it's as close as she can come to giving her beliefs a label.

> I remember the first earth-based ceremony-celebration that I had on my land here in Gig Harbor. I was scared to death that God was going to strike me dead. That was 20 to 25 years ago. I had a lot of fundamental Christian religion drummed into me that I had to wade through in order to get to where I'm comfortable. Today, I am comfortable where I am.
>
> I have a blatant pagan seven-circuit labyrinth. It's called a classic, or Cretan labyrinth. That particular pattern is based on the orbit of the planet Jupiter, which I find quite fascinating, and that pattern has been found in a great variety of places on the earth. Those patterns were discovered at about the same time, and archaeological studies show that the first ones were built at about the same time. Somehow,

*this pattern came into peoples' minds all over the world. It's
like the hundredth monkey. There are labyrinths in Siberia,
the southwestern United States, South America, Asia, Africa,
Australia, all over the world, with this particular pattern. I
use it as a meditation path. I don't walk very far anymore, so
it's a perfect walking path for me, because if I get tired I can
sit down on a bench and rest. I also find it a peaceful place
to go to pray when I am struggling with a problem, or when
sending energy to someone about something.*

As far as her love-life, women have always been important
to her. Gloria is a self-described serial monogamist, with her
longest relationship being nine or ten years.

*I've been attracted to women spiritually and physically
from as early as I can remember, babysitters, neighbors,
relatives, friends, probably from about the age of four. After
my botched attempt at conventional marriage, I dated a few
men, but the emotional pull continued to be toward women.*

Donna and Gloria, 2005, at Gloria's croning at Labyrinth Grove

Donna and I had known each other for 30 years. She was a social worker at the Child Study and Treatment Center in Tacoma, which is a children's mental health center. It's the kids' section of Western State Hospital. Her former partner, Carolyn, was a psychologist there, as well. They lived across the bay from me, out here in Gig Harbor, and I knew that they were lesbians. Donna insists that they did not know that I was a lesbian.

We met because I used to be in children's services. I used to take the case studies of some of our most disturbed kids out to them and say, "You have to enroll this kid because he's crazy, or she's crazy, and they need help." Donna's role was to cross her arms, frown at me, and say, "Not sick enough." And so that's our little joke. I never did succeed in getting one of my kids enrolled in that program.

Donna's former partner, Carolyn, died seven years ago of Lou Gehrig's Disease. I saw the obituary in the local newspaper. It was 1999, and I was single at the time, had been for a number of years, happily single and dealing as well as I could with my limited energy and ability. I saw Carolyn's obituary and thought about reaching out. "Well, you know, she has been so closeted that I'm not sure exactly how to make contact," I thought. So Donna was the one who made the first contact.

Donna was in an online group for lesbians. About a year after Carolyn died, she finally decided she had to do something, or she was just going to vegetate away. She found this closed list of older lesbians, and was able to join. She lamented to those folks, online, that there were no lesbians in this area. One of the women who then lived in Denver said, "Well, I can't believe that!" So she went online and looked for the lesbian organizations in this area. She found Tacoma Lesbian Concern, and our website. So she told Donna, and Donna said, "Well, I find that pretty hard to believe, but I'll

look at the website." So she did, and as she was going through
the information, she saw my name. She said, "Oh, my God, I
know her."

Donna e-mailed TLC, but she didn't know that I was
the one who did all the e-mails, and all the phone calls. That
was part of my job with TLC for years, and I wrote part
of the newsletter. So I was the one who responded to her.
She says she just panicked, because I wrote right back. She
figured nobody would get around to her for a few months, or
something. I wrote back to her the next day, and said, "Hi,
Donna. Been waitin' for ya!"

We talked by phone, and I invited her to come to an
event which was going to be at my home on the Fourth of
July. She said she was too scared to do that, so I said, "Well,
why don't we meet for lunch?" We met at a little restaurant
up the way here, and I finally talked her into coming to
that Fourth of July party. She came and parked where she'd
be able to escape, and she stayed for a while before she did
escape. She would come over to visit frequently, and I kept
sending her out to places where there were lesbians, so she
could go meet somebody, and she kept ending up back on my
doorstep. Finally she just wouldn't go home.

I told her that she really didn't want to get hooked up
with an old disabled lesbian, referring to my lung condition,
and she convinced me that that was going to be just fine. This
is a bit of a joke, because she will read this some day, but her
two dogs were living over at her house by themselves, and
she'd go home to feed them every day. Finally, I felt sorry for
the dogs, so I invited the dogs to come and stay here, too. So
that's how we all ended up over here together.

I'm a little ahead of myself, because, in the meantime,
one of the things I told her is, "I'm an activist. I am a lesbian
activist. Anybody who sees you with me is going to make
an assumption, and you're going to have to deal with that,

you know. You can either say, 'I'm not a lesbian, I'm just a friend,' or you can deal with the fact that you're a lesbian." So by the time she went to visit a friend in Denver a couple of months later, she was wearing a bright colored tie-dye shirt, and got off the plane with a bunch of rainbow stuff on. Her friend said, "I can't believe that this is the same woman that I've been corresponding with." But she did come out of the closet fairly rapidly.

We've been having a wonderful time. We have been traveling, doing things that I could never have done alone, or ever thought about doing. If there's something that's needed, Donna gets online and finds the resource or the best way there is to do that. She had had a lot of practice doing that with Carolyn.

You can't ask for a more concerned, resourceful, and caring partner. We live a busy and adventurous life. Life is good! I have not gotten stronger, but I certainly haven't gotten any worse, with 25% of my lungs working. My biggest problem is avoiding catching something that would debilitate the lung capacity that I have. But we have a lot of things that we do to take care of that, and so we're having a good time.

So. Yeah. I am happy and I am moving along. Gonna just keep on movin'.

Gloria continues to live where she can, on any given day, see the waters of the Puget Sound, hear the susurration of the wind in the huge trees that surround her home, and marvel at the pileated woodpeckers visiting her bird feeders. Her son, Chris, continues to write, creating dozens of plays that have been produced across the country. Gloria and Donna have now broken Gloria's previous ten-year record for a relationship.

Interviewer: Arden Eversmeyer

Among the many passions and interests that keep Gloria busier than she ever has been, Gloria contributes to the Old Lesbian Oral Herstory Project by serving as an interviewer, and helps shepherd a local OLOC chapter. Above, she is interviewing Eris Dreykus in 2009. Gloria joked later about feeling sorry for the transcriber who had to listen carefully for the story being shared while ignoring the sound of both her own, and Eris', supplemental oxygen running during the interview! Below, Gloria shares the couch and wi-fi signal with Mary Henry early one morning while they're on a Puget Sound OLOC leadership retreat.

Elizabeth 'Betsy' McConnell

Born December 1935 in New Jersey
Interviewed at age 73 in Colorado

We had a good marriage, except for the one detail.

When I was in the high school, going into the tenth grade, we moved from a bedroom community in New Jersey to Louisiana. I think what was happening was that the forests in New Jersey were becoming depleted, and my father's lumber mill caught fire and was destroyed. So we had to go elsewhere. But even through that, we did pretty well. I mean, it was hard for the family to make that adjustment, because we were moving to a totally different environment.

It was a different culture, and I was in the tenth grade. So it was a big adjustment. We moved to a community in Louisiana, Hammond. I was there for 10th, 11th, and 12th grades. They were happy years, but I never became a "Southerner." I was not a southern belle, although I did give it a good shot.

Hammond was the home of Southeastern Louisiana College, and Betsy was able to take some of her high school classes there. As soon as she graduated from high school, Betsy headed back east, where she enrolled in Wells College, located in the Finger Lakes area of New York.

It was pretty much a liberal arts education. I majored in sociology, and took a lot of psychology and philosophy courses. I didn't really know what I was going to do with it, but it was, at the time, an all-girls' school.

I met a man when I was in my first year of college, and dated him. He was a good man, and so we had plans to marry. That's what you did. I thought, this will all straighten out, you know, after that. We would get married and things will fall into place. Actually, things did fall into place very well. After my mother died, I did marry Bill, and we had three children together.

We had a good marriage, basically. I mean, except for the one detail. I wasn't even aware that I would ever go in a different direction.

I had no awareness of that. I will say that at some level I knew from adolescence what my feelings were, and they just weren't the way they were supposed to be, the way other people were. I couldn't understand why girls were so exciting. I had no vocabulary for this.

I'm a middle child. I don't know if it's middle child syndrome that compels us to always try to do what is expected of us. We try to please

At age 14

our parents, and I loved my parents very much, so I wanted to do the right thing.

I loved being a mother. I wanted to be a mother. I knew, when I got married, I was going to be a mother, and I loved it! I was so wrapped up in all that. For most of the years during that part of my life, I was content. I was very focused. But looking back, I realize that part of me, part of my very consciousness or awareness, was entirely shut down.

Like many wives, Betsy worked hard to get her husband through his medical training. Rochester, New York, was their home while Betsy had her three children, but they weren't to stay there long. The family spent two years overseas in Holland, where Bill did medical research, then two years in Maryland where he fulfilled his military obligation. Eventually, they settled in Denver, where he worked doing clinical research.

Life was going along fairly well. Betsy's oldest child was in college, and the youngest was in high school. Her middle child was struggling, and the family was working hard to understand her problems. Then Betsy started to have her own issues.

I guess I just started really looking at myself. We did family therapy, and we did lots of that kind of stuff, trying to figure out what was going on with the one child. Actually, we never did figure that out. However, I've had therapists give various theories about it: that a child, sometimes unconsciously, can see that there's something wrong in the marriage. We didn't fight, and that kind of thing. There weren't visible problems in our marriage.

I suppose I was beginning to really look at myself, and to feel when seeing the women together. "Those two women, that's really where I want to be. I can't do this anymore." It wasn't that my life was hard to live, or anything like that. I just couldn't be the wife anymore.

Betsy, age 20

Although it seemed not a real slow kind of thing, it probably was. It got to a point where I just couldn't do it anymore. And I became pretty depressed. I was going to therapy, and nobody quite had an answer.

Finally I said, "Well, I know what it is." I knew good and well what it was, and just wasn't ready to acknowledge that.

Betsy found herself drawn to a friend, who was helping them out while the family was trying to work through problems with their middle child. When she realized her feelings for the woman offering support had grown beyond friendship, Betsy told her. Her friend said, "We can be friends, but I can't reciprocate."

Betsy came out to her husband as soon as she was able to admit who she was to herself, and he seemed to take it fairly well.

He knew I wasn't functioning very well, so I guess he wanted something to happen. I don't think he ever suspected anything like that. I think he thought maybe it would go away. We stuck with the marriage for a little while. It just never, at this point, occurred to me that our marriage would have to come to an end.

We went to lunch one day, and he said, "You know, we're going to have to get divorced." I responded, "Oh, my gosh, we are?" This was my best friend. Except for work, we did a lot together. I thought about that, and I said, "Yeah, I guess so." He obviously didn't think there was any hope of continuing under those circumstances, and I don't know what I was thinking. I guess I thought maybe I could have it both ways.

I simply had to come out. I could not continue living as a rational, functioning person in that situation, playing the role. I don't think I could have done that. It was becoming oppressive to me. I didn't have a hard life. That's not it. I was just terribly conflicted, but needed to be free to express my true self.

I've always been able to understand the difference between 'wants' and 'needs.' Actually, my needs are pretty basic. I definitely saw that what I was feeling was not a 'want,' this was a 'need.'

The next big hurdle was telling the children what was going on. Both of her daughters seemed to understand, saying, "It's okay, mom, whatever works for you." Her son wasn't quite as accepting. It was harder for him, since he was still at home, and in high school. Also, there was the idea of mom leaving dad for another woman. But her son came around in time. Besides, Betsy had not left her marriage for another woman, she had left for herself.

I had a lot to learn. I had probably lived a pretty sheltered life. So I did have a lot to learn, and I learned it. I just went out into the community. I went to the bars, I went to various groups, and whatever I heard about that was going on. I met people, and I made some good friends.

I had a couple of relationships that lasted a year or so. Then I had a relationship with a woman that lasted two or three years, and that was a learning experience. That didn't work out, but we're still friends.

Then I met Gill, and I got to know her pretty well. It wasn't like, "Oh yeah, that's my woman there." But I was definitely attracted to her.

Betsy had been working for the local Girl Scout Council for several years, and continued to do so as this new aspect of her life bloomed. She also began to become more aware of the world around her.

Until I came out, and my life stabilized a little bit, the most active thing I ever did, probably, was to put a bumper sticker on my car. I was totally wrapped up in my family role, and in my career with the Girl Scouts. Before that, I had worked as a social worker. I did try teaching, too, but I wasn't cut out for that.

Once I came out and found myself in a relationship that was stable, I could put my energies elsewhere. I've been with PFLAG for maybe ten years. I've been on the Board for six years. Before that, we went to the March on Washington. I have pictures of that. I've been to the Gay Games as a tennis player. Gill has supported me in all this. Since I've been retired, I've been pretty involved politically. Definitely in the last few years, I've gotten much more active.

60 year old Girl Scout

By active, Betsy doesn't just mean politically and socially. She always loved sports, and regretted having spent her teens in Louisiana, where "girls didn't do sports." She participated in everything available once she was in college. Later in life, Betsy took up tennis, and began playing in leagues, even competing at the Gay Games. There, she won a silver medal, and had a very surprising bonding experience with her oldest daughter.

My daughter had been married and divorced. At the time, she was teaching at Yale University, in the French depart-ment. This was 1994. I had been to the 1990 Gay Games in Vancouver, British Columbia, and now I was getting ready to go to the 1994 Gay Games in New York City. So I called my daughter on the phone, and I said, "We're going to be coming to New York, because I'm going to play tennis in the Gay Games." I thought it would be great to get together, because she was living in New Haven, which isn't very far from New York. "It would be great if we could get together, or if we could see each other," I said. She responded, "Oh yeah, that's great, Mom. You know, I'm going to be in the Gay Games too." I said, "Oh? Tell me more." And it went from there. So, needless to say, we went to the Gay Games together, and we watched and cheered for each other. She played on the Connecticut women's soccer team.

Tennis wasn't Betsy's only sports passion. She was also interested in skiing, and did a bit of bicycling around town. Well, maybe "a bit" is not the right term.

One of the highlights of my life was my bicycle trip across the country. We went from San Diego to St. Augustine. This was a group of about 20 women. It was run by Woman Tours. A couple of lesbians founded this company and were running it, and now another younger one has taken over. But most of the woman participants are straight women. The trip is designed for women 50 and over. We stay in motels, and we have a cook. It's not camping.

When you look at women in their 50s, there are not too many single women who can take off for two months of their lives. And it's not cheap. Some were retired, and then a lot of them are married women whose husbands support them. These cyclists are a wonderful group of people. We've had a reunion every year since the trip. That was in 2005, my 70th year, and I have a whole scrapbook and video about it.

That was one of the best experiences of my life. I was not the oldest, I was the second oldest. But I was the oldest to pedal every mile. My goal was to pedal every mile. It took two months, 58 days. It was wonderful. I made all kinds of friends in that group. Our group just jelled. We're friends, we're still friends.

Gill encouraged me to do the trip, because I got interested in cycling. I was doing fundraisers around town, multiple sclerosis and things like that. I said, "I'm going to look at bike tours." I was looking at some shorter ones, and this Woman Tours thing got my attention. She said, "You know, just do the whole southern tier from coast to coast. Why should you wait to do that?" I was going to work up to it, you know. "Do it, do it while you can" she urged.

I can't thank her enough for getting me to do that, because I don't know if I'd do that now. I might. It was an adventure. It's not that I like pushing pedals so much. I like adventure. That was the wonderful thing about it for me, the feeling of accomplishment, and the support that I got from everybody was just incredible.

Betsy plays tennis regularly at a local club, and has become very close to many of the other players. When they asked, Betsy was up front about her relationship with Gill, and it didn't take long for others to see that there was very little that set them apart, to see Betsy as "a normal person!"

I just feel so absolutely, totally fortunate, because I do have people who have supported me along the way. My friend Lindsey, that I spoke of before, and her husband are still very good friends. I think some people have to struggle along with me to get comfortable. We've kind of struggled together. But I'm definitely comfortable in my skin now.

My relationship with Gill has just grown and grown over the years. And it doesn't stop. It keeps on growing and getting better. She has been so supportive of all the activities that I love to do and she is a loving partner. People have said, "I don't see how you two can be together for so long, as you've nothing in common." Well, we have a lot in common.

I think one thing we hit upon early on was that we have values in common. That is so important. What we don't have in common is our interests, or at least activities that we each like to do. But having common values is so important. She's gotten really interested in photography. She's excellent as a photographer. She loves birds. She takes picture of birds that you can't believe. And so, you know, it's so wonderful that she loves this, and I love that, because then we can share our things with each other. I can tell her about what I do, and she can tell me about what she does. You don't have to do things together.

We have quite a wonderful life together. Again, I am very lucky, and thankful that I am loved by such a person. Like any relationship, it doesn't happen without issues. It takes a lot of work. But we work on it, and it seems to be paying off.

The more I get to know her, I just love her more and more all the time. I still do. We have been together about 22 years now.

Betsy continues to thrive in Colorado.

Interviewer: Arden Eversmeyer

Betsy at 67, with Gill

Bobbie Knowles

Born December 1936 in Florida
Interviewed in 2008, at age 72, in Florida

I'm not over yet!

Bobbie is purely a product of central Florida, starting with her birth in St. Cloud, and growing up with her two brothers in Haines City. True to the southern tradition, she was known to everyone in Haines City as Bobbie Lee.

School was okay for Bobbie, but it never really held her interest like almost everything else did. Her elementary school was only a few blocks away, yet she found lots of reasons not to get there on time.

Two of the blocks between home and school were joined together, and it was a wilderness area that I always cut through. There was a period where I was late about three weeks in a row. Of course, it didn't bother me! The last day that I was late, I saw the principal getting out of her car in front of the school. I started to hide, and then I thought,

"Well, she's late too." So we walked in together. Instead of my going to my classroom, she had me go to the office with her.

Age 14

She sent a runner up to my classroom to get the register, and she counted up how many days I had been late in a row. She said, "How many licks will it take to get you to school on time?" Of course, I was scared of her and I held up a finger and I said, "One." I got one lick, and I was never late again. That's what I remember from elementary school.

School was easy for Bobbie, so she didn't spend much time on her studies. What captured her attention was sports, and in her high school that meant basketball.

I participated in the girls' basketball team. That's the only competition we had. Dad and my brother had put up a basketball backboard in the side yard. I had the best two-hand shot and jump shot, back in those days, that you could come up with. And I always beat my brother Toby at 'horse.' Our girls' basketball team won the Ridge Conference Championship, and our team was, throughout those four years, superior to the boys' team. The crowds would come to watch us play, and then they would go home after the first quarter of the boys' team, because it wasn't very exciting to see them lose.

Bobbie graduated third in her class in high school, but swears to this day that she should have been first. "The first two people cheated!" she maintains.

She didn't stray too far from home for college, attending Florida Southern College, in nearby Lakeland. While there, Bobbie joined the women's softball team, and when she had an experience with a teammate, four years her senior, she had a mixed reaction, since the woman already had a girlfriend.

That was very disturbing to me. "Why are you messing with me if you're going with Jackie?" I asked. Her answer was, "Well, it just happened." Well, now I know why I was never interested in boys. Kissing them was like kissing a ball, as far as its effect on me! In those days, you didn't know. How do you know somebody else prefers women over men?

Graduating from college, Bobbie took her first teaching position in New Port Richey, a small community on the Gulf side of Florida. There, she had an affair with a married woman that lasted until Bobbie left the area.

I was accepted in her family just like I was another wife, except I certainly didn't do the things they did. I went fishing, and all that sort of stuff, with them every summer.

I left New Port Richey because, my fourth year there, my principal said I had to teach half a day elementary school. My junior high classes were scheduled in the morning, and my afternoon classes were elementary level. I was not pleased with that situation. When he told me I had to continue it next year, I said, "I will not do that. You can start looking for a teacher now." From there, I went home and didn't even think about looking for a job, and then I thought, "Well, I guess I have to work."

So in July, I looked at the map and I picked out a couple places that would have access to good fishing. One of the places was Punta Gorda. I wrote a letter down there to the school board and told them I was interested in a position in junior high school, teaching physical education. I did not give

Bobbie at 24

any other information. All I wanted to know was do you have a position or not?

Bobbie got the job, but only stayed there two years. While she was there, she was given the task of working on an evaluation of her school. The committee member heading up the evaluation just happened to have been Bobbie's intern teacher from college. They hadn't been working together long at all, when she said, "Bobbie, it's about time you went on and got your master's degree. Do you mind if I make a couple of calls?" Before she knew what had happened, Bobbie had an internship arranged at the University of West Virginia, and she was resigning her current teaching position.

After graduate school, Bobbie ventured out to Wisconsin, where she took a job teaching at Wisconsin State College in River Falls. Before she'd hardly had time to settle in, Bobbie heard about an impending teachers' strike, and she opted to return to Florida, where she landed another position at Palm Beach Junior College.

Experiences gained while working at a summer camp had a large impact on Bobbie, probably more than anything else to that point in her life ever had.

I loved my time at summer camp. I was the first counselor they had ever hired without a personal interview, and I taught in the canoeing program. When the person who was head of tripping didn't come back, I was promoted to head of tripping. That means that I got to plan all of the canoe trips that went out of that camp, and decided which campers went and which counselors went with them, and stuff like that. It was very exciting.

There were four campers that went through the program, and then were coming back as junior counselors. This was the first time I ever drove to camp. Mrs. Isserman told us before we left, "Treat the junior counselors just like a counselor." So I wrote Judy, and I said, "I'm coming through St. Louis, and I'm picking up Dinkmeyer. Would you like to join us, and travel up to camp with us, instead of coming on the train?"

Well, evidently, Judy said something to Mrs. Isserman, who was the director. When I appeared at camp, I was there probably five days before she fired me, and paid me for the summer. Her reason for firing me was because she said I no longer abided by the rules of the camp, which was a joke to me. I was devastated. She said, "I've notified all the counselors. They're going to be in a meeting in the dining room downstairs, and I want you to be gone by the time we finish." So, I just went down, got my keys, couldn't talk or I would cry, and then packed up and left.

I went into Winter, which is a little town where the camp sent their laundry every week. I had sent some laundry in, so I got a room for the night and checked at the laundromat. They said, "We'll have it ready in the morning," and I said, "Thank you, I'll be back." Then along comes Carol Ladwig, my closest counselor friend. She came and found me at the motel. "What are you doing here?" I asked "Well, Mrs. Isserman sent me to go with you to Florida, to be sure you got there safely," she responded. I said, "You tell that son-of-a-bitch that I don't need a nursemaid."

She and her friend went out to dinner, and the friend returned to camp the next morning to tell the director that Bobbie didn't want an escort. Twenty-some years later, Bobbie ran into someone from the camp while at a professional meeting. Mrs. Isserman had recently invited all the rest of the staff and campers back for a reunion, but Bobbie had not been included. In talking, she learned that she herself wasn't the only one who didn't understand what had happened. The counselors were all shocked, and no explanation was ever offered.

As the camp director approached her 100th birthday, Bobbie got a call from a former Camp Chickagami camper, who talked her into attending a celebration. When an opportunity arose for her to do so privately, Bobbie (whose camp name was Billie) approached Mrs. Isserman, who was now in a wheelchair, and said, "Mrs. Isserman, I am Billie. And I just wanted to tell you that my years at Camp Chickagami did more to mold me as an individual than any other experience I ever had, and I was devastated when you fired me." That was all she said to her, and

Bobbie, second from left, with teammates

Mrs. Isserman didn't say a thing. Glad to have gone, Bobbie was able to put it behind her, even if she didn't get the satisfaction of understanding what had motivated Mrs. Isserman to fire her.

Bobbie's teaching career at Palm Beach College expanded to include working with women's intercollegiate sports on a state level, and then beyond.

> I was representative from the southern states of Mississippi, Alabama, Georgia, and Florida on the National Association of Intercollegiate Athletics for Women, which went by the acronym of AIAW. There was a lot of jealousy between the men there in athletics and myself. Nevertheless, I thought, 'screw them' and went on to do what I wanted to do.
>
> I had the support of my department chair, so that made it fine. Then, when they put women's athletics together with mens' athletics, under a male athletic director, things began to go downhill.
>
> There were two times I didn't even get paid leave to go to their annual meeting, so I took personal leave. That gives you some idea of the problems that I ran into there. The only way I could get out of athletics, under this jerk, was to take a sabbatical. So I did. When I came back, of course, they had another coach, a male with no college degree, no experience in volleyball, or whatever. So you can imagine how that program went downhill.

The inequities in sports in the school system wasn't something new to her. Back when she was playing softball in college, her team had won the state championship, something of which Bobbie was very proud. But even after winning at that level, the trophy the team was awarded for coming in first wasn't as large as the trophies men were getting when they won third place. Years later, nearing the end of her teaching career, the inequities were still well entrenched.

I had to teach full-time and coach, and the men had half-time teaching and coaching, which was typical in those days, but not at all schools in Florida. That's when I said, "Never again will I do anything in athletics for this school." So I retired after 37 years of teaching and coaching, and went back to full-time teaching.

With more free time, Bobbie got involved in carpentry, and spent considerable time finishing the inside of what had been a shell of a cabin, where she now lives.

Here in the kitchen, I did all the walls and the window trim. In the workshop, I did all the exterior outside paneling. I finished the roof, and I just had a good time doing it. I shamed my brothers into buying me a riding mower, because prior to that, I did it all with a push mower.

Bobbie had several relationships throughout her teaching career, some lasting only a short time, others much longer.

I went with a gal that happened to be a member of the faculty, but she was in the closet. She was in so deep, you couldn't even find the door. That was not very pleasant for me. I kept on saying, "Oh, I can change her." Well, forget that. That was a long-term, 19-year relationship. I finally just walked away from it. Just walked away.

It wasn't until she met the woman she's now involved with that she was truly happy. Bobbie lives in her cabin, and the love of her life has another place on a nearby river.

I'm in a relationship with the love of my life. We're going on nine years. We kayak, we go scalloping every summer. We bought a new boat that's a lot plusher than the one we had, so that we can take as many as two other couples out with us. We scallop at least three times during the summer, going out four days each time. During the year, if it's a beautiful day, we take the boat out, and just poke along the St. John's River in front of the wilderness area.

We play golf, and are in a league. We try to play at least one other time during the week, but it seems we're so busy, we don't always have time to do that.

I'm in retirement, and I don't know when I had time to work! Anybody that doesn't have more than one hobby is going to be sad.

As I look back on my life, I wouldn't have changed anything, except I'd have gotten out of that 19-year relationship after six months!

I have enjoyed my life, and I'm not over yet! These are the golden years.

Bobbie continues to live and play in Florida, and she now resides with the love of her life.

Interviewer: Arden Eversmeyer

Saundra Tignor

Born August 1937 in Washington, D.C.
Interviewed in 2008, at age 70, in California

Well, how are you going to do that?

Everyone is shaped to varying degrees by the family in which they were raised. In Saundra's case, those strong influences came not just from her immediate family, but from her grandparents, aunts and uncles.

My paternal grandfather was an attorney, a practicing attorney. He had three brothers, two of whom were practicing physicians, and the fourth one was an attorney, like himself. I want to mention that, because it was very unusual in the African-American community for men, let alone women, to be educated, and able to practice in that era, the 1920's or so.

They had several sisters, all of whom also went to college and were teachers, my great aunts. So my father was the son of an attorney, and he attended Minor's Teachers College and Howard University, got his bachelor's degree in education, and became a science teacher.

When he married my mother, he continued his
education. He went on to get a master's degree at Columbia
University, by spending four sequential summers in New
York City.

Saundra's mother also had a college education, and worked
as a substitute teacher while she raised her children. Later in
life, she became one of the first computer programmers at the
Pentagon. Her mother's family also contributed to building
Saundra's character. Some of them she remembers interacting
with directly; others she knew through dozens of stories passed
on to her.

Everyday actions that are often taken for granted taught
important lessons. Her maternal grandfather made a lasting
impression on Saundra by walking to and from work, five miles
each way, no matter the weather. He did this, not out of necessity
but by choice, saving money so that he was better able to provide
for his family.

Her maternal grandmother, a formidable woman, had lived
in Maddenville, Virginia, an unusual area populated by Africans,
Europeans, and Native Americans, that all mixed and mingled.

These strong personalities were a part of her everyday life,
and were as much Saundra's parents as were her actual mother
and father. Her family lived in Washington, D.C., with one set
of grandparents. She and her brother lived with her maternal
grandparents during the week to attend school, and went home
on weekends.

I went to the segregated public school system in the District
(D.C.). Caucasians were track one, and we were track two.
Nearly everybody went to Banneker High School, named
after Benjamin Banneker, and Dunbar High School, which
was the first college prep school for African-Americans in this
country. It just so happened it was in Washington, D.C., so
we went to it. And it was a wonderful place. Academically,

we had teachers who had masters degrees and doctoral degrees because they couldn't get jobs in the fields that they wanted to work in! So they came to teach at Dunbar, and it acquired quite a national reputation.

When I graduated from school, I attended Howard University for one semester, because I graduated at the age of 16. I could not enter nursing school until age 17. It was not an uncommon practice to skip students ahead in school early on. I had been skipped a full year. "Skipped" means you accelerate a grade. So, I went to Howard University for one full term, and then I went to Bellevue Nursing School in New York City. I completed the term there, and became a registered nurse.

I did all kinds of nursing. When I graduated from Bellevue, they made me a head nurse.

As she was training in the various aspects of nursing, Saundra was also maturing in her personal life, learning what personally worked for her, and what didn't.

When I went to nursing school, I did go out with this man for a couple of years, and we got married. The marriage lasted about 19 months. During our marriage, I moved out of the nurse's quarters, and moved to a place in Jamaica, Long Island. We lived there a little while, but it wasn't working. I didn't know what marriage was, and he had no idea, even less of an idea than I did. I wasn't feeling anything for women at that time, but I just didn't like what marriage was: cooking, cleaning and preparing a house. So I left the marriage. He would have, had I not.

Leaving the marriage, Saundra returned to the Bellevue nurses' dormitory. She had started a friendship when she lived there earlier, with a red-haired Caucasian woman. Moving back to the dorm, they resumed their friendship.

The Bellevue dormitory had a very large lobby, which everybody came and went through. It was the only way to get in and out of the building. One night, I was just sitting there by myself, watching people come and go. One time, she came in and said she had been out on a date with a man. She said, "Oh, I just can't stand it. He wanted to paw me. I just can't stand men anyway. I don't know why I'm going out with him. As a matter of fact, I like

Age 24

women." Well, we had never had that kind of conversation. I was a little taken aback by her remarks, but intrigued by them as well. I was maybe 19 or 20, and I was intrigued by what the ramifications of her remarks were, or could be.

I did not have a discussion with her about it, but we intensified our friendship, which, at this point, was still very platonic. We went to the movies together often, and went drinking a lot at the local bar. We arranged to have meals in the dormitory together on certain days, when our schedules would permit. Long story short, there developed an attraction between us, a physical, sexual attraction between us. So we ended up in my room in bed one night. We had a sexual encounter, shall I say?

Saundra had been aware that she'd had some attraction toward girls in her classes, but it was diffuse. She had no name for it, but instinctively knew she was different. For many years, she'd gone to camp every summer, and had had strong feelings toward female counselors, and for some of the older campers. She'd go out of her way to spend time with them and get their attention, but didn't recognize what was going on. When that first sexual experience with a woman occurred, all that confusion was resolved.

Throughout her childhood, which always involved going to one Baptist church or another, Saundra doesn't remember ever having heard anything negative about homosexuality, not from anyone whose opinions she valued. As odd as that was, it helped her discover this part of herself without having to deal with the more usual fear and guilt.

> We drove out to California together. For me, it was with the idea of staying. She came along with the idea of seeing what California was about, intending to return. By that time I was identifying as a gay woman. I knew my parents were not going to be happy about that, and I just wanted to be able to live my own life as freely as I could. But we did stay. We stayed together for ten years.

While they were living in California, Saundra's only sibling, her brother, died. Getting together with her family back in Washington, D.C., was an opportunity for her to come out to her mother. She'd been living in California with Edie for several years, but her mother said she'd had no idea. "Struck me as odd, but denial is more than a river in Egypt!" Apparently, having been married provided her "pretty good camouflage."

> I would have come out to my father, but he died early of cancer. He really suffered, so I was advised not to trouble him further by telling him that I was a lesbian. However, there's familial evidence to support the possibility that he already knew. One of his brothers knew, and his sister-in-law, and

*my aunt knew. There were family members who knew. I
didn't tell them, but they knew.*

Activism was always an integral facet of Saundra's life. In
the early 1960s, when the civil rights movement was at a turning
point in the South, she became involved.

*I believe it was the summers of 1963 and 1964 that I
went down to Mississippi, and then to Louisiana. I was a
registered nurse at that time, and I worked in a doctor's office
with three Jewish doctors. They joined a group, or formed a
group, called Physicians for Human Rights. One or two of
them said they were going to go down to Mississippi, using
their vacation time. They spoke to me and another African-
American nurse, to see if we'd like to go. Gilda was a family
woman. I said I was interested in going. I went down with
them by plane, and it was the most revealing thing that I had
probably ever done in my life.*

*I had not participated in sit-ins or marches, or anything
that put me in harm's way. What I did do was act as a
second line of defense administering first aid, and counseling
some of the people who were more active in the civil rights
movement. I remember teaching some sex education classes,
at least one or two.*

*I stayed in community homes, in the home of a family
who was very generous. They fed me every morning before I
went out, and let me sleep there during the two weeks I was
there. There were a lot of whites involved in the movement
down there, near where I was, and it was very dangerous for
them, as well as for us.*

*They gave us a multi-page leaflet that told us how we
were to act to maximize our safety. It stated things such
as not talking to any strangers (black, white or any other
race), always going outside in twos, not going out at all if you
didn't have to, not sitting in front of lighted windows, and*

elaborated on those. It just read like a manifesto of war. It
had all these do's and don't's, in order to stay alive and intact.
It was just amazing to me that this part of the country was
still in the United States. I'd never encountered anything like
that before. It made a big impression on me.

I did not tell my parents I was going down. I went
home to see them right after that, and told them. They were
horrified. Horrified that I could have gotten hurt, could have
gotten killed. They lambasted me for that. But, after that they
got pretty interested in how things were down there.

I felt generally unsafe the whole time I was in Mississippi,
but there was no time I felt overtly threatened. I had this
tremendous admiration for the students, other young people,
and not so young people that participated in all the marches
and sit-ins, and in all the other protests that were happening
down there. They were, indeed, risking their lives. It was an
interesting, thrilling, dangerous part of my life, but it only
lasted two weeks.

Then the following summer, I went down to Louisiana,
where we did some of the same things. But it didn't have
the same intensity that Mississippi had. It was dangerous
enough, and we got the same warnings, but it wasn't the
intensity of Greenwood, Mississippi. I don't remember where
we were in Louisiana.

Living in California, Saundra continued to work in nursing,
but changed her focus. For a while, she did private duty nursing,
then worked for Head Start as a school nurse, before going back
to school for more training.

I went back to school and got my bachelor's degree in nursing,
and then I started public health nursing. I did public health
nursing for the County of Los Angeles. I specialized in
communicable diseases. I did field visits to people who were
suspected of contact with someone who had a communicable

disease, and also counseled people in the clinics who had communicable diseases, or worse. I did tuberculosis work for two years, and was supervisor of that clinic, mostly doing TB prevention with people who were immigrants at that time. They had a team that went out and did mass testing, and those that were positive were invited into our clinics for preventative care. It was there that I counseled, and later was promoted to supervisor of that clinic.

AIDS became a health crisis in the late 1980s, and Saundra worked for the Minority AIDS Project as a case manager. In that role, she was able to help men who were not only dying, but who were ostracized by their own community.

In an effort to be more involved in the LGBT community, Saundra joined a local group of gay and lesbian people living and/or working in her part of the city.

I thought it was a good thing that it was a neighborhood-based organization. They tried to interact with the straight community on many levels: the police, Chambers of Commerce, and others. They tried to educate straight people about homosexuality, that we were just like them in every other respect, except that we preferred our own gender.

I learned a lot there about grassroots organizing, about organizational structure, how organizations are run, about committees, and the structure of an organization. It was very rewarding, very gratifying, and educational. I learned a lot from the guys, but there was a lack of women involved. Men and women, lesbians and gay men, were not getting along at that time. So I took it upon myself to gather the women from the neighborhood. My partner at that time said, "Well, how are you going to do that?"

What I did was just go back and get all of the names and addresses that the organization had. A lot of women were still living in the neighborhood, or working in the neighborhood, but had just not been able to get along with the men. Or when they came, there were no other women there. At two meetings, there were only two or three women, so they went away. I sent out a meeting notice, to be at my house, to all of these women, and about thirty women showed up that first time. That was pretty rewarding. It was a women-only meeting, and the board, being all male, came and spoke to them, asking if they would continue under the umbrella of the Uptown Gay Alliance (UGA).

That was pretty controversial. Some of them wanted to form their own independent and separate organization. Some of them were willing to work with the men. Most were not. They'd had previous experiences. Not just within that context, but all their lives. They didn't want any part of it. Parts of the two meetings held got kind of testy between the men and the women.

At that time, the organization was just calling itself the Uptown Gay Alliance. There were objections to that. It was a time when lesbians were reclaiming the name 'lesbian.' All of that lead us to get Ivy Bottini in on this. What a woman! She came to the meeting with the men, and she told them, "If you want lesbians in this organization, and you're saying that you do, and you have me telling you what the deal is, you have to have the word 'lesbian' in the organization. You are not going to get to first base with just calling yourself gay."

Some of them got it, and some of them got mad and left. We ended up, after much to-do, with the Uptown Gay and Lesbian Alliance. So having done all that, women came for a little while. The agreement between the men and the women was that the men would continue doing their own thing, having their own meetings, doing their own events, such as roller skating and a couple of other events. We'd also meet with the men about the neighborhood stuff. That would require two meetings a month. That lasted a good year, at the most.

After Saundra left the area, the group did continue under the leadership of a few other women for several years, before it reverted to the way it was before. But for Saundra, and a few other women, it had been important. For the first time, the group had a woman officer. Saundra herself served as its first female newsletter editor, and found it to be an incredible opportunity to learn about grassroots organizing, strategy, communication, and making contacts.

After parting ways with the Uptown group, Saundra put her newfound knowledge and skills to use within the Black Gay and Lesbian Leadership Forum. There, she played a role in putting on a conference, only to find that the conference and organization didn't offer much to the women in the group.

> It was one of those Thursday through Sunday conferences, and on Sunday night, one of the women, Christine Trip, called the women together and said, "I didn't get my money's worth. We need to do something else." There were about fifteen of us in the caucus that night. After she said it, a lot of women agreed, and we agreed to form a local black lesbian organization.

After a rocky start, the new organization did solidify under the name of United Lesbians of African Heritage, ULOAH. Saundra, as charter co-chair, entered what was to become the phase of her activism for which she felt the most passionate.

> I was invested in this! It was me. We did, indeed, put on annual conferences for about 18 years. That was here in Malibu, California. We drew women from places like the Caribbean, England, Canada, and South Africa. We did convene, and we talked about our needs and our differences, and all of the challenges that faced us. We covered not only homophobia, but racism, sexism, and for the older women, we discussed ageism.

At the 2008 National OLOC Gathering in Los Angeles

Saundra retired from nursing relatively young, when she was just 50. Since she was still young for full retirement, she cast about, looking for what came next. Moving from the Los Angeles area up to San Luis Obispo, she and a business partner ran a bed and breakfast for five years. "We did not become millionaires, or anything like that, but it was fun work." As anyone who has done such work knows, it can be overwhelming, and Saundra decided to try something else.

For several years, she ran another small business doing floral arrangements for special events, and marketing fruit, vegetables, wreaths and so on at local farmers markets.

Now, in her retirement, Saundra spends some of her time involved in Old Lesbians Organizing for Change, participating in the local Pride parade, and giving workshops at the OLOC National Gatherings regarding racism, classism, and other isms. However, in some ways, activism now almost takes second place to badminton!

> *It's the second most popular sport in the world, soccer being first. Badminton keeps your reflexes sharp. The more you move, the better your game is, too. So I'm working on moving a little bit more.*

Saundra stays busy, knowing that it makes a difference in her health. Staying busy motivates her to get on the computer, researching and learning, encourages her to listen to people, and helps her to reach out to others, as well.

> *I tell that to my friends, who are not nearly as active as I am, and they say, "Yeah. You're right." Then they go back to doing pretty much nothing. But the more you do it, the less effort it takes. There are days when I want to stay in a chair. But mainly, I'm out of the house by 8:00 a.m. during the week.*

Saundra continues to thrive, and play badminton, in California.

Interviewer: Arden Eversmeyer

Helen Kalcsits
and
Vivian Larsen

Helen Kalcsits

Born March 1937 in Illinois
Interviewed in 2006, at age 69, in Arizona

Oh, God. I'm a confrontational woman!

I wasn't a planned member of the family. My dad, nine months earlier, had just returned from a job out of town, and my mother told him, "No, it isn't the right time," and he said, "Yes." She wasn't exactly pleased with my conception. In fact, the story goes that she took a broom and chased my dad down the back stairs when she found out she was pregnant. She thought that "family time" was over, and she wanted to spread her wings a little bit. Now she had another child.

At that time, ten years was a big gap. I think my mom wanted to get back to work. She had only been to school six years, so it wasn't like she had a professional job. She loved cooking, and had worked at restaurants before the girls were born. Then, when I came along, she stayed home until I was in eighth grade; then she went back to work. I remember having a "lovely" conversation with her about how she was deserting her family.

Helen grew up in Chicago in an era when jobs were scarce, and most families were still trying to make it back from the Depression. The neighborhood was filled with children. Even though Helen's siblings were much older, she never lacked for playmates, but most of them were boys.

I knew I was different from others by age four or five. That was obvious. With my size and androgynous nature, I could have been a male or a female. You couldn't tell if I was a young boy or a young girl. In fact, when I was in sixth grade, we had a little football team in our neighborhood, and we were going to play another neighborhood. They didn't want any girls to play. So I had my hair braided and pinned up, wore a football helmet over my head and played. They never knew they were playing against a girl. It wasn't that hard, you know, just to be who I was. I never had breasts to conceal. When I was eight years old, I wanted a pair of spikes, baseball spikes, for Christmas. My mother cried, but got them for me so I could play.

I started on my first organized team when I was seven. I would have started earlier, but every time the young woman who was in charge of the playground would come out to talk to me, to ask me if I'd play with the midget team, I'd run home. I was so shy. Finally, she caught up with me when I came for a drink of water and got me to join the little midget team. So at seven years old I rode the street cars around the city of Chicago to other playgrounds to play softball.

There were very few girls Helen's age in her neighborhood, and she wanted to play sports, so she played with the boys. Her sisters were both so much older than she that it was like being raised an only child. Helen's entry into the family seems to have interrupted their previous way of life. The family didn't do things together anymore. She'd heard them talk of picnics in the park, trips to the zoo, and things her parents and all their relatives from Austria used to do together. By the time Helen came along, the rest of the children in the extended family were teenagers, and zoo trips and family picnics were a thing of the past.

Helen was, admittedly, more than a bit rough around the edges while growing up in Chicago, but Chicago was rough around the edges, too.

In the city at that time, particularly in the south side of the city, race was a big issue. More and more African-Americans were migrating from southern states into the city's land area, and they were coming further and further into our neighborhood. My family, coming from Austria, was extremely racially prejudiced. I don't even know how old I was when the first black family bought a home about a block and a half from our home. I remember all of us running over there because the neighbors had set fire to the porch and the garage. We were all standing in the street. Everybody was yelling, "Nigger, go home. Nigger, go home. Nigger, go home." It was quite an atmosphere to grow up in.

It wasn't long after that that my dad bought land further south, and started to build his own home. Typical of my mom and dad was the construction they were doing. It was done on weekends. Most of the guys who worked for my dad on the big job would come and do the work for him on the weekend, and my mom would cook.

It was kind of fun. We had a stone frame around the door. It was a typical little Chicago house. It was brick, with only the face and front common brick, because you didn't want to waste money on brick for parts of the house you couldn't see. Right around the front door, we had a stone-mason install the stone. He was the nicest guy, because he let me sit with him all day and pick out the stones. God, I felt so important. It was just the neatest thing to be up there. When they were putting the roofing on, I remember my dad let me climb out on the roof and help hand out the shingles.

While Helen's parents were in this process of building a different home to get them "into a better area," she had been temporarily living with her sister. This enabled her to continue going to the Catholic school she'd been attending.

I was a gang member. There were some of us kids in the neighborhood that were stealing. I was the only girl. We were mostly stealing bikes. My job was to file off the serial numbers, and to help with the repainting. In order to be initiated into the gang, you had to go out on a Saturday and steal lunch for everyone. They didn't care what you brought back, but you had to steal it. I still remember running out of a store with a loaf of bread under my shirt and lunch meat. Luckily, in those days, they didn't have the things rigged to set off alarms. Sometimes I'd walk eight blocks to someplace where they didn't know me at all. I'd steal, and bring it back to the gang, and they'd eat it.

My sisters informed my parents that I had gone bad, so they'd better take me back home. As soon as seventh grade was over, they shipped me over to the new house. I had been drinking and smoking for some time. Okay, I was stealing, too. I probably would have been pregnant within the next year or two, hanging out with the gang. I was young then, only 13, but when I moved into the new neighborhood, none of the kids smoked, drank, or even swore. I had to change my entire ways.

It changed me totally! For the first time when I moved there, that first year, I met two young girls my age, Anita and Carol. We got along very well. Probably Anita was my first love, but we would never have called it that, or dealt with it.

Helen and her friends loved basketball, and when a couple of young women asked if they wanted to go with them to play in a gym, they jumped at the chance.

The two women that were driving were older. In my mind, they could have been 30. To be closer to the truth, they were probably only 18 or 19, maybe in their early 20s. You know how it is through a kid's eyes, there is no concept of time or age. I met them at the school, and we all got into the car. We hadn't been on the road for five or ten minutes, and they were kissing. It just threw me for a loop!

I didn't know what to do. I was looking out the car window, as I didn't want to see them. They never made advances toward me. When they asked me if I wanted to go the next week, I said no. I wasn't ready. That was the first time I had ever seen two women be intimate with each other, and it was just kissing and hugging.

An unusual situation also played a role in Helen's formative years. Some of her extended family purchased two acres outside of the city, where they could get their hands back into the soil and grow vegetables. They'd all go and spend the weekend weeding, watering, and doing other chores.

We spent a lot of time out there, most of the weekends in my early high school years. As I got more friends, I didn't want to go. It became an issue between my parents and me. I would want to go somewhere with my friends, rather than go with them. One day, I said I didn't want to go with "two old fogies." What a whipping I got! I might have been 15, but I still got a whipping, and went with them.

High school became a refuge away from her home life for Helen, partly because it was an all-girls school, and partly because of sports. Both maturing and going to the girls' school had Helen thinking about her self-image.

The only time I ever felt like a girl was when I became a teenager. Then, boys reacted differently to me. I couldn't play football with them anymore, and they didn't want me on the baseball team. They wanted to know if Anita, my best friend, liked them.

High school is when I really took off in sports. It was a Catholic school, and they had organized teams that played the other Catholic schools. There were at least six all-girl high schools that competed together. We competed in softball, basketball and volleyball. I started when I was a freshman. I had a wonderful lesbian gym teacher, Miss Morgan, who never admitted that she was a lesbian.

If I'd gone to a public high school, I don't know if I would have had the same sense of belonging that I had in an all-girls school. I could be the top jock. I could be the one that some of the other girls looked up to. I didn't have a male image in front of me all the time. I was allowed to flourish.

Although Helen flourished as an athlete in Catholic school, she also absorbed a heavy burden of Catholic guilt. Helen's family didn't actively participate in church, but they made sure they reinforced that sense of sin and guilt in her.

When you're brought up in the Catholic church, you grow up with lots of don'ts, and a lot of guilt. I masturbated from when I was very young. I didn't know what I was doing, but I masturbated. And it didn't take me too long to realize that this was wrong, a "Do Not Do." When I got to Catholic school, it was considered a sin. But I didn't stop doing it.

As a Catholic, you get caught in "double-edged swords." I didn't want to confess it, but if I don't confess it, then the whole thing snowballs. As far as the Catholic religion is concerned, if you commit a mortal sin and you don't confess it, and you receive the sacraments, that's a sacrilege. When you do that from the time you're seven until you're seventeen, you are guilt ridden!

I was condemned! I mean, I believed that I was going to hell! It didn't matter if I could hit a good shot or if I even had a hook shot. I was just a filthy, rotten, dirty person.

In my senior year, I finally broke down and went to one of the nuns and confessed. She said, "Go to confession, that's all. There's nothing wrong with this. Just go to confession." So I did, and felt so relieved that I joined the convent!

I can look back now and tell you that I had all these wonderful reasons for going in. I wanted to dedicate my life to something. But in the back of it all was that I was a sinner, and I had just been saved. I knew I was a lesbian, although I couldn't put a label on it, and I didn't

As a postulant, with her parents

know where to go with that knowledge. I had a scholarship to college. I was so afraid, because it was to Illinois State College. It was a state teachers college with strong lesbian representation in the P.E. Department. I went straight to the convent after graduating in June, and I entered in August.

I stayed in the convent 11 years. It takes me a long time to give up on something, to admit that I've gone the wrong way. I take gradual steps. I can't look back at the steps now and say it was the wrong decision, because I was in no way equipped to be a lesbian when I entered the convent. And I was much better equipped when I came out. I learned a lot about myself. I had a very, very difficult time in the convent.

What Helen considers her first "real lesbian relationship" occurred while she was in the convent. Unfortunately, it was with her Mistress of Novices, a 51 year old woman. She put 19-year-old Helen in a very difficult position. Resisting the older nun's attentions made things even more confusing for her.

It was a mess. I was a young kid. I wanted to please her. She was the person who was in charge of me. It was sheer hell for most of the next two and a half years. You can put all kinds of religious connotations on it: "I want to be your best friend. I want to be your friend in Christ." But when she keeps me up until 1:00 a.m. because I won't kiss her, there's something wrong.

When people said later, "Well, you asked for it," maybe I did. Maybe I did want her to look at me, and to notice me. But the rest of it, I didn't want. I didn't want special treatment. I didn't want anything else that came with it. And when I refused her intentions, it put me in a terrible situation. So, during that time in the convent, probably the first six months were wonderful, and after that it was sheer hell for the next two and half years.

They made me speak Lithuanian, and I didn't know Lithuanian. We had to stop having ordinary conversations, because you cannot speak normally if you have to translate everything in your head first. The hardest thing is to try and tell a joke, and not have the words for the punch line. Sometimes it's funnier because you may have the wrong words for the punch line.

Not all of her stay was bad, however. The convent was a teaching community, and Helen studied to become a teacher.

I always liked mathematics. I was a member of the math team when I was in high school, and enjoyed getting ready for competitions. When I entered the convent, one nun had the idea that it would be great if they trained me in counseling, and then let me get a degree in physical education. That way I could be the nun/gym teacher/coach, who could get to know the girls on a different basis, and do a great job. That way they would take advantage of my athletic interests and abilities, and still have me do a real job with the young girls I would be working with. It was a great idea, except that they wouldn't let me take my habit off to do any of the P.E. work. So that idea quickly went down the drain.

There were some things that were so hurtful. There was one year when the Mistress of Novices wouldn't allow any of the other novices to speak to me. I went through one year without anyone talking to me, as punishment for not responding to the older nun. She thought for sure there had to be someone else I was interested in.

We had this big beautiful yard behind the convent, and as novitiates, we used to do these wonderful gatherings, where we'd go outside and we'd get the benches together in a circle and practice singing. We would have three-part harmony, and sing some of the new hymns together. It was really good fun, doing everything a capella.

One woman was a new novice. She'd been in a year as a postulant, but this was the first time she was a novitiate, and we were going to sing a song in three-part harmony. She hardly knew me, and she came over and sat next to me so she could hear me. As a result, she was placed on her knees and given a ten-minute reprimand, right in front of all the other nuns, for having a particular friendship with me. She never understood.

There was no way to prepare them and say, "You don't talk to this one." But the word got around very quickly that you don't go near. There was another nun that was a first year novitiate, Sister Regis, who was almost as tall as I was. From the back, with the long habits on and everything,

*you couldn't tell the difference between us. I remember two
young first-year novices running up to tell me something,
and then realizing it was me. They said, "Oh. It's you, Sister
Eugene," my taken name, and just walking away knowing
they couldn't talk to me. I went through hell that year. That
was a very difficult year.*

Eventually, Helen was able to have intellectual discussions
with the other women, which opened her mind in many ways. In
the end, some positive things did come out of her experiences in
the convent.

*I don't think I ever would have gotten that kind of education
if I had gone to Illinois State and become a gym teacher.
I have a degree in theology that I got while I was in the
convent and I have a degree in mathematics. I would have
been playing ball at the state college. I still play ball, I'm
still an athlete, but there is another side to me that never
would have developed if I hadn't gone into the convent.
So I'm grateful for that. I came to realize that the convent
community was not going to grow with me.*

Several factors played into Helen's decision to leave. She
knew, if she wanted to continue to grow, she would have to leave.
She had learned to stand up for herself while in the convent, and
that didn't make life any easier. When another nun she was close
to told her she had been forbidden to talk to Helen because they
were having a "particular friendship," Helen went straight to the
Reverend Mother to demand an explanation.

Reverend Mother told her that theirs was a "dangerous
relationship," and that she thought it was better for everyone if
they didn't spend time together alone.

*"Well, thank you so much! I'm getting ready to make my
perpetual vows in August. I know now that I can't make
them," I said. "Why can't you make them?" Reverend*

Mother responded. "Well, I'm dangerous. Are you going to be with me all the time, with all the nuns that I meet and live with? If I'm considered a danger, and you have to be there to say who can talk to me and who can't, when I can be alone with someone and when I can't, I don't think I'm the kind you want to make perpetual vows," I stated.

Oh, God. I'm a confrontational woman! I became that in the convent, as I was growing, and maturing. It became obvious that I didn't want them to be in charge of my life. I could teach, and I could have more influence out of the convent, than I could by staying in.

Once she'd made her decision to leave, the convent couldn't get Helen out the door fast enough, adding another hurt to the already considerable list. The day before she was to officially leave the convent, Helen was returning all the habits, shoes and other clothing. It happened to be lunch time, and she saw this as a chance to tell the other nuns what was going on, and to say goodbye. These were women with whom she had shared her daily life for over a decade, so she sat down to eat with them. Within minutes, the Reverend Mother saw her there, and had another nun come to the table and tell Helen she was to go see Reverend Mother immediately.

Reverend Mother began, "You shouldn't be here. Can your parents come and get you now and take you?" "Mother, they're not ready for me today. They're planning on coming tomorrow," I said. Reverend Mother insisted, "You're to leave immediately." I think the reason was she didn't want me to talk to anybody about leaving. As soon as I pulled out of the convent grounds, at the first street, I just parked and cried. Eleven years, and I couldn't even stay there!

I wasn't a troublemaker, and I hadn't done anything wrong. They didn't have any reason for me to leave. I was a good nun. I was a good teacher. I got along with everybody.

I had just decided to leave the convent. I guess they were afraid. If they thought you were a troublemaker, they wanted you to go.

Helen found out right away that, while she definitely didn't want to stay in the convent, neither was she prepared for life on the outside. She felt completely lost. Even clothes were an issue, because she had none of her own. When people addressed her as "Helen," she didn't respond at first. For years, she'd been "Sister Eugene." Her situation was further complicated by the lack of a job, and a credit history.

By then, her parents owned and lived above a tavern, so Helen went to stay with her sister, however she didn't fit in there either. For the past eleven years, she had been told when to awaken, when to go to sleep, and when to go to chapel. After only one night at her sister's, she felt too anxious to stay there once her sister left for work. Helen went over to help her mother prepare for lunch time at the bar, but her mother wouldn't let her do anything. "I was supposed to relax and enjoy myself. She didn't realize how much I needed to do something."

Living at home wasn't going to work. Helen moved out and stayed with friends temporarily. The convent had given her $100 when she left, her dowry from when she entered the convent, and that was all the money she had. They had also tried to give her a check for $200 from the community, to help her get started. She refused to accept it, ripping up the check and telling Mother Superior, "What I needed from you was kindness and consideration. And you give me money!"

After she left the convent, the first friends to contact Helen were the women she'd played ball with in high school. Her friends took Helen to get some clothing. Her dad co-signed a loan for a car, and she got a job teaching at a Catholic school. "I wasn't sure enough of myself to go to the public schools. Also, despite all the math I had studied, I didn't have a real math degree." Helen began teaching in Catholic schools, until she got a master's degree. After that, she spent the rest of her teaching career in public schools.

Helen also quickly sought out and joined both a volleyball and a basketball team. "Most of the people that I played with were lesbians." Some of her athletic skills were still there, but to keep up with her friends, Helen had to learn power volleyball. In the convent, she had to play volleyball in her full habit, with her skirt pinned up, and the sleeves rolled back.

> It was through the basketball team that I had my first real lesbian relationship with one of the other women. Much to my mother and father's regret, she was an African-American woman, a beautiful woman and a great basketball player. We played together and we were together in a relationship for approximately six years. Marva was very hidden about her sexuality. She didn't want her family or anyone else to know. When we would go out someplace, she would never go any place that was strictly lesbian. If it was a party or a dance, Marva would always bring a man along with her as her escort, and I was there, also.

Her family had some sense of the nature of her relationship with Marva, but Helen had never really come out to them. Her parents had a fit about Marva, but other than mean-spirited comments about Marva's race, they had never really talked about it. "The only conversation we ever had was after my mom died. My father couldn't say I was a lesbian, or anything like that. All he said was, "I know you're different, and there won't be anybody there to care for you. So you'll have to take care of yourself."

Marva was also dating men while she and Helen were together, and even became pregnant twice during the time they were involved. When Helen needed someplace cheap to stay while she took some classes, she fixed up a little apartment for herself above her parent's tavern. Helen's father found out that

Marva would spend some nights there, and his deep-seated racial prejudices came into play once again, and Helen left. A month later, she was called to her mother's sickbed. Basically, her mother said that if having Marva come there was the only way Helen would come back, it was okay. Helen agreed to return, but, since Marva was aware of what had happened, Helen insisted that her family had to deal with the racial issue openly. The atmosphere was predictably tense, but liquor helped bridge the gap. Helen's relationship with her parents didn't last much longer.

Six years after Helen left the convent, she and other women who had left for various reasons were invited back to a Mass. It was to be a celebration to show how much the women who had left still belonged there. Helen knew that this was something that could happen only after the "old guard" was gone, and that the nuns were truly trying to reach out and reconnect. "They only made one mistake; they asked for a donation before we left!"

Eighteen years after Helen left the convent, she again went back, this time to confront the Mistress of Novices who had made her life so difficult.

> That was a very unusual visit. We just talked for a little while. She wanted to show me the new addition they had put on the Mother House. Then we sat down, and I started to talk to her about some of the things that had happened when I was there. I then realized she was in her late seventies. For her, it never happened.
>
> She walked me out to the car. She gave me a hug, and I hugged her. She stood back from me and held me by the shoulders, and said, "Still the same." Then she turned around and walked away. I thought, "Why didn't you just come out? Why stay in?"
>
> I wasn't the first one she had fallen in love with. But I was the last one she had in the Mistresshood, because I went to the head of the young sisters the day I got out. I went to Sr. Aloise,

*and said, "Get her out of there. She does not belong in there."
And they took her out the next year.*

Another turning point in Helen's life was reached when she attended the Michigan Womyn's Music Festival. Someone had gotten together a meeting of teachers and educators at the festival. In the group were young women looking for ideas about how to deal with being lesbians while also being teachers. "I felt embarrassed, because I had been teaching for so many years, and all I could do was warn them. I couldn't say anything positive."

Helen had also recently attended a consciousness-raising event that had challenged her secure, closeted life. With this new sense of self, Helen understood her life would never be the same.

The Michigan festival also provided another motivation for Helen to make some changes; her name was Vivian. Helen knew when she met Vivian that the long-avoided discussion with her family needed to happen.

*When I met Vivian, I realized that there was no way
Vivian could be hidden. You have to meet Vivian. She's an
"out dyke," I tell you. I knew the first thing I had to do was
call my sisters.*

*So I called Gert, the matriarch of the family. Years
before, when I'd been tending bar on weekends, Gert came in
with somebody. She was higher than a kite, and she started to
lay into me about Marva, and about me wanting to be with a
black woman. "You tell me that's just friendship; well you can
stick that up your ass, honey." So I knew that she understood
what my relationship with women was, but we had never
talked about it, other than when she was in a drunken rage.*

*When I went there to tell her, I said, "I don't want
your girls coming around." They were always in and out
of her house every day. "For this visit, I want to come and
sit and talk with you." So we sat and talked, and I said, "I
wanted you to know I'm a lesbian, and I'm with Vivian." It*

was really funny, because the first thing she said to me was, "Helen, that's fine. Let me call Patsy" [her daughter]. I said, "Why?" "They think you're dying of cancer!" she replied.

For the first time in their lives, they went on to talk, and Gert shared personal things about her own life. "I guess my talking about my sexuality allowed her the freedom to talk about hers."

Vivian and Helen also felt she needed to come out at school. They were living in Oak Park, a small community that, at that time, did not have a human dignity policy for the town. A lone gay man had spoken up on behalf of adding a new policy, claiming he represented the Oak Park Gay and Lesbian Organization, something that didn't even exist. Everyone called everyone they knew who was gay or lesbian. Next thing you know, they were a force, sitting in and testifying at city council meetings. "In my life, I had never heard two straight hours of

Helen and Vivian, flanked by Helen's niece and niece's husband

bigotry spieled before. Then there were two straight hours of support that followed."

It took some effort, but the Human Dignity Policy was adopted by Oak Park. Then the next step was to get it adopted by the high school. Several small meetings were held before making a proposal to the school board, and the word went out to find a teacher within the system who would speak out on behalf of the proposal. When no one else came forward, Helen volunteered.

> *There are so many of us that are hidden; we're just woven into the fabric of the educational system. Because it was so dangerous, we felt we couldn't come out. I thought I had done a disservice to my students in the past by not letting them know who I was. Just to let them know, because I had known at least one gay boy who had committed suicide. I'm sure there was more than one young lesbian who had a harder time because they didn't have a role model, or at least someone there that they could say, "See, she is and she's okay." It's important to feel that it's all right to be gay.*

Word of what had happened made it to the Superintendent of the school district before Helen even returned to school after testifying. There was going to be "action" taken against Helen. This led to a four-month personal battle with the Board of Education in Cicero-Berwyn, where Helen was teaching.

Two more open meetings were held in the auditorium of the Oak Park-River Forest High School. Those in opposition to the administration's policy change applying throughout the school district were now even more determined to put a stop to it. They were distributing leaflets filled with their vitriol all over the area. A big meeting was held, and people were given three minutes each to have their say. About a half hour into the meeting, a man "came in his fancy suit and brought the leaflet with him."

He took the microphone and said, "Before this whole thing started, I couldn't have cared less. I had lesbian neighbors, and I had gay neighbors. I didn't think we had to put anything in a written policy. I didn't think we needed it in the village, and I didn't think we needed it in the high school. I figured things were just going the way they should be going. And then last night somebody put this thing on my door. Now you've got to pass it. This is just like Hitler's Germany. This is just like what happened to the Jews. You cannot let this kind of poison influence a vote."

At the end of this meeting, the Board voted unanimously in favor of the new human dignity policy.

Helen's personal battle with the Cicero-Berwyn School Board was just getting started. That "action" the Board had promised turned out to be a letter letting Helen know she was not allowed to speak to any student about her own sexuality. Trying to work within the system, she expressed her objections to all the appropriate people, but they wouldn't budge. Feeling she had no other recourse, Helen took her complaint to the lawyer that represented the Teachers' Union.

The lawyer sat at her desk, with a photo of her family on it, and questioned why Helen felt making a statement about her sexual identity was important. Helen said, "Why do you have this picture? That picture tells every one who comes here, 'Look, I'm a mother, I'm a wife, I have kids.' You make a declaration automatically with that picture, and I'm not supposed to say who I am." The lawyer was still baffled, and again asked if it was really important. Helen responded, "Well, is it really important to you? What would it be like if you came to work every day and could never say anything about the people you live with?"

"They don't get it," Helen realized. She went back to the local union rep and, on his advice, waited. Their contracts were coming up for renewal, and the Union had decided to take a stand: they would refuse to sign their contract until the letter was removed from Helen's file. Still, Helen refused to just sit and wait. They may have effectively kept her from talking to students, but there had been nothing said about her talking with staff.

> *I started to set up visits with teachers I knew at school. I'd have coffee with them in the morning. We'd have lunch together, and we'd go out after school. I saw every group of teachers that I could, sitting down and coming out to them. I told them that I had been silenced, and I said, "You all know me well enough to know that I would not start talking about my sexuality in the middle of my calculus class. It doesn't fit in pre-algebra or in my honors geometry classes either. So, where exactly I'm going to discuss this, I don't know. But if a kid comes to me after school and says something, I don't see why I'm not allowed to say whatever I need to say."*

When the contract was finally ready for ratification, and the Union had won all of its major issues, except the removal of the letter from Helen's file, the 200 or so members of the Union rejected the contract. The letter was removed the next day. "In fact," Helen affirmed, "they said the letter never existed, although I had ten copies of it."

Life wasn't really always so full of drama and challenges, yet in August, 1988, Helen embarked on another big adventure she had never expected.

> *Viv always wanted a commitment ceremony. We waited over three years before we came to the point that we really wanted one. I wanted to make sure that we could bargain, that we could have difficult times and come out the other side, that we could process differences together, and that we could really make a life together. Before that, it didn't make any sense to have a commitment ceremony. Finally we did, and it was wonderful!*

Viv always wanted a ceremony, and I didn't want it. And then somebody asked me afterward how I felt about having commitment ceremonies. The way I saw it, before the ceremony, it was like Viv and I holding hands, and it was us against the world. After the commitment ceremony, it was like there were a hundred other pair of hands surrounding ours, and over ours, helping to bind us together.

That was the first time my sisters ever saw me dance with another woman. Men were dancing with men, women were dancing with women, and men were dancing with women. It was really an eye-opener for my family, because they had never been around gay people before.

Retirement was coming up in the next few years, and Helen and Vivian started exploring their options. After ruling out quite a few other places, they found themselves falling in love with Arizona. They bought a piece of property, and made a deal with a local man who built adobe homes.

It was not delightful the first year. Our two dogs that we moved in with both got ticks, and their feet started to bleed from the rough ground. All the windows weren't closed in, so we had bugs all over the house. It was 118° the first day we moved in, and that summer we had 99 days of 100° or more. One of the worst summers in history. What a mess.

We learned to stick with it, however. It has just been a joy. We learned that in the summertime you get up at 4:30 a.m., and watch the sun come over the mountains.

Part of their Arizona adventure included opening a bed and breakfast, and focusing their advertising to draw as many lesbians as possible to keep them connected with the lesbian community nationwide. "I've been very grateful for the guest house, which has brought a variety of people here, gay, lesbian, and straight. Everybody comes here."

Helen had yet another totally new experience waiting for her, too. The neighbors adopted a newborn baby, and Helen agreed to babysit several days a week.

I didn't know which end was up, you know! It was the most fantastic experience in my life! I just marveled over his mind: the way it worked, his problem-solving ability at one month, two months, trying to figure things out already! It's been one of the best experiences of my life.

At age 70, Helen is still a jock at heart. She loves Arizona, the incredible sunrises, her new friends and neighbors, the guest house, playing grandma, and, of course, Vivian.

Helen and Vivian continue to live in Arizona. Helen is now 74, and Vivian, 78. They now live in a two-bedroom, two bath apartment in a lovely retirement home with their dogs and cats. Helen says, "Life is good!"

Interviewer: Arden Eversmeyer

Vivian Larsen

Born August 1933
Interviewed in 2006, at age 72, in Arizona

There are a lot of wonderful men,
but it isn't the same.

One might have thought, looking at Vivian's childhood, that she was born to a family of nomads! Instead, she was born into a band of strong Norwegians who, living through the Depression, had to go wherever they could find work that would sustain the family. By the time Vivian entered her teens, she had lived in 22 cities, in five different states. When she was ten, Vivian's father, who was then nearly 40, was drafted into the Army, leaving the family behind in a small town in Ohio, on Lake Erie.

The population was only 3,000 and it was a safe place to live. But those were very difficult years for me, and for my mother. She was desperately lonely, she began drinking, and dated other men to fill her loneliness. She also worked, first as a riveter in a war plant. But she had to quit, because she lost too much weight. Then she tried to tend bar, but her drinking got in the way, so she went to work as a security guard at the Diamond

Magnesium plant. I was alone a lot, and still experience startle reactions and hypervigilance from those early days.

It was only after her father came home from World War II that the family settled down into their first unfurnished home, and stayed in one place for several years.

When my father came home, we moved to Cleveland, Ohio, and my brother was born. I attended a junior high that, at that time, was predominantly black students, maybe 80%, 19% Jewish, and me. My high school was predominantly Jewish, maybe 80%, and 19% black, and me. Those were wonderful experiences for me, as they widened my world, and I am grateful.

For me, that was a long time in one place. I dated the captain of a football team from another high school. Yet, I knew from the time that I was seven years old that I preferred girls to boys. I fluctuated between being attracted to boys and girls.

When I was 15, I had a mad crush on a girl that I met at a summer Lutheran volunteer camp. We wrote, and visited as often as we could. I do remember being aroused by a neighbor boy when we were 16. However, my crush on Nancy lasted until we met again at Valparaiso University, where I went to study to be a Lutheran deaconess. She had attended her first year at Toledo University, but transferred to Valpo to be with me.

She got there earlier than I did for our sophomore year, and she had a brief kissing affair with another girl. They got caught. By the time I got there, they wouldn't let me near her. She was forced into counseling, and not allowed to be alone with any other females. The last I heard, she left Valpo, married the counselor, and had a slew of children. I never heard from her, and I don't remember anything but her first name, so I couldn't even try to look her up.

19 year old Vivian

Norwegians are traditionally strong Lutherans, but neither of Vivian's parents attended church regularly, or encouraged their children to do so. When Vivian began to be confused by her sexuality, she looked for a church that might help her deal with her inner turmoil.

I needed something. A group of girls I was friends with belonged to a Missouri Synod Lutheran Church, so I joined it. I dropped out of Valparaiso University after my second year, because my grades were terrible.

On my way home to Cleveland by train the Christmas vacation before I dropped out, I met a young man who was also Lutheran, and he was from Swedish descent parents. He was tall and good-looking. Since I thought I had to get married because that was what all 'good' girls did, I married him the summer after I dropped out of school. I was 20 years old by four days and a virgin, as was he. He was in the Navy, and we lived together in San Diego for three months. Then, when he went to Korea, I returned to Cleveland to live with my parents, and work. It didn't take long before I was again involved with a woman, so I filed for divorce. The attorney advised that I wait for two years, so when he returned safely from Korea, the divorce went through.

The poor man had terrible luck. His first wife, me, turned out to be a dyke.

Vivian had married in 1953 and divorced in 1955. Now what? In high school, a counselor had talked with her about career planning.

Mr. David, my counselor, was about six foot three, a big man. He said, "What do your parents want you to do, Vivian?" I said, "Well, my mother wants me to go to college, and my father thinks that I should take home economics and things like that." "I think you should do what your father says," Mr. David advised. I had taken a test which indicated that I wasn't bright enough to go to college.

In 1955, I fell in love with Jeannie, who was the coach of the telephone company basketball team. She wasn't actually a coach, she was a referee. Jeannie was a college graduate. She said, "That's nonsense. You're very bright, so you're gonna go back to college. Now, what kind of work do you want to do?" I said, "I don't know." She said, "Then be a teacher."

Taking advantage of a chance for a fresh start and her friend's encouraging words, Vivian went back to college at Ohio State University, and finished a four year degree in three years.

I went to Ohio State in Columbus, and fumbled around for a couple of years before deciding what I would teach, ending up with a double major. I had a major in speech education, and health education.

I took a job teaching in the largest high school in Ohio, Parma High School, which had forty-seven hundred students. I taught there for one year, teaching speech, drama, fencing, and health education. But by then, Jeannie had another girl-friend, somebody that she had loved before me, who returned to her. I only lived with her for one year. Then I went from one person to another. Those were the 1950s, and we were foolish, free-loving and reckless.

In that year that I was teaching, my high school debated a lot of Catholic schools, and I met a lot of nuns. I was kind of confused about who I was, because I was attracted to some men and yet I knew that the stronger pull was toward women. I think I must have had a little psychotic break, because I converted to Catholicism, Roman Catholicism. I say that because both Lutheranism and Catholicism are religions full of guilt and shame, making people feel bad about themselves, in my opinion. But then most religions do that as their control tactic.

Then a staunch Catholic, Vivian found herself joining an institute called Regina Mundi, which means "Queen of the Universe," and she actually took vows.

I think what I was trying to do was to fight two things: my lesbianism and my alcoholism. My mother had been an alcoholic, her father had been an alcoholic, and I'm an alcoholic. But the Church didn't really protect me from anything in myself. I applied to join a convent, and the wise Diocese denied me entrance, because they said I was still married. They wouldn't honor my divorce. They said that, in my appeal for an annulment, I had written that I had a crush on a girl when I was 15. Therefore, "Don't let her in the convent." Well, they were very smart.

The head of this religious group said she wanted me to get a master's degree, and asked, "What do you want to do with it?" I said, "I don't know. What should I get a master's degree in?" "Well, you could either be a Montessori teacher, or you could be a social worker like me." When I asked what social workers do, she said, "You could be a therapist, an administrator, or a community organizer."

That sounded good to me, so I applied to five universities, and Loyola University in Chicago granted me a full federal fellowship. It was called a National Institute of Mental Health (NIMH) grant. I moved from Cleveland to Chicago in 1960. At the end of the first year, they said, "We don't have a grant again."

Without any grant funds to continue her studies, Vivian went to work as a social worker, taking a job in the juvenile court in Cincinnati. She had only worked there for a year, when she was offered another NIMH grant, which she quickly accepted. She returned again to Chicago, finished her studies, graduated in 1963, and stayed in the area.

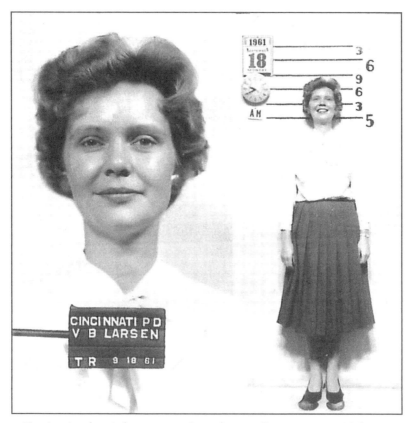

Beginning her job as a social worker in Cincinnati in 1961

I took a job as a medical social worker at Northwestern University, which also gave me a faculty appointment. Within ten months, I received a new job and became Chief Psychiatric Social Worker of the Katherine Wright Mental Health Center in Chicago. I went into therapy with a psychiatrist, and told him about my feelings about women. He said, "So? Why don't you live your life and enjoy it? Go find a good woman." And I said, "Well, thank you, Dale Loomis. What a good man you are."

I'd also gone to an analyst, Beulah Bosselman, and I remember thinking that I was sick, because the American Psychiatric Association called homosexuality sick, at that time.

She had never said it was a mental illness, but she encouraged me to leave the Catholic Church and become a Quaker.

Experience had taught Vivian that simply switching to another religion, one that she felt was all about controlling other people, was not the answer for her. She opted not to join the Quakers, or any other religion.

Over the next few years, Vivian had liaisons with women, but felt a lack of emotional security. Once again, she tried the alternative and dated men.

I became engaged to Roger and I thought I was going to get married. But we had an argument, because he had set up a tango lesson, and I was exhausted. I did not want to tango. So I broke it off with Roger. It was a good thing because I would have ended up divorcing him. He wouldn't have known what happened, you know? And Roger was a sweet man, a nice man.

Unencumbered, Vivian capitalized on another opportunity, and became the Executive Director of the Mental Health Commission for Proviso Township, a suburb of Chicago. It was a big job involving a large district, and kept her busy. Slowly, Vivian started to find other gay and lesbian friends, and ten years later fell in love. She and Bonnie moved in together as Vivian continued her career climb. She was now a Regional Director for the City of Chicago Mental Health Division, with seven mental health centers in her charge.

Vivian felt, during her professional life, that she needed to keep the lesbian side of herself well hidden.

We were never 'out.' We were frightened, because they were raiding bars and publishing names. I remember very clearly, in 1968 they raided a bar and arrested seven men. They put their names on the front page. One was a school principal, and the rest were teachers. One of the men hanged himself. It was so tragic. So when we would go to bars to be with other women, I was always 'Natasha,' a student. I would carry a clipboard, in case we were arrested, so I could not be pegged as a lesbian. I had already had a high security clearance, because I was Regional Director of Mental Health. My brother, at that time, was a Lieutenant in the United States Army Signal Corps. They had cleared me for him, because he had a high security clearance. So I was very cautious and very careful.

In 1970, her boss, who had always shielded her from the politics of the job, resigned. Vivian decided she didn't want to stay either. He had taught her to "never get into a pissin' contest with a skunk, and never fight with somebody who's got more power than you." It's a lesson that has lasted her her whole life.

I applied for a fellowship through the National Education Department, and I received that fellowship. The name of the program was the National Program for Educational Leadership. There were fourteen men and three women chosen from around the country, and we were going to become inner city school superintendents in education. A couple of the men had doctorates already, and some of them decided they were going to get them through the program. It wasn't actually an in-school training program. We could travel anywhere in the country to study educational systems, and interview people. We were paid $18,750 a year from 1970 to 1972, and that was a lot of money then. I was only earning, I think, $17,000 at the Board of Health as Regional Director. So it was an increase, and my expenses were paid.
    They sent me to New York, where I studied negotiations, and they sent me to California. I had thought about going to Claremont College to get a doctorate in education, and then my father became very very ill and died. I dropped out of the program before finishing.

As life became more and more stressful, Vivian began to drink heavily. She couldn't sustain a relationship, and decided she might be better off going back into mental health, a field she felt she knew well. Instead of taking a regular position, Vivian began to work as a consultant, working with the juvenile courts and police departments. She also took two appointments: one as an assistant in the psychiatry department at Loyola University, and another as an associate professor and supervisor of students in social work at the University of Illinois. Both were challenging and satisfying, but she still felt something was missing.

> *What I really thoroughly loved was when I became a psychotherapist. I did that when I became sober. In 1980, I stopped drinking, and opened my own private practice. That's when I really learned about doing therapy. From 1960 until 1981, what I'd primarily done was community organization, and administration. It was great. I was able to help a township of 200,000 people vote to tax themselves for mental health, and to develop a mental health center. We had a wonderful community mental health program going. In 1981, however, when I started my private practice, I learned what therapy was. My practice was always about 25% lesbians, 25% gay men and 50% straight people.*
>
> *I came out in about 1981. I was, at that point, very open. A year earlier I had said, "I can't keep going back and forth. I have to make a decision. I'm either going to be with men, or I'm going to be with women. One or the other." My penchant was always toward women, so I decided, "Definitely I'm a lesbian. That's it." And I came out. I know I'm bisexual, and that is okay, but my penchant is toward women. The emotional leaning is a much stronger pull. I like men, there are a lot of wonderful men, but it isn't the same.*

Vivian had several female partners over the next few years. But when she met Helen, in 1984, that was it.

We began living together in June of 1985, and we were married in August of 1988. We have been together ever since, and true to each other. We never had another thought.

We joined a small Unitarian church in Oak Park, Illinois, at my urging because I wanted to be married. They were a marvelous community of open-minded, educated, wonderful human beings, who welcomed us with open arms. There were a few other gay and lesbian members of that group. Before us, there were two gay men and two lesbians, and they lived together as husbands and wives, as a front.

Sometimes two people in a relationship are at different places in their evolution of accepting themselves and coming out. To a degree, this was true with Helen and Vivian. She was more out than Helen, but they both had work to do on that front.

I was out to my mother. My father did not know, because he died before I came out. He would have accepted it. He may not have fully understood it, but he sure would have accepted it, because he loved me. My mother was wonderful. When I first told her she said, "Oh my God, why did God do this to me?" And I said, "Well, Mama, God didn't do anything to you." She said, "Oh, but I don't understand."

Well, within two weeks of my coming out to her, she was on a panel with me at Northwestern University, for parents and friends of gays and lesbians. She said, "This is my daughter, and my daughter had to tell me, because she didn't want to lie anymore." She was wonderful. She loved Helen, and she was very accepting. She said, "Vivi, are all your friends gay or lesbian?" And I said, "Yeah, most of them are." "Oh, no. Not Dr. Delfin, too?" she asked. I said, "Oh, yeah, Mama. He's been with Julio since they were 18!" "No kidding. Well, I guess he's not AC-DC then!"

She was a woman ahead of her time. She used to always say that if these kids today would treat a marriage like an

expensive coat, and try it on before they buy it, they wouldn't
have so many divorces. They should live together for a year,
to see if it fits.

Vivian and Helen started looking for a place to retire, and in 1990 they fell in love with the Tucson area of Arizona. As they looked at their options for housing in the area, they bonded with a young couple, Lyle and Karen. Lyle had degrees in sculpture, watercolor, and educational psychology. But best of all, he also built homes, incorporating a wide variety of artistic touches. Lyle and Karen sold them five acres of land, and he built their new home. Over the next few years, the couple became an important part of Vivian and Helen's extended family. So much so, that they immediately took on the role of grandparents when a son, Andre, was adopted into Lyle and Karen's life.

Activism had been a part of Vivian's life for many years, working in mental health. Together with Helen, her activism has broadened, and they have started to include working with LGBT issues. Yet, Vivian is a bit resistant to calling herself a gay activist.

Helen and I both served on several panels back in Chicago,
educating policemen, and talking in public about being out
as gays and lesbians. Helen came out to the school board in
Oak Park. We went to Washington, D.C., for the LGBT
March on Washington in 1993. We also did some activism
here, when we first got to Arizona. We went with Wingspan,
a gay and lesbian, bisexual, transgendered community group,
and talked with groups of people.

I think I've been a gay activist, in that I'm out to every-
body in my life. I'm out at work. I was out when they hired
me. I wouldn't be hired without being out. And I call myself
'the old dyke' at work.

Retiring to Arizona didn't necessarily mean retiring from activism, and neither did it mean retiring from work. Vivian continues to work as a licensed clinical social worker in a nearby psychiatric hospital, where she does some crisis intervention and group work. But she can't work every day, since taking Andre to and from school is a priority.

Vivian loves her life in Arizona.

I wouldn't live anywhere else again. And we certainly have got to get rid of the horrible administration of this country, that's trying to put us all back in the closet. The Bush administration. Assholes. It's just ridiculous.

I think I might retire when I'm 75. Helen and I have been together 21 years. It's been a good life.

I have no complaints. I'm pretty active and healthy, and I have it in my mind that I can live into my mid to late eighties. I'm tryin'. I'm tryin'.

Vivian and Helen sold their remotely located B&B and have moved into town, but continue to thrive, together, in Arizona, in a wonderful retirement facility.

Interviewer: Arden Eversmeyer

Elizabeth 'Deedy' Breed

Born October 1922 in New York
Interviewed in 2001 at age 79 in Massachusetts

I tried to look it up. I didn't know the word 'lesbian.'

When I was about seven, an amazing thing happened, at least I thought so. My father and another man bought a sail boat. They named it "Kim." They originally called it "Kim" because it had been named "Buccaneer," and that name was too long. When they painted over the transom, they had to choose a shorter name with straight letters. My father was a great Kipling fan, so he picked the name "Kim" because it was short, all the letters are straight, and they didn't have an "s" to deal with!

One of the first times I went out with them I got sea sick, so I wasn't allowed to go out the next time. I would practice in front of the mirror, putting on my sailor hat, and weaving back and forth, back and forth, to get used to not getting sea-sick. I am sure it was just something that happened that first

Deedy, age 7

time, because afterward I was just fine. To this day, I don't really get sea sick. My father said he figured he had salt water in his veins, and I think I inherited that, because sailing, and the water, have always been very dear to me. I have enjoyed it my whole life. That was the first chance I had to do something that every-body else didn't do. It kinda set me apart.

I have just one younger brother. I was an only child for about eight years. My brother was born in the same year that the Lindbergh baby was kidnapped, 1930. Then my sister was born in 1934. That was during the Depression, after the stock market fell. I think my parents weren't happy to have another child at that point. My mother had multiple sclerosis, MS, which we did not find out about until a lot later. When my sister was born, my mother was not really well. I ended up sort of taking care of my sister, Pat, and I would bathe her and carry her around. I thought she was the cutest little thing. It was like having a real live doll. I didn't play with dolls that much, because I was more of a tomboy.

My mother's medical condition was eventually diagnosed as MS. I am the only one of the children that remembers her walking, standing, or doing anything mobile. By the time they had memories of her, she was in a wheelchair to start with, and then sitting in another chair, and not being able to be mobile at all.

Deedy's school years were a mixture of helping her mother and raising her siblings, as well as the usual childhood school experiences. She attended a nearby public grammar school, less than a mile from home in Hartford, Connecticut.

I had three friends, and we walked to school together. It was about three quarters of a mile away. You went to morning session, then came home for lunch, walked back again in the afternoon, then came home again for good. So, four times a day we did this trek back and forth all winter long, in the rain, snow, and sleet.

My friend, Lori, would start out first, as she lived the farthest away. She would pick up Natalie, who lived about a block away, and they would come and pick me up. Then we would go pick up Betty. The four of us were like the "Four Musketeers."

Those are the girls I hung out with. They all joined the Girl Scouts with me. Because my father had a boat, we became Mariners when we were in senior Girl Scouts, and we used to do things on the boat. We all were in Junior Choir, and we were all in the Youth Fellowship. I think we all went away to Northfield together, so I had pals.

The biggest thing we would do for entertainment would be to catch the trolley, go into town, and go to the movies every Saturday. I think movies cost 15¢, and we would have an extra nickel to buy a soda, or something. For about 50¢ you could do everything. I grew up on those movies that they had back in the 1930s.

When Deedy graduated from high school, she went straight to work. Her father helped her get her first job at an insurance company. She also began to take night classes in advanced mathematics at Trinity College, and then went on to a local junior college connected with the University of Connecticut. There, she studied physics.

That was a rough period, and World War II was just coming on. In 1941, I got a job as an Engineering Aide at United Aircraft, in the research department. The reason I was hired, with only a year of college, was because there were no men around. It was similar to being a "Rosie the Riveter." I was in the research department, which I loved. I stayed there 13 years, and by the time I finished I was a full Aeronautical Engineer. I took courses on the side, and all that sort of thing.

My memories of the war are more pleasant than a lot of people's are, I am sure, just because of that job. It was so wonderful. I was running a small wind tunnel by myself.

I had been there for about five years or so when the personnel director was calling everybody into his office. He talked to me and said, "Well, Deedy, United Aircraft is just starting a pension plan for its employees, but you won't be interested in that." He said, "You're a woman, and when the war is over you will get married and have children, and your husband will take care of you, so you don't need to be involved in this pension plan." Not having any feminist sensibilities, I let that pass. Of course, I can rue the day that I didn't insist, because for 13 years I could have been paying into a pension plan.

All through those years, Deedy continued to live at home. She dated a bit, but during the war years there weren't many men around that she found interesting. She did, however, meet one man at work who'd caught her interest, but not until after she'd had an experience that made her question just who she was.

A woman came to work in the same department where I was. She was an ex-WAC, and she kind of took a fancy to me. We had a brief relationship. Of course, at that time I figured, "Wow! We were the only two people in the world." I tried to look it up. I didn't know the word 'lesbian.' I looked up the word 'homosexual,' and found out it was this horrible thing, and the only book I read was The Well of Loneliness. *I thought, "Well, even in fiction they can't make it any better, so who wants this? Not me." So that was that. It was a very brief relationship that I just put out of my mind. I decided I wanted nothing to do with anything that had 'lesbian' attached to it.*

Shortly after I had broken up with this woman, I took a three month leave of absence. I went with another woman I liked as a friend. She was a skier and I was a skier. We had an incredible adventure. We visited 24 states on this trip, going to all the National Parks and National Monuments, and things like that. We skied for the first six weeks of that trip. I had won a trip to Aspen because I had sold the most tickets to something, so we started out there. We went from Aspen to Sun Valley, then to Alta, out to Squaw Valley, then worked our way back. We went south to Laguna, and tented on the beach for three days. We also went to Reno and hit five jackpots, and then to Las Vegas.

We came back through Yosemite, Bryce and Zion, Mesa Verde, and the Grand Canyon, where we took a mule ride down to the bottom and back. We could hardly get off the mules when we got back! In fact, I wondered why all those people were standing around there. It ended up that they were waiting to see if we could walk! Well, I don't think we disappointed them at all. Then we drove to Niagara Falls, and came back through Canada. We took a boat on the Great Lakes, and ended up in Canada. We didn't do much in the South. It was a great experience. The only way you are going to see the United States is by car. I have flown over it many times but you just don't see anything. This was an important part of my life. It just kind of opened my eyes. I had grown up pretty sheltered, and had not had the advantage of traveling at all.

Once you have a boat, you don't do anything but go on that boat every weekend. Not that that wasn't fun. My mother, bless her heart, could get around on the boat and spend two weeks there. Within a small area, she could hang on to things and move around on her own. We had some wonderful times on that boat. It did not go very fast. It had an auxiliary motor, so if we couldn't sail we could get into port with it. My father had a huge awning that stretched from the mast back over the transom, so we could all sit there under it in the shade, eat, swim and fish, if we wanted to. There were a lot of good times on that boat.

Some of Deedy's earliest memories were of being dragged along to Daughters of the American Revolution meetings by her grandmother. Her family was very proud of its heritage, and even though they had very little financially, they had a pedigree. When Deedy met a man at work that "had good breeding," that made a difference.

David came to work, and one thing led to another. I thought, "Well, he comes from good stock. He comes from Maine."

His father is a professor of Civil Engineering at MIT [Massachusetts Institute of Technology]. He was schooled at Deerfield and MIT. I really enjoyed his family, and I liked his sister. Of course I liked him, but I don't think it was a great all-consuming love affair. At least I was not experiencing being swept off my feet. We had a lot of fun together, and I enjoyed his company. His

Engagement photo at age 30 *family had a lovely place in*

Camden, Maine, and we would visit his family there, right on the water. His sister and I spent one hilarious weekend in New York, and she and I just went from one bar to another. She was a real neat person.

David and I got married in 1953. In 1956, my first daughter was born. Two-and-a-half years later, my second daughter was born. Five years after that, my son was born. So, I ended up with two girls and a boy. Of course, we were really anxious for that boy to arrive, because David's father could see the end of the family line, and wanted to make sure there was going to be a male heir. That is so important to some people, that the family name gets carried on.

One of the first things I learned when I married into that family was that the Battle of Bunker Hill was not fought on Bunker Hill. It was fought on Breed's Hill. Today, you go to the Bunker Hill Memorial and they do give credit to Breed's Hill. Here again, that is something about the "Yankee-ness" of the old Yankees. You may not have any money at all, but if you've got some relatives that did something, or who were here early enough, that seemed to compensate for it. A kinda' peculiar idea, I think.

I worked the very first three years we were married. David was planning to go to Harvard Business School, so we banked his income and lived on my salary for three years, to have enough money for him to go. He eventually did go, and we moved up to Arlington, near Cambridge, Massachusetts. I received my own diploma from the Harvard Business School, called a PHT. "Putting Hubby Through." Somewhere, I have that written in script, with my name on it!

I was part of what they called 'The Harvard Dames,' because we were the wives of the guys who were in the Harvard Business School. We even had a class. It was a special class taught by one of the professors for wives of eventual male CEO's and top management, on how to behave. We were never to put our interests ahead of the interests of our husbands. If he had to change jobs, which we were assured would occur probably five or six times, we were not to say, "Well, the kids are in school, and we don't want to move." You were to just shut your mouth and go wherever he had to go. Talk about a whitewash, absolute indoctrination.

That happened to me in 1957. Of course, David did get a good job after that back in Connecticut, and I was happy to be there. I really liked Connecticut. I spent most of my life there, fairly near my sister and my brother. So we settled in Branford, Connecticut, which is just east of New Haven. We moved into a typical mid-to-upper-middle class suburb, and joined the country club. I eventually became the women's golf champion for two years. My kids learned how to sail, they were on a swimming team, and they learned how to play tennis. It was not as ritzy a club as a lot of clubs around there. This was a real family club, where a lot of interest was paid to the kids. They made sure the kids had things to do in the summer to keep them out of trouble.

I had some good years there, as I look back on that part of my life with fondness. I still like to play golf, although I don't play as much now because of my hips.

That is when I took up birding. We had a lot of trees around, and David bought me a pair of binoculars. I didn't know anybody in town who didn't belong to the club at that point. So, I spent one whole winter looking out at the birds, and found this was something I really enjoyed doing. So I got some bird books. I got Roger Tory Peterson's bird guide so I could identify them. Then I started keeping a log, which I did for the next fifteen years. Every calendar year I would have a log of when I first saw each type of bird, and it became a real avocation which I really enjoyed. It's something you can take with you. Wherever you travel there are birds.

I had married in 1953, when I was 31. That meant that after I had children, I would be with other parents who were at least ten years younger. Most people got married in their twenties. I had my first child at 34, and the last one at 39. I was usually associating with younger people.

I thought my marriage was probably a good marriage. I mean, what did I know? This is what they had told me I had to do at my last place of employment. I was supposed to go and get married, have children, and live in a house with a white picket fence. For a lot of people, this is what happened after the war. This is how new towns started. We lived in a really nice house, one that we built ourselves. That was fun, because I helped design it. I like to do things like that. We built the house, and that's always fun, to build your own house. As kids came along, we needed more room, so we built an addition. It was a very nice house in a nice neighborhood close to Long Island Sound.

We always had a boat. I had a small sailboat for the kids. We did a lot of sailing and a lot of cruising. I chartered a friend's boat a couple of times, and took everybody for a two week cruise around Long Island Sound.

Some friends had gone overseas, and they left their son in charge of their boat, about a 32' sloop. He managed to sail it over to Port Jefferson, across Long Island, and then he got arrested on a drug charge. So he was hauled off to jail, and the boat was left at a marina. I went to rescue the boat and took my oldest daughter and my son. We got a ride over from somebody from the club that had a fast boat. I also took Captain, who kind of handled the boats at the club. He was an old guy, not a sailor, more of a motorboat person.

We started back, and all of a sudden I see these clouds appear on the horizon. I said, "Oh, we're gonna have some bad weather. I think we should take in a reef." "Oh, no," says Captain. "We'll be fine." Well, we weren't fine. The blow hit

*us and my son, Charlie, started getting seasick. I had the
tiller, and I had hold of Charlie by the seat of his pants, as he
was leaning over the side of the boat, heaving. My daughter,
who was forward in the boat, put her head through the hatch
to see what was going on, just as we hit a really bad wave.
The hatch came down, and hit her on the head, causing her
to bite her tongue. She was bleeding, and she came back up
the companion way with blood coming down her face. In the
meantime, we were in a really bad storm.*

*We took the sail down and tried to start the engine, but
it wouldn't start. So things were really kind of hairy for a
while. Eventually, we did get the engine going. The storm
blew over, Charlie stopped being seasick, and I was able to
take care of Lisa's bloody mouth. We got back to the dock at
Pine Orchard where we had started from. My husband was
waiting there. The first thing he says is, "What are we going
to have for dinner?" That was my marriage in a nutshell.*

Staying at home with her young children, and her binoculars,
kept Deedy busy, yet she still had time to get involved in
the community. She served as the chair of the Conservation
Commission for several years, and she ran for a local public
office, as well as other activities.

*By the time I was in the middle of my marriage, involved
in the local government of the town, going out to meetings
there, I was also getting very involved with the Girl Scouts. I
had a troop for about three or four years. Both my daughters
were in a Girl Scout troop. Then they wanted me to be on the
board of the Council. I served one six year term, was off for
about three or four years, then went back on. I spent a good
twelve years with the Girl Scouts. It's a group for which I
have great admiration, and think they are doing their part in
giving young girls self-esteem for whatever field they wish to
participate in.*

Life was flowing along quite nicely, and Deedy would have confidently assured anyone who asked that she was very happy. Then she happened upon the book *The Feminine Mystique*, by Betty Friedan, and the book literally changed her life.

I called a friend of mine who is in the League of Women Voters, and I said, "Betty, have you read this book?" She said "Yes!" So we started to talk about it, and then we called a couple of other friends. What have we all been missing? You know, there is a life out there. There is something else out there besides the diapers, the cooking, the cleaning, the washing, and the shopping. Then, we do it all over again the next day. This would have been 1968, or 1969.

Luckily, I lived not far from New Haven, where there was a hotbed of feminist activity. Young graduates had started a women's center in one of the old buildings. I heard about this and friends of mine were volunteering over there as some sort of counselors, rape crisis counselors, or some-thing. They started a six weeks course on 'Growing Up Female,' which I took. Here were all these young, vibrant, well-educated, vocal, feminists talking about other things that life could hold for women. They pointed out the second class citizenship women had in this particular culture.

My eyes were opened. I could not get enough, so I enrolled in a women's studies course at the local college. I took one course, liked it, and took another course. Then I got involved in all sort of things that had to do with the women's center at Yale.

Deedy's mind was reeling with all she was learning. Armed with a new way of thinking, she began to look at the life she was living with David, her children, and her political activities.

I would come home from some commission meetings, and my husband would start quizzing me on why I voted this way, why I voted that way? I thought, "I was the one that was elected. Why is he telling me how I should have voted?" With what I was learning at the women's center, and I was seeing how, right in my own home, there was a power situation, and I am the one that is supposed to follow the male lead.

Once her eyes were open about what there was out there for women, friction began to build in her marriage. Not only was David trying to tell Deedy how she should be voting in her role as commissioner, he also wanted to control what she taught their daughters. All the tension led to a divorce. It was messy, like most divorces, but Deedy was given the house, custody of the teenage children, and David left.

In the process of becoming a feminist, after meeting all these wonderful Yale lesbians, I had a relationship with one of the women who taught one of the courses. I'll never forget. It was on the eve of my 50th birthday. I was thinking to myself, "I need to find out about myself before I turn 50." That is what I had in the back of my head. Well, I waited until the day before turning 50 to find out. That was my second awakening, about women being in a relationship. Going along with my new-found sense of who I was as a woman, and the power that entailed, it all seemed to fit.

Shooting a hole in one, age 50

Over the next few years, Deedy became deeply involved in several projects that fed her new sense of self, and served her new community of women. She helped a group of poets at the New Haven Women's Liberation Center publish a compilation of their works, and provided some financial support to the New Haven Women's Liberation Rock Band, a group that played at women's dances in the Boston area. Deedy also spent several years heavily involved with Women's Health Services, working to make sure safe abortions remained available. Like many women, Deedy hated the idea of abortion, but passionately believed in women being able to make their own decisions.

The other thing I got involved with was the Connecticut Feminist Federal Credit Union. "C Fuck You" we called it. This was because, first of all, married women could only have credit as worthy as their husbands'. If their husbands had lousy credit, the wives didn't have any. When you divorced, you had to start all over again, and try to get some credit. If you were married, you couldn't get credit on your own.

It started in New Haven, and then we had a branch in Hartford. At the opening ceremony, we had a big chain with two women holding it, and somebody came with a welding torch in a mask, and cut it, cutting the chains of economic injustice. It made all the papers, and the TV news that night. Two of the women had gone to Detroit, where the first feminist credit union was started in this country. They came back and trained some of us who were on the board. Then we hired somebody to be there all day. We had a credit committee that decided who could get credit. We had a relationship with the Women's Health Services. If a young woman came in for an abortion and needed some credit for that, we had a special message that they would write, and then send her to the credit union to get the money to pay for the abortion.

Good, strong feminists that they were, the credit committee found it hard to turn any woman in need away. Unfortunately, they didn't really give due consideration to whether or not a woman would be able to repay the loan. An auditor from the National Credit Union questioned this practice at the end of their first year, and advised them to change their criteria for making loans. Feminists had rallied to make sure there were adequate deposits to make the loans, foregoing dividends to help other women. Still, they didn't want to turn women away. Instead, they began to falsify records, and by the end of their third year the feminist credit union had to shut down.

Deedy had been attending college classes at the University of New Haven since her divorce, and accumulated enough credits to get her B.A. She also earned an M.B.A., writing her thesis on the concept of feminist credit unions. Her experience had taught Deedy that being a feminist wasn't enough. You had to run the credit union like a business, too.

> That was a very valuable lesson for me. As much as we might want things to be a different way, and try to do it, it doesn't always work. The only good thing that came from that was that Congress finally passed the Fair Credit Act. That meant that Mrs. John Doe could now get credit as Jane Doe. They were not going to deny women credit because of their former husband's, or present husband's, bad credit. Women could stand on their own and qualify for credit. So, we did manage to get that passed. We felt very good about that one.

In 1981, Deedy and a group of her friends were asked to work on putting together a women's music festival in their part of the country. They'd all been to the Michigan Womyn's Music Festival and loved it, but wanted something closer to home.

> We started a Northeast Women's Musical Retreat, NEWMR. I was a founding mother. It was an exciting

thing. For three or four days, a group of women got together on a piece of land, usually at a scout camp. I had some connections to finding camps that weren't going to be used at the end of the summer. We had the event on Labor Day weekend. We had performers, and we all had jobs to do. Everyone involved had something either to do with the day stage, the night stage, the food, security, the waterfront, the camp store, or disability. I was the treasurer, so I was there to keep the books. It was really a lot of fun.

Our first retreat we held at a ski resort. I knew the owner's wife. She was a Girl Scout leader like me and she said, "Oh, you can use our ski place in Connecticut." It was wonderful. It had plenty of parking, lots of johns, and a big room where we could feed everyone. The only thing it didn't have was flat land. But, if you went up a ways, it leveled off a bit, so that's where people tented. They tented around the base camp. We had over a thousand women that came to that first retreat.

There was such a need for this, that people just flocked. Lesbian was not in the title, but it was called a women's festival. I don't think anyone would have rented us a campground if we had said we were lesbians. Obviously, the people who came were all lesbians. A few straight women friends of mine came and enjoyed themselves. After all, women's music is women's music, and if you like that, you will like it no matter what. And it's a camping experience. We always had programs during the day. Somebody would have a topic they wanted to talk about, and they would have a little class. We had various topics that people could go to, and then we had the day stage every afternoon. At night, we had the night stage. Music was the predominant reason people came.

Of course we made all sorts of mistakes. The food was a disaster. We had somebody that was going to help cater. We had an awful macaroni and cheese dinner one night, and I

Sailing in 1995 and inset, sailing in 1932 at age 10

*don't remember what we had the other nights. We just didn't
know how to do all this. But it was a roaring success. We
danced on the tables. I remember, all of us who were on the
planning committee, dancing and saying, "We did it, we did
it." We hadn't really believed we that we could do it.*

*I can't even remember who the performers were at that
first one. It could have been Margie Adam, because she's sort
of an old favorite. She might have been there. I know we had
a lot of trouble with the electricity, because power needed to
run a ski lift is much more than we need to run an amplifier
system. So they had to put in some kind of transformer that
knocked the power down. It cost a lot of money, and we
ended up leaving it there because once it's there you're not
going to undo it.*

*It left us off with all these ideas so that the next year we
could do better. I must say that each time, we never had over
a thousand people, but we have had as many as four or five
hundred. And our production skills have gotten better. It
runs very smoothly now. And as we bring new people on,
and some people leave, I think many women have had the
experience of being part of putting on a music festival, and
the excitement that goes with it. This is twenty years now.
We've also been looking for our own land for a number
of years. But, I think at this point, in the evolution of this
organization, probably that won't happen. What we will do
is disband and dissolve the corporation, and give money to
other worthy 501(c)3's. With that gift we can say, "Okay,
for 20 years we had a good thing. It's time to fold our tent."
I don't feel that sad about it because things do end. There's a
time for things to start, and a time for them to end.*

One of the many joys her involvement in the music festival
brought to Deedy was an opportunity to meet Shevy Healey and
Ruth Silver, some of the founding mothers of OLOC. Ruth and

Shevy gave a workshop on ageism at one festival, and after getting to know Deedy, encouraged her to join the OLOC Steering Committee. Being a part of OLOC took Deedy into a whole new world, once again.

Deedy traveled to Atlanta in 1991 to participate in the National Lesbian Conference, and two years later marched down the streets of Washington, D.C. as part of the OLOC parade contingent. OLOC was placed at the front of the march, and garnered a huge amount of attention as they chanted, "Two, four, six, eight. How do you know your grandma's straight?" That may have been the most public venue at which Deedy came out, but it wasn't the only public experience she had with the process.

> *The coming out process is something you don't just do once. You do it in many different places, and in many different ways. The most recent time that I have come out is with my congregation at the UU Church in Chatham. First I did a sermon on ageism. Then, just recently I did another sermon, titled "Authenticity: How To Grow and Thrive Out of the Closet." I had started coming out during the ageism sermon, but this one was definitely coming out. I find that every time I do it gets easier, and makes me more authentic. This is why I picked that title.*
>
> *The other time I recall coming out was to the Girl Scouts. They had a group called The President's Team, which was made up of key people on the council. One day we were having a meeting, and they were talking about some diversity: how they were trying to do more in the inner city. I announced to everybody, "You want to have some more diversity? Well here I am. I'm a lesbian." It was taken quite well. It's funny the reaction I got. I don't suppose anybody would act horrified that I said this. Most people, depending on the circumstances, especially if they know you in another context, when you announce that other part of yourself, think*

Birding while in her 80s

"Oh, well. It's still the same old person." It's important for those of us who have these other groups where we are known, for whatever reason, that we make it clear to people we're also lesbians.

My hope is that eventually coming out is going be one of these "ho-hum, so what" type of reactions. Then we'll be done with it. It's always been a positive thing, and I think that is what gives me the incentive to keep on doing it. Maybe it is because I go to a church where coming out is so expected, but I don't feel there is any reason for anybody to stay in the closet anymore.

The fresh air is great out here, out of the closet.

Deedy suffered with Alzheimer's disease the last few years of her life, and died in Florida in 2009, at 86 years of age.

Interviewer: Arden Eversmeyer

Joann Jones

Born January 1932
Interviewed at age 75 in Ohio

I didn't fall out of love with my husband, I just fell in love with Bev.

Asked how she came to identify her feelings as possibly something other than heterosexual, Joann calmly answers, "I can look back now and tell you, better than I could have at the time it happened." By the time this new revelation came to Joann at age 48, she had already fallen in love with a woman. She was married, had adopted five children, then gave birth to five (two with special needs), and was foster parent to seven more. It's hard to imagine life presenting her with a more complex set of circumstances, or the journey she traveled to get there.

I was born in the house where I now live, and my father and his four brothers were born here before me. Grandfather bought the house and the land in 1892. So it's been in the family for several generations. I've never lived anywhere else. I had a sister who was two years older than me, but she died

*in a tragic tractor accident as a young child. A couple years
after I was born, my brother was born, so I grew up with a
younger brother, and shared the home with him. He went
into the armed forces in 1952, and was discharged in 1954.
Six weeks later he was killed in a tragic plane accident here
on the farm. I have been the only member of the immediate
family to continue to live here.*

Joann spent her youth much like every other child growing
up during the 1930s and 1940s in the heartland of the United
States. Life revolved around family, church, school, and farming.
She attended the same country school from first grade through
the twelfth grade. Once Joann graduated, she began attending
Earlham College in Richmond, Indiana, only 30 miles away.
When, during her second year of college, an opportunity came
along for her to go abroad, Joann was intrigued.

*I applied to become an International Farm Youth Exchange
student. You had no choice as to where you were to be sent.
There were four representatives from Ohio that were chosen.
All of them were students at Ohio State University, except
me. We were each sent to a different country. When I found
out I was going to Finland, I had to look it up on a map
to see where it was. I knew that it was somewhere around
Scandinavia, but in 1952, the most shocking part for me was
that it bordered Russia. There was a mile-wide strip of land
between Finland and Russia that was a No-Man's-Land,
and you had to get a passport to go into that area. We were
also warned that sometimes people came up missing in that
area of the country, and there was no way that the government could help us out if that were to happen.*

*I was assigned to four different farms in Finland over a
period of time. My second farm was next to Karelia, which
was the land that Finland had to cede to Russia in the
Second World War. So that was an interesting aspect of the*

trip. It all worked out fine, and I was able to stay the whole six months before I came back home.

We worked on farms. We cut wheat and formed wheat shocks. They have a lot of trouble with water drainage in the fields, so when they shock their wheat, or oats, they have to put it on stakes above the ground, to hold the wheat off the soil. Those stakes were already driven into the ground by the men on the farm. But one of the jobs I had during the summer was to go through, with the horse and wagon, and pull those stakes out of the ground. I would take them in and put them in the barn for the next season. Earlier, before I took the stakes out, one of the chores was to actually put the wheat on these stakes. The stakes were about as big as a fence post, about four inches in diameter, probably five or six feet tall. You took a two pronged fork, stuck it into a bundle of straw, and then aimed it so that it came down over each post.

One of the other things I did was to help milk cows. I was experienced at doing that because we had to milk cows at home, just for our own use.

There were young people my age, or near my age, on every farm but one. One of the biggest barriers was not being able to speak the language. I never did acquire that ability, other than to convey my immediate needs. I carried a small English-to-Finnish and Finnish-to-English dictionary. I would hand the Finnish person the Finnish to English version, and they would find the word that meant something to them. They would convey to me what they were trying to say, and vice-versa. I learned to count, to say greetings and thank you, and those kinds of things. But it's a very difficult language, and I didn't learn very much of it.

Before I left Ohio, the Dayton Daily Newspaper farm editor came out to our farm and asked me if I would be willing to write a series of eighteen articles, over an eighteen week period of time, for the Sunday paper. Each week I sent *the article, as well as black and white film, to the newspaper to be published in the Sunday edition. I agreed to do that and, as a result, the Dayton paper paid the 4-H foundation, I think, $600 toward my trip.*

Part of my responsibility was to carry not only the little black and white camera for the newspaper, but a color slide camera to use for making presentations when I got back from Finland. I was to convey the Finnish lifestyle to the American people, as to what was going on in Finland. Sort of a peacemaking effort. I made over two hundred presentations in two years, after I got back from Finland. I was pretty busy. Sometimes I had one presentation in the morning at a school auditorium, one at noon with the Rotary, Lions, or Kiwanis groups, and one in the evening.

In between traveling around the area to give presentations about farming in Finland, Joann was working on her own family farm. She also made time to square dance on a regular basis with a group of her friends. It was at one of the dances that a young man caught her attention, and within three months they were engaged. Six months later, they were married.

Lewis was a farmer who lived about ten miles from Joann's home. He continued farming at home, and began helping Joann's dad, too. His role on Joann's family farm grew over the years, especially after her brother was killed. The family operation raised feeder pigs, cattle and laying hens, as well as cultivating grains and hay.

The family obstetrician told Joann that she wasn't likely to have any children of her own, but she and Lewis wanted a big family. When they had been married less than three years, they adopted their first child, a baby boy. A year later, they adopted a girl. Next came twins from Korea, one of whom died of a brain aneurism later that same year, and then two more. Now that they had a family of five, Joann became pregnant. In addition

Joann and Louis in 1956

to adding another child to the mix, Joey's impending birth was the beginning of a whole new phase of Joann's life. She became active in the field of mental retardation, and began to take in foster children.

The family home, where Joann had spent her whole life, had lots of room and, as her older children matured and left home, space became available, and they began to care for other children with needs like Joey's.

There were no options available for Joey except institutionalization. The only school was not an option, because Joey was not potty-trained and could not walk. I got very involved in starting programs for children such as Joey in our county. The state of Ohio wanted foster homes for other retarded children. Many of the foster children came to our house to live when they were three, four, and five years old, and have stayed here ever since. We had some who were able to live on their own, independently, when they came of age. One is married, and has a son. Two of them are living independently in their own apartments.

Joey was only the first of Joann's biological children, as she soon had four more. One is Jessica, another child with needs very similar to Joey's, but with one major difference. "Joey doesn't talk. Jessica never stops talking!" Adding Jessica's needs to the mix spurred Joann on, and she became even more involved. But unlike most people in her situation, not only did Joann ask questions, she became one of the answers.

Life was complicated, no question about it. It was also very rewarding. With her family's support, Joann was now managing a residential care facility for individuals with limited mental abilities, limits that often were accompanied by physical disabilities. Joann couldn't do it alone, so some staff was hired.

Lewis and Joann Campbell Jones, '54, write, "We are very happy with our adopted family and feel that in our own little way, we have proven that love can be an even stronger bond than blood." Left to right, Jamie, 3½ (Apache Indian), Mark, 5, Toney, 8 months old, Kim, 4, Tammy, 11 months old and Tommy, 3½ (Korean). Lewis Jones manages the Home Farms, R.R. 2, Camden, Ohio.

Article from newspaper in 1963

I was on the Board of Mental Retardation at that time, and the county had hired a pre-school teacher so that some of the young children, who were coming into the county program, could have more of a regular education. The teacher that the board hired was Bev. I got to know Bev, and her partner Becky, at parent-teacher conferences. I was also engaged in the operation of the center which hired Bev, and it gave us an opportunity to get acquainted, and to understand each other in different roles. I recognized that Bev and Becky had a relationship that was very special.

My husband and I took them out to eat on occasion. Once, when we took the older kids to Disney World in Florida, we needed someone to come and stay with those who didn't go, and Bev and Becky did that for us. I was always intrigued by the lifestyle of the two women living together.

It didn't take long for me to recognize that I was falling in love with Bev. I didn't fall out of love with my husband, I just fell in love with Bev. But that didn't work for him and, shortly thereafter, he wanted to get away from the farm for a few days. He went to visit the pastor who had married us, and stayed with them for a couple of days. Then he visited another former pastor who lived in Maryland, staying there a couple of days. I can only guess, from what happened when he got home, that the advice from them was to make it as difficult as possible for me to make this choice. If he threatened custody of the minor children, that would be the way to get me to change my mind. Which is what he did.

He came home from his trip by bus. I picked him up at the bus station in Richmond, and asked him if he had had anything to eat. "No," he said, so we stopped at McDonald's and got something for him to eat. In the course of our lunch together, he said that I would have to forgo my relationship with Bev, or he would file for divorce and take custody of the children, which was quite a threat.

At that time, I didn't feel that I had any choice in the matter other than to continue with the recognition that I was gay. I had not dealt with that all my life. I had not recognized before what those feelings meant. As our psychologist put it, the experience moved a simmering pot off the back burner onto the front burner of the stove. There was no way of getting around the fact that I needed to deal with who I was.

I came out to the minor children, because I felt I needed to be honest with them about what was going on. Bev had moved in, and was living in the household with Lewis, myself, and the younger children, and they needed to understand what was going on. Lewis continued to live there from January through June, and my father, who had retired but was still living on the farm, died in June. At that time, Lewis went to live with a friend, but continued to farm the land and operate the farm.

It wasn't until the following October that he actually filed for divorce and custody of the children. At that time, we were going through some very painful recognitions of Joey's need for surgery. He had developed severe scoliosis. Lewis wasn't here to make those decisions. I tried to consult with him, but he wasn't interested in making any decisions of that nature. I had to file for temporary custody of the children so that I could go ahead and make the arrangements. Bev and I took Joey to Gillette Children's Hospital in St. Paul, Minnesota.

Bev and Joann found people to stay and care for the rest of the children at home, while they took Joey to St. Paul. It wasn't an easy surgery, and required that they stay in Minnesota for a while. The worst possible timing prevailed, and Joann's divorce hearings necessitated her flying back and forth, so she could both testify in court and be in St. Paul for Joey.

Lewis asked our neighbors and friends to testify that I was an unfit mother, because I was now homosexual and shouldn't be granted custody of the minor children. On the sixth day, I

Twenty-six room home where Joann has always lived.

had to come back for a brief testimony from the psychologist and our church pastor. Bev and I moved from the Methodist Church to the Quaker Church, and the Quaker pastor was willing to testify on my behalf at the hearing.

Lewis' attorney had come out of semi-retirement to take Lewis' case, because he was considered to be a very homophobic attorney. He had both Lewis and me go to Dayton for a full psychological evaluation, as well as the children, including the two handicapped children. During five days of testimony in court, that material never was presented. It was never brought up, on the advice of Lewis' psychiatrist. My attorney sought that record. They hadn't used it because the psychiatrist had said that all the children seemed to have a better relationship with their mother than their father. The psychiatrist made the recommendation that I be given custody of the minor children. Naturally, Lewis' attorney didn't want to use that. He had to pay for all that, but he didn't use the material, which was really interesting.

*We all had to wait several months after the testimony
in court before the judge made the award of custody and the
disposition of property. That was another big issue, because
my father had died in the meantime, and left land that was
not settled in the estate. I was living in a house that Lewis
and I jointly owned, on property that we jointly owned, and
we just didn't know how that was going to turn out.*

*In fact, Lewis owns a higher percentage of the land. He
was also granted twenty acres on the east side of our land,
across the road. Dad had deeded it to both of us before he
died. The remainder of Dad's property did not enter into the
divorce. Therefore, I got the home place. I got the house and
the farm buildings and the two houses across the road, which
were my dad's retirement home and the one where we have
the second group home. So it didn't mean having to leave the
land or the property. Lewis has continued to farm the land,
still owns that portion which was given to him at the time of
the divorce, and which he intends for the children to inherit
at the time of his death.*

Before the divorce, Bev quit her job and became a full
partner with Joann in the operation of Home Farms, the two
residential group homes. For some of their neighbors in their
community, acceptance of Joann and Bev as a couple, caring for
children, was just too much to take.

*There were two petitions circulated. The first one was that
I would lose the license at the Home Farms where I live,
because of my homosexual lifestyle, and that made me a
detriment to the individuals who live here. That petition
was signed by sixty or seventy people in the immediate area,
and was sent to the Department of Mental Retardation
in Columbus, Ohio, to the director of the department. The
director then assigned licensure to come out and inspect the
home, and review with us what we were doing. When they*

came, I didn't have outside help, and they said they would give us more money to operate on!

The second petition was an effort to keep me from getting a license for a second home on the farm. It, likewise, failed, and we've been licensed ever since. Bev's name continues to be on the license. We felt really good about that.

Shortly after I came out, I was asked to resign from the Board of Mental Retardation for the county, where I had spent twelve years trying to get good schooling and programs started. I said, "On what basis?" They said because of my lifestyle. I said, "You'll have to find a different reason to get me to resign than that." I went home in tears. I went to the next meeting, a month later, and they apologized. So I stayed on the board. Those things are all part of the picture of what it was like to come out when you are almost fifty years old.

Back when Joann was still married, she and her husband had donated an acre of land from their farm, so that the United Methodist Church, in which they were very active, could build a parsonage. Living so close, the pastor and his wife were frequent visitors, and the pastor's wife became their most dependable babysitter. When the rumor mill got into gear, and the pastor heard what might be happening, the pastor came by, asking Joann if he could speak to her in private.

We went out to the office, and he said that he understood Bev had moved in, and that I was having a relationship with Bev, and was that true? I said, "Yes." Then he wanted to know if it was sexual, and I said, "That's true, but that's just part of it." He immediately stood up and said to me that he could no longer be my pastor, and that his wife could no longer babysit.

He left the office and left the house, and I didn't exchange another word with him after that. I did hear, however, that at a visitation for one of the church members who had died,

he told my husband that he and his wife had held a mock funeral for me in their parsonage, after he had returned home.

Quickly resigning from the Methodist church, she and Bev began looking for one that would welcome them for who they were. Bev was friends with a Quaker pastor in a nearby town and they started there. In fact, the man told Bev, 'You won't be alone.' Even with his assurances that they'd be welcome, some members left when Bev and Joann started attending together.

Bev and Joann in 2006

After the divorce was over, one member of the Quaker church even went to the courthouse and got a record of the testimony that the pastor had made during the divorce trial. Some members asked the pastor to resign, but he refused.

The district for the Quaker church then got involved, evaluating whether or not the pastor should be "defrocked" because he had testified on Joann's behalf during the divorce. The district left it up to the local congregation to decide. After heart-wrenching discussions, the pastor stayed and many of the members withdrew from the church.

*We both feel very fortunate that the community has had a
change of heart over the twenty-five years that Bev and I
have been together. One family, in particular, who signed one
of the petitions at the time of the divorce, let their mentally
retarded daughter move in to live with us. Although we never
discussed the issue of the petition, my life style, or anything
like that, I consider us good friends.*

*The same is true of many of those in the community who
had signed the petition, or who had refused to wave back as I
drove by, or to speak to me when I met them in town. Many
of them seem to have had a change of heart. It isn't that we've
sat down and talked about it, it's just that over a period of
time, we were able to continue to live a normal life together.
And we are who we are, without apology.*

*I think our children have grown up to become good
members of the community, and don't reflect anything
negative caused by our lifestyle. We have been able to re-
establish a fairly decent relationship with my ex-husband,
and he comes to see the two handicapped children once a
week. I furnish transportation for him to use the van. He
and his wife take Joe and Jess out to eat once a week, and we
also occasionally gather together at Thanksgiving, sometimes
at Christmas time, and other celebrations in the family. Over
the years, two of the children had weddings on the farm here,
and Lewis and his wife were very present at those times.
We've had pictures taken together. It has worked out over a
period of years, for which I'm very thankful.*

Whether or not to come out as a lesbian to all of her family
was never an option. When Bev ended her previous relationship
and moved in, Joann and Bev's relationship very soon became
common knowledge.

*There was no hiding it. Everyone knew. I'm not sure that
I would have been willing to make some of the choices I'd*

made at the pace I did, had I recognized the fallout. But it's a good thing I didn't recognize what was coming, because I don't know how I would've handled it. However, I didn't have to do it alone.

The "big house," where Joann and Bev were living and running the group home had been built and added on to by Joann's grandfather, who farmed and needed more room for his extended family, and hired help. It is three stories with twenty-six rooms that can be used for living quarters, plus a full attic and basement. There was plenty of room, yet they realized they had to have someplace that they could get away from it all. The state had recognized how much work Joann and Bev were doing alone (basically working 24-7), and allocated enough funds that the home could hire some outside help. Once getting away was an option, they had to decide where to go. Neither of them wanted to go far, so they had a small getaway house built on the farm. The move, while not far, was a welcome relief.

Joann and Bev also carved out time to hike and travel some, and to build a circle of friends within the lesbian community. "It's just so important to be able to share time and space with those of the same lifestyle. It's very lonely without it."

I feel very fortunate in many respects. Things that have occurred in my life have not always been easy, but I feel stronger for having experienced them. And it has directed my life in a way that I would never have expected it to go.

Joann continues to live in Ohio, on the same property where she has always lived. She and Bev both still devote much of their time to Home Farms, where Joey and Jessica live.

Interviewer: Arden Eversmeyer

We deeply appreciate the women who shared their stories with the Old Lesbian Oral Herstory Project, and then allowed us to share them with you, the readers. We can only hope they know what a gift they have given to us all.

Addenda

October 11, 1994
National Coming Out Day for Gays and Lesbians

To: My family
From: Charotte L. Avery, sister and aunt

In need to tell you that I was born a Lesbian.
I do this to be true to myself. What you do
with it is up to you.

I will not debate the Bible with anyone. My
relationship with my loving God is my personal
business. I feel I have lived my life as a
Christian, serving God, my fellow man, and my
family.

I no longer have room in my life for ANY people
who cannot love me unconditionally. This is a
basic principle of Jesus' teachings.

I love you all,

Charlotte L. Avery

Marcia Perlstein, an OLOHP interviewer, book beta-reader and all-around Project Cheerleader, encouraged us to include both the coming out letter that Charlotte Avery mentions in her story on page 194, and the letter Arden sent to Tre, mentioned on page 166, so here they are. As Marcia said, "The letters are so special, and so powerful, they should be set apart and included in their entirety."

December 1986

Dear Tresse,

Out of your ancient past comes an unfamiliar name. No need for you to remember, so I will get on with the purpose of this letter.

Summer 1949 - a sophisticated lady arrived in Denton on her bicycle from New York City. Awsome! I had come out the previous year with senior P.E. major Barbara "Andy" Anderson. A lovely lady and still my friend. I no longer have any recollection of how I met you. I do remember a couple pair of shoes you made for me. But most important, I remember an all afternoon/evening bull session in your room that has profoundly affected my life. We discussed the lifestyle that had always been mine, but I had so recently discovered. As a result of that day there has never been one minute of regret, doubt, or guilt for me.

Summer 1952 - I came to Houston to visit a college roommate. I had quit my job in West Texas and was looking for another. I met and fell in love with a wonderful lady - Tommie. Many wonderful qualities - funny, kind, gentle, wise, respected by everyone, and a fine athlete. So the good life goes on.

Summer 1981 - I took a medical retirement after 30 years in public school work - 11 in physical education and 19 in counseling. The problem was severe job burn-out. My health improved a million percent.

May 1982 - Tommie and I sold a quite large home we had lived in 26 years and moved into our new retirement home. In July, on our 30th anniversary, Tommie was diagnosed with cancer.

October 1985 - my sweet lifemate lost her long battle. Because I was retired we had some true quality time those last years. I miss her, but I do not wish her back.

Bottom line - in the many years I was in contact with young people I often said it would be wonderful to know if I had made a positive impact on just one young life. The only way we ever know those things is if we are told. So it became important that I say these words to you. Myenduring relationship with Tommie was related to the peace of mind about myself and my lifestyle. And that same peace has helped me in the months since Tommie died. I am changing and growing - almost like a new coming out. Maybe there will be another nice lady in my future - maybe not - I expect I'll be rather choosy. I have thought about you and that session so many times over the years. Then the article in People Magazine gave me the tool I needed to say these words. I hope this reaches you. I am very grateful to you, Tresse Ford, and I hope your wisdom has touched others as it has touched me.

Merry Christmas to you and yours.

Sincerely,

Arden

Arden Eversmeyer
3311 S. Primrose Meadows
Pearland, Texas 77584

Without Apology
Women by Year of Birth

1917	Eleanor 'Ellie' Schafer
1918	Jess McVey
1919	Kathryn 'Kittu' Riddle
1922	Elizabeth 'Deedy' Breed
1923	Louise Cason
1923	Ruth Taylor
1924	Bessie Morris
1925	Elaine Weber
1926	Pat Durham
1930	Charlotte Avery
1931	Jacqueline 'Jackie' Mirkin
1931	Arden Eversmeyer
1932	Lucille 'Lucy' Frey
1932	Joann Jones
1933	Vivian Larsen
1934	Joan Meyers
1935	Gloria Stancich
1935	Shaba Barnes
1935	Elizabeth 'Betsy' McConnell
1936	Delores 'Dee' Austin
1936	Bobbie Knowles
1937	Edith 'Edie' Daly
1937	Helen Kalcsits
1937	Saundra Tignor

To learn more about
the Old Lesbian Oral Herstory Project,
visit www.olohp.org

To learn more about
Old Lesbians Organizing for Change,
see page xiv or visit www.oloc.org

To learn more about the Sophia Smith
Women's Archives at Smith College,
go to www.smith.edu/libraries/libs/ssc/

The Future of the
Old Lesbian Oral Herstory Project

Every generation has a story to tell. For now, the OLOHP continues to focus on life stories of lesbians born early in the 1900s. Lesbians who fit this demographic lived through decades of tremendous change, change in opportunities that were afforded to them as lesbians, and in the laws affecting their daily lives. During their lifetimes, lesbians went from risking institutionalization in psychiatric facilities where they were subjected to inhumane treatments to "cure" them of their homosexuality, to being able to legally marry in several states.

Arden has devoted the past fifteen years of her life to making sure there is a lasting record of these unique lives. She is rightfully proud of what she's accomplished and hopes she has built a foundation on which others will build, moving forward to gather the stories of the next generations of lesbians as well. The stories of women born in the mid-twentieth century will be distinctly different, but they, too, will be well worth gathering and preserving.

Having personally reached the milestone of 80 years of age, Arden continues to serve as Director of the OLOHP. When asked about what she sees for the Project over the next decade, she first says, "I'm not done yet!" Arden continues to devote several days a week to the work of the OLOHP and hopes to do so for years to come. She's also thought about what happens when she is no longer involved and has taken various steps to help ensure the Project's future. Arden has trained other interviewers, shared the process she developed for gathering and preserving herstories, incorporated the OLOHP with a strong Board of Directors, and gained non-profit status. The Project has now entered into an agreement with Smith College. All the records and the collection of herstories of the OLOHP will become a part of the Sophia Smith Women's History Archives at Smith College in Northampton, Massachusetts.

OLOHP Website: www.olohp.org

Sharing some of the insights, adventures and experiences revealed in the many stories of the Old Lesbian Oral Herstory Project has always been an important goal. One of the ways we have accomplished this goal is through our website. The site, found at www.olohp.org, has a wide array of information about the OLOHP itself as well as a sampling of profiles, photos, and audio clips from some of the Herstories.

The OLOHP Books

A Gift of Age: Old Lesbian Life Stories was the first book to come out of the stories of the Old Lesbian Oral Herstory Project.

Without Apology: Old Lesbian Life Stories, is our second offering. There are tentative plans for a third book at some point in the future. Look for our books in your local women's or LGBT bookstore, if you're so fortunate as to have one, or order them at www.olohp.org

A Gift of Age: ISBN 978-0-9823669-6-7
Without Apology: ISBN 978-0-9823669-0-5

The OLOHP Newsletter

As a vehicle for sharing information about what is going on in the OLOHP and sharing bits and pieces from specific stories, we have developed a newsletter. The *OLOHP Insider* is produced quarterly and is available as a PDF via e-mail. If you would like to be added to our mailing list, please send us an e-mail request at info@olohp.org. Back issues can be downloaded by going to www.olohp.org and clicking on 'Newsletter' in the sidebar.

"Every old lesbian has a story.

And they don't need to climb Mt. Everest in order to have one.
— Arden Eversmeyer

This quote appeared on the cover of a brochure from Astraea Lesbian Foundation for Justice.

If you are an old lesbian who would like more information on sharing your own story with the Old Lesbian Oral Herstory Project, or if you know someone who might be interested, here is our contact information:

OLOHP
PO Box 980422
Houston, TX 77098
e-mail info@olohp.org
www.olohp.org

Order Form

Three Easy Ways to Order:
- ◆ Order online at www.olohp.org
- ◆ Download an order form at www.olohp.org
- ◆ Mail this order form with payment information to OLOHP

Make checks payable to OLOHP **OLOHP** **PO Box 980422** **Houston, TX 77098**	Shipping Inside US: $4 for 1 book $2 each additional book Out of US: varies, ask *Usually ships in 48-72 hours*

Bill To (as it appears on check or credit card)

Name:		
Address:		
City:	State:	Zip:
Phone:		
E-mail:		

Ship To (if different than above)

Name:		
Address:		
City:	State:	Zip:

☐ Check	☐ Money Order	☐ MasterCard	☐ Visa

Credit Card Number	Expiration Date
☐☐☐☐ ☐☐☐☐ ☐☐☐☐ ☐☐☐☐	☐☐☐☐

Item	Unit Cost	Quantity	Total
Without Apology	$19.95 (US dollars)		
A Gift of Age	$16.95 (US dollars)		
	Sales Tax (TX residents add 8.25%)		
	Shipping & Handling (see rates listed above)		
		Order Total	

Discount available for bulk orders. Contact us at info@olohp.org

Old Lesbian Oral Herstory Project • www.olohp.org
PO Box 980422 • Houston, TX 77098 • info@olohp.org